Persuasion
The Litigator's Art

MICHAEL E. TIGAR

PROFESSOR OF LAW AND EDWIN A. MOOERS, SR. SCHOLAR
Washington College of Law, American University

Persuasion
The Litigator's Art

SECTION OF LITIGATION
American Bar Association

© 1999 American Bar Association.
All rights reserved.
Printed in the United States of America.

02 01 00 99   5 4 3 2 1

Tigar, Michael E., 1941
    Persuasion / Michael E. Tigar.
        p.   cm.
    Includes index.
    ISBN 1-57073-637-5
    1. Trial practice—United States. 2. Forensic oratory.
3. Persuasion (Psychology) I. American Bar Association.
Section of Litigation. II. Title.
KF8915.T55 1998
347.73'75—dc21   98-47122
                                                CIP

Discounts are available for books ordered in bulk.
Special consideration is given to state bars,
CLE programs, and other bar-related organizations.
Inquire at ABA Publishing,
American Bar Association,
750 North Lake Shore Drive,
Chicago, Illinois 60611.

www.abanet.org/abapubs

*This book is dedicated to the memory of
Edward Bennett Williams.*

Contents

Contents

A Note on Citations

Notes are at the end of chapters, except for a section of Chapter Two and all of Chapter Three, Part II; Chapter Five, Part II; and Chapter Six, Part II. For those chapters, I have put my annotations in running commentaries to Edward Bennett Williams's words to discuss the techniques of argument he is using.

Citations to *Examining Witnesses* are to my 1993 book, also published by the American Bar Association Section of Litigation.

The entire transcript of the Nichols trial is on the Internet and in a Westlaw database, OKLA-TRANS. Openings and closings in that trial are also available as part of a series of trial materials reprinted by the Professional Education Group, Minnetonka, Minnesota, all of which may be ordered directly at 612-933-9990.

PEG also sells a series of books that are annotated transcripts of lawyer arguments to juries and courts. It is called Classics of the Courtroom. These books are well worth owning.

Some of the material in Chapter Four is drawn from the brief we filed in *Gentile v. State Bar of Nevada,* 111 S.Ct. 2720 (1991).

Preface

Edward Bennett Williams and the Art of Advocacy

This book is about persuasion—how we convince judges and jurors through argument to find for our clients. It is about a study that once dominated legal education, then died away, and now is reborn. This book is about ideas that every law school once made the centerpiece of its teaching and to which few law schools today pay much heed.

Most lawyers have, at one time or another, read the elegant and persuasive words of Daniel Webster, Abraham Lincoln, Mark Twain, Clarence Darrow. Many have studied the arguments of other great advocates in the common law tradition. What marks their arguments? What makes them memorable? A lawyer in Houston once showed me his collection of books about great trials. "I keep reading these things in my spare time," he said, "and I keep finding arguments that I have wanted to use and that I thought were original with me. We really are part of a tradition."

On the way to writing this book, I was appointed counsel to Terry Lynn Nichols in the Oklahoma bombing case. In the three years that followed, I learned again what Edward Bennett Williams had taught. I had already begun work on this book and had chosen to use the *Connally* and *Alderman/Ivanov* cases as examples of persuasive advocacy to juries and to judges. As I prepared for the Nichols trial, the significance of Edward Bennett Williams's work in those cases was borne in upon me. Connally was charged as the result of a cynical and misguided plea bargain. His acquittal after trial was based on a trial record that spoke volumes about prosecutors forgetting their objectivity. The *Alderman* and *Ivanov* cases, as they came to the United States Supreme Court, were about whether government should be accountable in an adversary hearing when its agents deliberately violate the law and invade privacy.

I began to reflect on Williams's work in a new way. We are tempted as lawyers to regard our persuasive skills as simply "tools of influence," as Professor Martha Nussbaum describes them, with no higher justification than that they produce results. But the well-lived life of the advocate must include concern for how we use those tools. Their highest and best use is against government attempts to stifle democratic rights and to use state power in illegitimate ways. Edward Bennett Williams was not simply a "hired gun." The cases I have chosen as examples prove that. A political leader, a Mafia figure, a Soviet spy—what did they have in common? All three were the targets of unlawful or unethical conduct by government.

I have more than thirty years in the law. In the case of Terry Nichols, I saw a desire to get a death sentence at any cost that led advocates and those who worked for them to engage in some of the most unprofessional conduct I have witnessed. The intriguing thing was that much of this conduct translated into trial strategy that the jurors found repellent. A contest between adversaries with such disproportionate resources can never be an even match, but I was again struck by how our tools of inquiry and influence—rooted as they are in a long tradition—rightly are seen as valuable in the quest to defend democratic rights.

As the dedication says, this book is for Edward Bennett Williams. I discuss principles of advocacy, the study of which I began in Ed's office. More than thirty years ago, he hired me at a difficult time in my life. Shortly after his death in 1989, I wrote a column in *Litigation*. I tried to capture some of the qualities of Edward Bennett Williams's advocacy. He was educated in the tradition of classical rhetoric. He understood and loved to discuss the elements of our art. This is what I wrote, with just a few notes added:

It is hard to say what makes a great trial lawyer. Those we celebrate have been students of society, quick to resent injustice, eloquent in defense of freedom and fairness. I recall telling my father, when I was about 11, that I was thinking of becoming a lawyer. He thought for a time, then went back to his room and came back with a copy of Irving Stone's *Clarence Darrow for the Defense*. This, he said, is the kind of lawyer you should be. Through high school and college, I devoured books on Darrow: his autobiography, the Weinberg collection of trial excerpts, *Attorney for the Damned,* the fictionalized *Inherit the Wind.*

In college, I began to read of a Washington lawyer who had defended Frank Costello, Jimmy Hoffa, and even—though this was harder to understand—Senator Joe McCarthy.

Edward Bennett Williams had also written a book, *One Man's Freedom.* Unlike other lawyer books, it was not self-glorifying. It was a series of arguments for progressive change in the system of criminal justice, coupled with such things as the duties of a lawyer and the prospects for international law.

My first week in law school in the fall of 1963, I picked up an issue of the *California Law Review,* and there was an article on the Teamster monitors and more about Ed Williams.

By the end of my second year, I was putting together a résumé, asking that he consider me for a job when I finished my clerkship. The time for job interviews came sooner than I expected, and I went to the offices of the ten-lawyer firm that Ed Williams headed. He offered me a job that day, and I accepted.

During the years we spent together, I learned what it means to be a trial lawyer. I learned technique, discipline, passion, honor, and humor. And I grew a lot trying to match his stride.

At a technical level, Ed's cross-examinations, summations, and oral arguments are the finest example of the lawyer's art. They are like symphonic poems that excite awe in other composers and give understanding to the audience. The typical cross-examination of a major witness began with "clearing the underbrush," a process that Ed described with a gesture of wielding a machete. He had to make sure how many prior statements the witness had given and match that against the log of material provided by the prosecution. Any small concession would be won here, and ambiguities resolved.

Then the examination would march through its themes: the witness's bargain with the government, prior inconsistent statements, extensive preparation with the prosecutors, and record of peculation. Ed always held two complementary insights about these cross-examinations: First, he would keep on until the witness made the concessions compelled by the facts—and in the very words Ed needed for his closing argument. Second, Ed never forgot that cross-examination cannot do the work of closing argument.

In the *Connally* case, for example, he confronted the witness Jacobsen, who had testified on direct that Connally counted money with a "glove or gloves" in order to leave no fingerprints:

> Williams: You told us that Mr. Connally and you had a meeting in his office alone, that he excused himself, left his office for ten minutes and came back with a cigar box and a rubber glove or rubber gloves on top of a pile of money in the cigar box, is that right?[1]
> Jacobsen: Well, it was something like that.
> Williams: No, tell me what it was, Mr. Jacobsen, not whether it was something like that or not. You tell us exactly how it was, Mr. Jacobsen.[2]

Jacobsen: I believe the rubber glove was on the side of the money in the cigar box. The rubber glove or gloves was on the side of the money.

Williams: Now, when you told Mr. Tuerkeimer in your interview with him back last year about this episode, you told him it was a rubber glove, did you not?[3]

Jacobsen: Yes.

Williams: And when you testified before the grand jury on March 23rd, you told the grand jury it was a rubber glove, did you not?

Jacobsen: Yes, sir.

Williams: But when you testified on Thursday here in this courtroom, before His Honor and this jury, you said it was a rubber glove or gloves; is that correct?

Jacobsen: Yes, sir.

Williams: When did you decide it might have been a glove or gloves?

Jacobsen: Between the time I testified before the grand jury and the time I testified here.

Williams: What was it that changed your recollection from it being a glove to it being a glove or gloves?

Jacobsen: Just the logic of it being gloves instead of glove.

Williams: It was the logic of it, is that right?

Jacobsen: Yes.

Williams: Was that because, Mr. Jacobsen, the prosecutors pointed out to you that nobody could count money with one glove on one hand and a big pile?

Jacobsen: No, sir.

Williams: Well, what was the logic of it that changed your mind . . . and caused you to testify on Thursday that it was a grove or gloves?

Jacobsen: Well, the fact that you couldn't hardly handle money with one glove.

Williams: Well, that was what I just asked you, Mr. Jacobsen.

This cross has it all. Control: "You tell us exactly how it was." Pace: We get each prior statement and the witness agreeing to it. Preparation: The prior grand jury testimony *and* the prosecutor's notes—produced after a hard fight—are deployed. Daring: There are at least four nonleading questions in the series, including the ones laden with the most significance. Closure: Ed does not stop until he has the devastating admission that this witness kept working on his story until it was "logical," and then Ed moves on to another topic. This cross, like all of them, was sharp and clear.

The Jacobsen cross was one of a series of these episodes, each one based on the most intense study of the case and frequent heated discussions with those of us privileged to be second-chair. There were times during the examination when the news reporters would comment on how labored it sometimes seemed. Connally's friends would communicate these sentiments. Ed's impatient reply illustrates the second principle: Cross-examination is not closing argument.

Ed worked on the *Connally* summation, as on the summation in every case, from the moment he was retained. We were always talking in terms of goals, the better to see the path.

Work on the *Connally* summation intensified during the weeks just before the trial and during the trial itself. Ed changed the organization of it as he rethought the Jacobsen cross and the Connally direct. While Ed was always alert for the unanticipated, each unit of the cross was constructed to fit its proper place in closing argument. Making Jacobsen eat each prior inconsistency created a stack of court reporter's transcripts that Ed brandished and sampled throughout the closing. Then, in his closing, Ed made best use of the concessions patiently extracted during cross.

He knew the courtroom. It was his territory. He taught us that by his example. He had an imposing physical presence, made more so by his ability to use movement as a form of comment on the proceedings. He could even take paces backward from the witness box without looking, because he had measured the space in his mind's eye.

With technique went discipline. It was more than being at the office before any of us and more than his rigorous insistence that he would know every document, every prior statement, every relevant argument, before he stepped into the courtroom. It was more than his patient work to prepare a witness to testify.

Ed taught us that discipline requires you to test yourself before you are tested by others. Those of us chosen to be his sparring partners learned our lesson. I recall, just a few years ago, stopping to have lunch in Ed's office. I had been away from the firm for several years. Ed had been representing Victor Posner, and there were whispers that the illness that finally brought him down had slowed him, or eroded his powers.

The whisperers were wrong. He sat preparing an argument for the court of appeals. "Listen to this." I listened. "The government puts Posner to trial with another defendant. We moved for severance. The government has a document, admissible only against the codefendant but"—he paused for emphasis—"*lethally* prejudicial to Posner." "Lethally" may have been Ed's favorite adverb. "The judge has promised that if they offer it, he must grant a severance. Three days into the trial, they offer it."

Now Ed was on his feet. He did a perfect imitation of the judge's ire, the prosecutor's wheedling. His hands sawed and chopped the air for emphasis, those expressive hands that were always in service of his advocacy. He recounted his motion for severance and mistrial. Motion granted.

"And the question is," cocking his head to one side in a familiar gesture, "would a retrial violate double jeopardy?" I had not come to do this work, but was honored.

"Sounds a little like *United States v. Martinez*[4] to me," I said. A Tenth Circuit case, but written by an Eighth Circuit judge. I told him the facts. Ed leaned over and punched four buttons on the telephone. "Hello," he said softly to whoever answered. "How about the *Martinez* case?" A pause while the other party replied. "I know it is not in the brief. The question is why it isn't." Another pause. "Meet me in the library."

We took the elevator to the library and got out the case. We read it. Ed thought the associate who joined us had been through enough. He turned on me. "This case doesn't get us there. The district judge was in on the misconduct."

Ed continued to debate, arguing first on one side and then the other. Supreme Court cases came off the shelves. At last, he was satisfied that he had explored every crevice of the argument, and we went back upstairs to eat the remains of our tuna sandwiches.

The discipline was for clients as well. He demanded candor from them, and when trial rolled around, hard work. Before going on the stand, the client was forced to confront the evidence piece by piece and be ready for the ordeal of testifying.

Ed's discipline was physical as well as mental. I have spoken of his hands and his courtroom mien. He had internalized the idea that every nuance of movement or gesture in a courtroom may be observed by the jury and considered in some measure significant. He practiced control, and demanded it of those who shared the counsel table.

Beyond discipline was passion. Ed made his reputation by the vigor and eloquence of his defenses, not just of people but of the principles of fairness in an adversary system. What other major figure in American law so eloquently described the values inherent in adversary justice, and so wisely adumbrated the constitutionalization of those values? I say none, and I offer his book *One Man's Freedom* as an exhibit.

In *Ivanov v. United States,*[5] we had persuaded the Court to grant *certiorari* on disclosure of wiretaps. Ivanov was a Soviet citizen convicted of espionage. Some of the taps were of his apartment, and there were rumblings that some of them had been at the Soviet diplomatic premises. Ed was asked during oral argument whether it was his position that wiretapping in national security cases was always illegal. He paused and made what was for him, the most crucial distinction the law can know. The national security, he replied, might require or permit any number of things. "But I have always been taught that the federal courts, sitting in criminal matters, are a kind of sanctuary in the jungle."[6]

I saw the passion summoned again and again, and I am sorry that I missed his last oral argument, where it was in full flower not long before his death, arguing a first amendment case for the *Washington Post.*

Ed's passion for justice led him to approve jaunts of mine that would have given other senior partners pause. I undertook the defense of an alleged saboteur pro bono. I was three weeks in trial, and more weeks on appeal of the counts on which the jury did not acquit. Ed shared my joy at our victory, declaring the Sabotage Act unconstitutional.

With technique, discipline, and passion went honor. Ed had struggled to redeem the image of the criminal lawyer, and his work endures even the baseless assaults of today's new crop of deriders and detractors. He was, however, more than an eloquent advocate of honor. He was honorable. I recall vividly a shouted argument about one of the firm's valued clients, on a certain Friday afternoon. Sunday morning the telephone rang. It was Ed. I began to apologize for some of the things I had said. He brushed that aside. "I called to say I've thought about it. I owe you an apology. We can't say in court what the client wants; the facts aren't there. Come in tomorrow and let's figure it out."

My first day in the office, he had warned me in terms that Watergate figures and inside traders should have heard: "Just remember, when times are tough and it looks like someone's going to jail, make sure it's your client."

Then there was humor. Ed's fund of stories about clients, politicians, judges, priests, and others was inexhaustible. The humor of these stories was irrepressible. It bubbled up as the story went on and spilled out over the assembled group. And at the punchline Ed always looked like an altar boy caught with the wine on his lips.

Underneath the qualities of a great trial lawyer were those of a best friend and mentor. And there was courage. As he battled with cancer from the moment he announced his first surgery to a meeting of partners, down through the years that remained, he fought that battle as he had every other.

The day Ed went to the hospital and asked for the last rites of the Church, I was in South Africa. I had gone to work with the Black Lawyers Association of South Africa in teaching trial advocacy, principally for use in political cases. I knew I was in a place that my years with Ed had pointed out to me. But I sat, alone in my hotel room, and wept.

Learning to be a trial lawyer is through example, which is a shared and vicarious experience. Vindicating the fighting faith of our profession is also through example, a striving to be worthy of those who have gone before.

Good night, Ed.

NOTES

1. Contrary to the "commandment" not to repeat the direct examination, Williams does so because only then can the jury see the contradiction that is about to be sprung.

2. Never let the witness define the terms of engagement. But note that Williams is now letting the witness loose to repeat the story. All the better to let the jury see the witness's difficulty in the questions to follow. And note that Williams moves from "tell me" to "tell us." Many times, you want to remind a witness that the jury is watching, that you want the witness to tell it to the jury.

3. The defense had moved for and obtained the prosecutor's notes of interview, to the extent they contained "statements" of Jacobsen within the meaning of 18 U.S.C. §3500. Thus, we had Jacobsen not simply with a contradiction between the grand jury and the trial, but with two prior inconsistent statements. One such statement can often be explained as inadvertence. Two or more pose the witness more difficulty.

4. *United States v. Martinez,* 667 F.2d 886 (10th Cir. 1981), *cert. denied,* 456 U.S. 1008 (1982). Martinez was being tried for sending letter bombs. During his trial, the district judge met secretly with prosecutors to urge them to commit conduct that would provoke a mistrial so that the case could be tried again. The court of appeals held that the mistrial, which did occur, was improperly obtained and that the double jeopardy clause precluded a retrial.

5. Reported with *Alderman v. United States,* 394 U.S. 165 (1969), and on remand as 342 F. Supp. 928 (D.N.J. 1972), *aff'd,* 494 F.2d 593 (3d Cir.), *cert. denied,* 419 U.S. 881 (1974).

6. The precise exchange, and the rest of the argument, are in Chapter Six, Part II.

Acknowledgments

I have been shown many kindnesses by many people. Judge Timothy Corcoran, John Segal, and Priscilla Anne Schwab of the Section of Litigation's Book Publishing Board believed in this project even when my trial commitments delayed its completion. Jennifer Bell did heavy typing under difficult conditions.

My wife, Jane B. Tigar, read and edited the manuscript with her customary love and her considerable expertise.

My most fervent thanks must go, as before, to all the clients whose life or liberty I was permitted to defend and to all the great lawyers with whom I have worked. Major Debra Meeks remains, for me, one the best examples of courage and principle that I have ever known; I am glad I could help. Harold Haddon of Denver has stood with me through many struggles, always with wise counsel, great advocacy, a sense of humor, and love. All my colleagues at Haddon, Morgan & Foreman deserve special thanks. Most recently, Ronald G. Woods of Houston, Texas, shared with me the duties of lead appointed counsel in the case of Terry Lynn Nichols, accused in the Oklahoma City bombing. One could not have a finer friend and colleague than Ron Woods.

Chapter One

The Elements of Persuasion

This book is a sequel to *Examining Witnesses,* which I wrote in 1993. I began that book by noting that an architect first imagines a complete house, then uses experience, skill, and artistry to devise the components that will become the completed project. I divided trial preparation and presentation into parts—direct examination, cross-examination, demonstrative evidence, and presentation of expert witnesses.

Now I want to take the analysis a step farther. Most of this book deals with trials, but its themes are relevant to appellate practice as well. This book goes farther in one sense because it deals with argument as well as witness presentation. In another sense, it moves behind the elements of trial presentation to the elements of persuasion itself. This is not a new undertaking. For 2,500 years, lawyers, orators, philosophers, and teachers have analyzed these elements. Their studies are entitled *rhetoric* or *semiotics.* I have freely borrowed, and will often credit, their insights.

A NOTE ON THE ORGANIZATION OF THIS BOOK

Chapters One and Two are about the advocate as storyteller, and they refer to the classical rhetorical tradition in which Williams was educated and of which he was a master. Chapter Three, Part I, talks about opening statement, and Part II is a fine example: Williams's opening in *United States v. John Connally*. I have "split the screen" for Part II, to comment on the techniques he is using as the opening proceeds. In this way, I try to make this fine example teach us how to accomplish the same goals that Williams did.

Chapter Four talks about tactics during trial. Chapter Five, Part I, considers closing argument. Using the same technique as in Chapter Three, Part II, is the annotated closing argument in *United States v. Connally*.

Chapter Six, Part I, talks about argument to judges. Many lawyers think that the principles of argument to the court are entirely different from those for jury argument. It is certainly rare for an advocate to have the mastery of both forums as did Edward Bennett Williams. But I am convinced that his techniques are in fact based on the same principles. In that spirit, Chapter Six, Part II, is an annotated version of two Supreme Court oral arguments he made on the same day in 1969.

THE DIALECTIC OF ADVOCACY

A trial is an exercise in dialectic, in the clash of opposites. I encountered these words *dialectic of advocacy* my first day in law school, from Geoffrey C. Hazard and from the casebook that he and David W. Louisell wrote. Advocates present two, and sometimes more, opposing versions of events. A trier—judge or jury—decides. In this book, I speak mostly of jury trials until Chapter Six, when I add some thoughts on persuading judges. The jury's decision—its speaking of the truth, its verdict—is sometimes "general" and sometimes "special." Most special verdicts simply answer some general questions, such as "Do you find by a fair preponderance of the evidence that John Smith proximately caused the death of Lisa Jackson?" The essential opacity of verdicts is a hindrance when we want to think about persuasion. Jury verdicts are evanescent, to be interpreted fleetingly by the participants, but leaving no firm and permanent record that tells us how the jurors parsed the evidence and decided what was true.

By contrast, think of the judicial opinion. Appellate judges write at length about their reasoning—in most cases. Even trial judges are compelled to issue findings and conclusions, though these may be party-drafted and not give us much insight into the actual process of deciding. Studies of the judicial opinion abound, along with theories about how opinions should be parsed. Scholars write books, symposia consider the meaning and interpretation of "text," and schools of jurisprudence form over whether the categories of judicial thought contain anything at all. The point, however, is that there are texts that permit such study.

When we ask how to persuade jurors, we are forced to rely on secondary sources. We can read psychological studies of juror behavior. We can hire trial consultants to match the demographics of our prospective jurors and then "test" themes for trial. We can draw upon our experience from living and working in a community, to know the attitudes and values that jurors are likely to bring to court—or if we are strangers come simply to try a case, we can ask others to share their insights.

In writing this book, I assume you have some or all of these tools available to you. I assume that you will use juror questionnaires, effective *voir dire,* and all the other tools the judge will allow. Making that assumption puts my writing at a certain level of generality. I am talking about trials—and, in Chapter Six, appeals—in general.

Talking about cases in general is useful, because there are enduring ideas about persuasion. These ideas took shape beginning in ancient Greece and have been refined in use ever since. I will not trace the history of classical rhetoric, nor pay more than the customary passing homage to Aristotle. The ideas I share are valuable for their living power and not for their lineage.

By noting that trial is an exercise in dialectic, we are using another word for "adversary system," or "clash of ideas." Of course, the inequality of resources between opponents, or decider bias, or any number of other things, may make the adversary contest unequal. But our job is to understand that contest so that we may participate in it most effectively.

After all, the process assumes equality of resources. Sometimes a fair judge in a criminal case will actually see that the resource balance is as equal as the system can make it. But the rhetoric of trials is filled with references to equality—giving each side a fair hearing, listening to all the witnesses, not making up your mind until you've heard it all: "You have been sworn as jurors to try the case between John Smith and Priscilla Jones," or "Do you solemnly swear or affirm that you will truly try the cause now on trial between the United States of America and Terry Lynn Nichols, and true deliverance make?" Everybody knows that Terry Lynn Nichols doesn't have anything like the resources that the United States has, and even intoning the ritual oath seems to put him in a bad position. Judges confirm that the ritual and pomp of the courtroom may indeed give jurors the idea that the accused must have done something wrong, rather than conditioning them to be fair and impartial.

If your side is light on resources, then you must seize the advantages that the ideology of adversary procedure gives you. You act "as if" you really have a chance at victory. You try your case so that the jurors may seize hold of their duty and really go behind the facade built by unequal resources. To say this is not to deny the inequality but to suggest a means to rise above it.

If you make a habit of defending underdogs, the system is always ready to lend you an ideology, the better to deny your client justice without the slightest regret. This is a paraphrase of one of Roland Barthes's most trenchant observations, in his essay on criminal justice, "Dominici, or the triumph of Literature." Barthes writes, characterizing the Kantian "as if":

la Justice . . . est toujours disposée à vous prêter un cerveau de rechange pour vous condamner sans remords, et . . . , cornélienne, elle vous peint tel que vous devriez être et non tel que vous êtes.

That is, the system that calls itself Justice is always willing to lend you a spare brain, so as to condemn you without remorse, and in the manner of Corneille, to paint you as you must be and not as you are. We treat the accused, no matter how poor and deprived of understanding, as though he were the conscious and willing author of his acts.

In its fundamental sense, dialectics underpins Darwin's theory of natural selection, materialist theories of history, and indeed many visions of human progress. We speak colloquially but accurately about new ideas opposing old ones and about the social change that comes from such a confrontation. In the dialectical clash, the new synthesis contains elements of both opposing forces that have collided.

It is important to understand dialectics in this more general sense, because many advocates make the silly mistake of assuming that being an adversary means opposing every contention the opponent makes. I say "silly" because in almost every case the two competing versions of events overlap significantly. You don't want to attack at every point. Rather, you want to find the points of identity and difference. You will probably find a somewhat different point of reference from your adversary, from which the same events take on a different meaning.

In social life we can illustrate this by talking about the American Revolution. Never mind the skeptics who say it wasn't a revolution at all. The colonists overthrew the monarchy and established a constitutional system that became the envy of the world. As the Revolutionary War song had it, "the world turn'd upside down." Yet the "new" system traced deep roots in the one it had replaced. Almost every provision of the new Constitution and its Bill of Rights echoed claims for justice that had been in circulation for at least a century. The system of justice itself carried forward most elements of the English one. We called it a revolution, but what we got was a synthesis of the new and the old.

So it is with trials. The jury's verdict gives a victory to one side or the other—or maybe a little to both. But the story that the jury credits must take into account elements of the stories told by both sides. Asking the jurors to reject the opponent's case utterly, with not a single thought to any merit it may have, is to assume an unnecessary and probably impossible burden.

THE PRIMACY OF STORY

Legal literature these days is filled with paeans to "the story," or "the narrative." Everyone has one. The jurors will find one. The advocate had better tell one. The judge will buy into one or make one up to provide a context for decision. The jurors are waiting for one, and once they have locked on to a tentative version of events, they will receive and process all later information with an eye to making it consistent with the story's framework. Does all of this talk about story represent a new insight? No. For thousands of years, writers on rhetoric have insisted on the primacy of topic, of invention.

In this history, dramatists have an easier time than lawyers. When Sophocles wanted to tell a story about just deserts and good intentions, he could move his characters around and put his chosen words into their mouths. A lawyer has to work with evidence of the past facts, limited by an ethical obligation and by the practical sanction that if the jurors (aided by your adversary) catch you telling a fib, they will punish you and your client for it.

In the most fundamental decisions of our daily lives, we put the story first—it has primacy—and from it draw conclusions about results and reasons. A few examples will make the point. In the Judeo-Christian tradition, the Bible begins with the story of creation. It continues with the Jews' sojourn in Egypt and Moses's leadership. We are well into Exodus before God makes a covenant with his people and Moses receives and transmits the law. The collective experience of a people—that is, their story—precedes resolution and revelation. The power of that story is shown again and again, and aspects of it are examined and reexamined to validate claims about morals, ethics, and law.

In the New Testament, Jesus puts himself into the biblical story as the promised Messiah. His work on earth is the culmination of the same story, told differently. Jesus illustrates his teaching with stories that also form part of a basic cultural identity shared by many prospective jurors. Christian principles are, in short, also based on a series of stories. On a somewhat parallel track, speaking of the Western cultural tradition, Greek philosophy begins with an interpretation of nature—*physis*—and continues by overlaying norm—*nomos*.

In other cultures, this primacy of story is also apparent. Young Prince Siddhartha travels, mingles, and endures for years before he is ready to announce his teachings. The prophet Muhammad puts himself into the monotheistic New Testament tradition as the last in a line of prophets.

I am careful not to generalize these insights into a supposed universal collective consciousness. We are talking about jurors in the United States at this moment in historical time, with all of their diversity, yet united in ways that the advocate must discover to persuade twelve of them. Other jurors, in other times and places, are socially conditioned in different ways. In each community where you try cases, the mix of jurors in the venire will be different, and from each venire will come a group with its own particular characteristics.

The classical studies of persuasion are vindicated by modern learning about human perception. I have expressed a central premise of that learning as "Deciders Perceive Whole Stories." Jurors and judges decide cases based on a gestalt, or total picture, from which the decision occurs to them as a just resolution.[1]

For the advocate, the task of persuasion involves several distinct skills. In classical rhetoric[2] these were invention, the choice of topic or story; arrangement; style; memory (which includes using mnemonic devices and demonstrative evidence);[3] and delivery. As Professor Balkin has said, "People attempting to solve a problem need a preexisting framework to get started. They need a way of characterizing a problem and a way of approaching the problem once it is identified."[4]

We can also see the power of story by looking at trials in American history. True, some big cases in the television age blur this insight. Millions of Americans watched *People v. O. J. Simpson,* and Court TV has given gavel-to-verdict coverage of other trials. Some of these cases may qualify as cultural signposts, but they are tainted with elements both bathetic and boring—*soapoperific* might be a good word.

No, I am speaking of trials that affected their generation and in some measure shaped our vision of events and issues. In the Anglo-American tradition, trials have told enduring stories. Let me recall some of these to introduce the next theme, which will of course be "How can each advocate discover in each case the point of reference from which a persuasive story is told?"

STORIES IN FAMOUS TRIALS

In 1735, a colonial newspaper editor named John Peter Zenger published articles criticizing the colonial governor, William Cosby. Cosby got Zenger prosecuted for seditious libel, for it was a crime to criticize government. Zenger could have paid a fine, or perhaps issued an apology, and gone about his business. Zenger's education and background suggest that he did not even write the offending material. The probable authors were his New York lawyers, John Chambers and William Smith. When an arbitrary judge disqualified the local lawyers from the case, Andrew Hamilton of Philadelphia undertook the defense.

Hamilton used a tactic later used by the English advocate Thomas Erskine, in the libel trials of the 1770s.[5] He admitted that Zenger had published the articles and called on the jury to take unto itself the issue of whether they were libelous or not. At that time, English (and colonial) judges believed that the libelous (and therefore seditious) character of the publication was a matter of law and that the only jury issue was whether the defendant was responsible for the publication.

Hamilton's theme was that—for the liberty of the subject—the only safe way to decide libel cases was by the jury's general verdict. He thus spoke over the heads of the judge and prosecutor, urging the jurors in their own self-interest to decide the case and in that interest to recognize that criticism of government was valuable.

> The question before you, Gentlemen of the Jury, is not of small or private concern. It is not the cause of the poor printer, nor of New York alone. No! It may in its consequence affect every freeman that lives under a British government on the main of America. It is the best cause. It is the cause of liberty.

The jury acquitted, and of its verdict Governeur Morris said, "It was the morning star of that liberty which subsequently revolutionized America." Even though we may not remember the participants' names, we recall the colonial struggles over a free press at some level—they form part of our modern sensibility about freedom of expression.

Another historic trial was that of John Brown.[6] He made his reputation as a guerrilla leader of antislavery forces. On October 16, 1859, he led a small "army of emancipation" against the federal arsenal at Harpers Ferry, Virginia, seeking to obtain arms for a slave revolt. His force took hostages but was finally dislodged and captured by a Marine detachment under General Robert E. Lee.

Brown was tried in a Virginia court for treason, murder, and inciting slaves to rebel. He was convicted, and Virginia hanged him on December 2, 1859.

Brown knew that he would not be acquitted. He determined to use his trial to dramatize the irreconcilable division between the forces of slavery and those of freedom. He used the rules of evidence to exclude much consideration of his own personal, business, and political past. He obtained leave of court to present his motivations and objectives. By the time of his trial, Brown was already known to abolitionist leaders and had been praised by some of them, including Frederick Douglass.

Brown showed that he understood to whom he was speaking and how to manipulate the symbols and devices of the courtroom. He was speaking over the heads not only of the judge and prosecutor, but of the jurors as well, to the broad audience of antislavery opinion. He denounced his captors and anyone who would endorse their cause as tools of a sinister force that held people in slavery. One could not, he argued, expect justice from anyone in that courtroom. Brown saw that the legislative and judicial developments of the 1850s had put the slavery issue beyond any hope of compromise. The slave states would secede, or the free states would impose an end to slavery. That was a historic inevitability, seen and preached by many.

Brown portrayed himself as symbolizing and prefiguring that historic inevitability. He did so eloquently. His self-portrayal elevated him to a shared place with Zenger and others. He became the symbol he sought to be.

Professor Robert Ferguson, who wrote a brilliant study of Brown's life and trial, has also described more generally what lawyers and parties are doing when they seek to persuade jurors to accept a story of events. He writes that "the struggle of attorneys to find the best accounts for their clients turns courtroom transcripts into excellent barometers of what is said and thought in a culture at any given moment of time."[7] He notes that "jurors must first recognize the developing contours of a story to accept it."[8] This theme—the historically and culturally defined relationship between speaker and listener—will be treated in Chapter Two. For now, we acknowledge that as advocates we must both study and embody the basic understanding of the world shared by most jurors. Sometimes we do that to ask jurors to validate that understanding; at other times we will ask them to look beyond it. But whether we accept or challenge, we are speaking in a context of shared meaning.[9]

Clarence Darrow and Dudley Field Malone, in the historic Scopes trial, knew they had little chance of a jury acquittal. They tried their case to the audience beyond the courtroom. William Jennings Bryan tried his case to that audience and to the jurors as well.

Professor Ferguson notes that sometimes the story an advocate or party wants to tell is so challenging to accepted views that it is suppressed. In 1800, a group of slaves were tried for insurrection, convicted, and hanged. The surviving record of their trial shows that their leaders were literate students of revolutionary rhetoric. They confronted the tribunal by acknowledging that its decision was inevitable. Yet their leader made clear where he stood by saying "I have nothing more to offer than what General Washington would have to offer, had he been taken by the British and put to trial by them."

In the Oklahoma City bombing case of Terry Nichols, the defendant had been condemned by the media within hours after he was arrested. No juror in Colorado, where the case was moved, was unaware of the main outlines of the proposed government proof. The trial and death sentence of co-defendant Timothy McVeigh had generated more publicity in Colorado than in any other media market, including Oklahoma City.

The jury's acquittal on the main counts of the indictment[10] was the result of formulating a theme—a story, if you understand that means something based on evidence and not imagination—that put the evidence in a certain perspective. "Terry Nichols was building a life, not a bomb." From there we had to cross-examine every witness, blunt every bit of forensic evidence, and build a plausible alternative to the government's theory.

You may tell me that your cases will never risk sundering a fragile American Union, as did that of John Brown, nor point toward a revolution, as did that of Zenger. Hardly the point, I say. And these cases illustrate what I am saying. John Brown's case could be seen as simply the trial of a desperate, bankrupt man who committed an ordinary crime and deserved to be punished for it. Indeed, one wonders why the prosecutors and judges did not make more of an effort to portray it so. Brown's genius was to transform his criminal trial into a morality play about the most basic issues confronting the American people.

Every case you try should be about issues that move jurors. The plaintiff in your torts case seeks a fair deal from a corporation that ignores public health and safety. Your sexual harassment client wants corporate America to bring decent conditions to the workplace. If you are defending, the jury is the institution that can protect all of us from the expense of needless lawsuits and inflated claims. If you cannot summon up a moral to your story, better to settle the case or not to bring it at all. I am reminded of Mark Twain's dedication to Huckleberry Finn:

Notice

Persons attempting to find a motive in this narrative will be prosecuted; persons attempting to find a moral in it will be banished; persons attempting to find a plot in it will be shot.

ELEMENTS OF CLASSICAL RHETORIC

We understand the primacy of story in human communication, perception, and persuasion. We also know that jurors are moved to accept one story over another by emotional elements in the narrative. Rather than rely on trial consultants to help us shape the story we will tell, we can profitably return to a classical understanding of persuasion. Great advocates, including Edward Bennett Williams, were schooled in classical rhetoric and applied the lessons well.

We all employ "rhetoric" in the classical sense of persuasive discourse. This is what we do every day. We are in this regard like the man in Molière's play who exclaimed: "My goodness! For more than forty years I have been speaking prose without knowing it."[11] When we speak, we are, like it or not, condemned to signify. Our words, gestures, and exhibits in court mean something to the jurors, just as they do in ordinary speech. But to become better persuaders, we must deconstruct or dissect our presentations. To do this usefully, we need a taxonomy—words to describe what we are doing. We can then give those words content and meaning as we analyze the process of persuasion. By such analysis, we can do better as participants in the process. The utility of classical rhetoric is that the words lie ready to hand.

In the Western tradition, the study begins with Aristotle,[12] but its roots can be traced even earlier. Then Roman disciples such as Cicero and Quintilian enlarged on the subject. Aristotle's treatise on rhetoric contains an extensive discussion of emotions—all to the end of understanding the role they play in persuasion.[13]

Classical rhetoric is divided into five parts, some of which we have already encountered. They are:

1. Invention—*inventione* in Latin, *topos* in Greek— referring to the topic, point of view, and structure of argument. We might call this the choice of the basic story and its elements.

2. Arrangement, or the order in which the argument will be presented. In Chapter Three, Part II, we reproduce Edward Bennett Williams's opening statement in *United States v. Connally*. Williams worked on the opening over several weeks, beginning with a planned order and then filling in details. Arrangement is important because you want your hearers ready for the main message at the time you deliver it. In a symphony, the first movement generally is in sonata form; this convention helps the hearer to identify and trace the composer's themes as they are introduced and as they reappear.

3. Style. From Roman times until early in this century, rhetorical "styles" were the object of detailed study. Writers thought that various styles—varying in formality and mode of expression—fit different set-

tings and circumstances. It remains true that a jury trial calls forth a different style of discourse than an oral argument to a court or a dinner-table conversation. However, a proper style begins with the advocate's own personality, rather than being engrafted by study or imitation. In contemporary America, a more informal and direct style is appropriate than was the case even fifty years ago. Thus, the study of style for its own sake is self-defeating, for one may be tempted to adopt mannerisms that put barriers between the advocate and the jurors. Style may involve gesture and placement as well as figures of speech.

4. Memory. The classical writers regarded memory as subsidiary to invention and arrangement.[14] A part of memory has to do with the speaker, who must have learned the discourse well enough to pronounce it effectively. To assist, one might use mnemonic devices, from the Greek word for memory. Some speakers think to avoid the issue by writing out their openings and closings, or even all of their questions on direct and cross-examination. This is always a bad idea. *Memory* can also refer to being memorable or remembered or retained. In *Examining Witnesses,* I referred to ways in which a lawyer might put down markers that could later be recalled in argument, by using demonstrative evidence, vivid words, or particular forms of expression. This is the more important sense of memory—fashioning the argument in ways that its main elements can be recalled. In jury trials, the jurors vote only after deliberating. Usually this takes some time, and your champions in the jury room must have something to hold on to, to recall, and to present to their opponents.

5. Delivery, the presentation. One unites the other four elements at a specific time and place.

In Greece and Rome, at least among literate free citizens, the study of these principles was regarded as essential to participation in public discourse. Those who represented people or points of view in public forums studied these principles intensely. Their reported speeches, such as those of Cicero, still repay our careful study. There are many possible reasons why such study has lost pride of place in modern legal education. Perhaps the retreat of rhetorical study into formality and mannerism hastened its exodus. Perhaps the "case method," which turned attention to appellate opinions rather than the process of persuasion, played a role.

The disappearance of education in rhetoric from law schools has robbed a generation of lawyers of tools forged long ago and honed in dutiful service. Properly understood, the study of rhetoric illuminates the intrinsic connection between discourse and reasoned decision. More precisely, we can study the ways in which reasoned decision is helped or hindered by certain forms of argument.

We have all heard *rhetoric* used in a pejorative sense, often modified by *mere*. To say that a speaker uses "rhetorical flourishes" may not be a compliment. Neither this book nor the proper study of rhetoric itself provide recipes for exaggerated speechifying, much less for intentional distortion. It is true that the study of persuasion may be used to conceal deceit as well as to illuminate truth. In that sense, rhetoric may be value-neutral. Whether it is "good" or "bad" will depend on the purposes for which it is used. Identifying and defining "purpose" is one function of legal ethics. In the dialectic of adversary advocacy, the study of rhetorical principles helps truth to emerge through rigorous testing.

INVENTION: PRINCIPLES OF THE STORY

I have often urged lawyers to map out a closing argument in the very first stages of working on a case. I have received some irate letters from lawyers who wonder how one can do that without having all the facts in hand. Isn't it irresponsible to be working on a closing argument so early? The answer is no.

Unless you are appointed by the court in a criminal case, you will make a decision to accept a client's matter, or to file litigation. Inevitably, you do not know all the facts when you make this initial decision. You know only enough to commit resources and to have a probable view of the theory on which relief is available. That is the point to imagine you are summing up. You will identify the holes in factual or legal research that need to be filled. Then every time there is action in the case, take a quick look and see that the overall theory you have developed still works. In working the case, you say its story over and over.

Let us look at an example of finding, developing, and then telling the story.

The Air Force major sat in my office with tears in her eyes. She was about to be charged with sodomy and conduct unbecoming an officer and a lady. Conviction would ruin the career she had spent twenty-two years building and might forfeit the pension she had earned and even send her to prison. The felony of sodomy, under the Uniform Code of Military Justice, includes any oral-genital contact between people of the same or opposite sex, whether married or not.

The Air Force proposed to charge that the major had carried on a two-year affair with a civilian woman, Pamela, who lived in her home. When the affair cooled, so the allegations went, the major demanded that the woman move out. When the woman refused, and instead threatened legal action, the major allegedly brandished a pistol and threatened her life.

Two lawyers—one military and one civilian—had urged the major to plea bargain. They couldn't think of a story that might raise a reasonable doubt before the military officers who are the "jury" in a general court-martial. Of course, we made the pretrial arguments about equal protection, privacy, and a Department of Defense policy that made private consensual sexual conduct none of the Air Force's proper concern. We made those arguments to protect the record in case an appeal was necessary. But at trial those issues would not be our story, our moral drama.

The first lawyers on the case rightly saw that the testimony of the alleged lover/victim was, if believed, conclusive. The lover/victim, Pamela, had made consistent statements to civilian law enforcement officers about the alleged assault and after several sessions with Air Force investigators had told the story of alleged sexual liaison in great detail.

We first had to ask to whom we would tell this story. In a general court-martial of an officer, the "jury" consists of up to nine officers who outrank the accused. So we would see colonels and lieutenant colonels. Each of these career officers would have a college degree and some postgraduate work. Each would have served in the Air Force for at least twenty years. They would all have some interest in military history and customs. They would look across the courtroom and see the major, with her medals, and see reflected a distinguished service record. Or, the military base being a fairly tight community, and the case having been covered by the media, they would already have some idea of the issues.

You will notice in all these historic cases that "to whom" must have been on the advocate's mind early on. To be sure, John Brown knew that the "in court" judgment would go against him. He was talking to somebody other than the roomful of deciders. In most cases, however, you will want the more immediate pleasure of victory. Andrew Hamilton wanted both the immediate and the long-term win—and he addressed the jury in terms that helped gain both.

In the usual case, you will anticipate facing a jury whose demographic composition is in a general way predictable. If that prediction displeases you, choose another forum to begin with or seek to undo your adversary's choice.

In the major's case, we doubted that a gay rights approach would avail us. We were confident that the jurors would agree that privacy in sexual matters deserves respect, by the military itself and by individuals keeping their sexual preferences to themselves.

The standard of proof was "beyond a reasonable doubt." We might have made the classic defense error of analyzing the weaknesses of the prosecution's case, deciding how best to reveal and emphasize them, and stopping there. That would have been a mistake, as it is always a mistake for a defendant to rely solely on weaknesses in the plaintiff's case. The jurors will, one must assume, apply the burden of proof. However, they will want a context—a how and a why.

The heart of the prosecution's case would be testimony by Pamela, the alleged victim and sexual partner, describing in the same detail as at the preliminary hearing her sexual liaison with the major in Virginia, followed by Pamela's moving to San Antonio to share the major's house and bed. The prosecution would produce letters and cards allegedly from the major to Pamela. Some of the letters were affectionate. Others were suggestive ("I can't wait to see you face to face. Or face to . . ."). One card was rather graphic and spoke of tongues. A handwriting analyst was scheduled to testify.

In addition, the Air Force investigators who took Pamela's statement would produce a prior consistent statement if necessary, and a San Antonio police officer would testify that Pamela had called and complained that the major had brandished a gun at her. A former (and perhaps current) lover of Pamela's would say that she saw the major and Pamela being affectionate and that the major said at a public gathering that she was going to "marry" Pamela.

If we could undermine Pamela's credibility, we could win. We would also have to deal with the corroborating evidence. It would not be enough merely to show that Pamela had some animus, bias, motive to falsify. It never is. All witnesses are biased, if only in favor of their own prior version. That prior version becomes "their truth." We must show why the witness is not to be trusted on a point—we must develop a reason.[15]

As we pondered, we received a gift. The prosecution produced Pamela's journal for the year in question. The journal corroborated the brandishing charge—for it contained an account consistent with Pamela's present story—but it proved the prosecution's undoing. Here in Pamela's hand was nearly a year's worth of reflections—the year leading up to her leaving the major's house and a few weeks beyond. In the diary, Pamela confessed her hatred and resentment of the major. She described her dream as being able to live off someone else's earnings. She explained that she wanted to live in the major's house rent-free until she could get around to applying for medical school, and that by having a Texas residence she would avoid out-of-state tuition. She described filing a false insurance claim and forging a signature on a medical school recommendation letter. She wrote of threatening to ruin the major's career by "exposing" her as a lesbian. The diary was written in a hand that resembled in many ways the handwritten portions of the more salacious of the correspondence Pamela claimed the major had authored and sent.

I said that we needed to undermine Pamela's credibility. Not quite. We needed to do that while maintaining the major's dignity as a military officer. We were not going to put the major on the witness stand. In criminal cases, that is an acceptable option—tactically and legally.[16] The major sat throughout the trial in uniform with her medals on her chest. She faced the court members—the military jury. Her response to the testimony being offered was visible. She did not shake her head, laugh, or otherwise display emotion. She was attentive, respectful, and at times dourly and subtly dubious.

In opening statements, I told our story. The major, having served for more than twenty years, was being accused by Pamela. Pamela's story did not make sense, was contradicted by her own diary, and was motivated by a demonstrable desire to inflict hurt. Perhaps knowing that Pamela's story was not convincing, the prosecutors would bring other witnesses, whom they would claim would add to Pamela's version. Not so. Everything these witnesses would say depended on Pamela's credibility. Pamela's friend repeated what Pamela told her, using the excited utterance hearsay exception. A police officer summoned by Pamela days later could not repeat Pamela's story but admitted that Pamela did not ask him to search the house for a gun and that he had not done such a search. He had checked and seen that in fact the major did not have a gun registered in her name. Photographs of Pamela and the major did not show them in any compromising positions, and the only one slightly suggestive showed the major—fully dressed—with her arm around a man.

The handwriting expert from the Texas Department of Public Safety would not, I said, be able to add anything. I left that part vague, because the expert's report was riddled with errors, and we did not want to reveal the defense theory about the letters and cards.

Pamela's direct was predictable—describing sexual encounters with the major and purporting to tell the story of their living together. Cross-examination took longer than the direct. I took Pamela one by one over the relevant parts of her diary.

One of Pamela's friends took the stand to describe a party in Virginia at which the major supposedly told the guests that she was going to marry Pamela. There were some pictures of the party, which showed fully clothed people of both sexes smiling. The friend had not told this story to investigators the first few times she spoke with them.

The handwriting "expert" did not do well for the prosecutors. He had mixed up the handwriting samples, showing some as being both the major's handwriting and not identifiable. He had made elementary errors in evaluating the handwriting sample given by the major. He had to acknowledge that the most provocative writings—on greeting cards that Pamela claimed the major had sent—were done with a different pen and in a different style (hand-printing rather than handwriting) than the letters from the major to Pamela.

Eventually—in closing argument—I wanted to argue that Pamela and not the major had written the inscriptions on the cards, but I did not ask the expert about this. After all, handwriting comparison can be done by the lay fact finder as well as by expert witnesses. A prosecution expert was not likely to agree with our assessment of the writing.

To find a theme, we cast our minds back to an oration of Cicero, *Pro Murena.* Cicero defended General Murena on charges of corruption. The themes were military versus civilian accusers and the dignity of military service. Of course, any civilian accuser may destroy a military career with a true tale of wrongdoing. But Pamela had threatened the major's military career with extortionate demands for money and lodging long before she told a story of a lesbian affair. The parallel with Murena's case, where civilians jealous of the general's power had made their accusations, was therefore clear.

In any jury case, one wants to have a theme with which the jurors will identify. One casts the case as championing a set of agreed values against an adversary who threatens those values. Sometimes the values are simply those of fairness, burden or proof, and neutral application of accepted principles. In the major's case, the ill-motivated civilian accuser was one strong element. Another element was the threat to military careers from allegations so easy to make and so difficult to dispel. If statistical evidence is any guide, most of the officers on the panel would at some time have had sexual relations other than with a spouse. Similarly, it is likely that most of the officers—in or outside their marriages—had engaged in some form of oral sex. The Uniform Code of Military Justice provision criminalized as "sodomy" all oral-genital contact, consensual or not. A sexual partner would therefore have a powerful weapon—the threat to report that he or she had been kissed below the belt.

Relying on our theme, I cross-examined Pamela on her admitted hatred, her admitted threats, and her admitted wrongdoing. I examined the officers who had questioned her on her delay in making the central accusation, and from the police officers Pamela had called I brought out that Pamela had not sought to have the major's house searched. From Pamela herself, I showed that after allegedly being threatened she came back and lived in the house for a few more days.

Then in closing argument, we could weave these elements around our central theme. After all, one could not cite Cicero in the opening statement, lest one be thought too argumentative. One could not refer to principles of law about credibility, for the fact finder had not yet been instructed.

The major's case illustrates all the decisions you must make in choosing the story. A basic decision must be based on the theory of minimal contradiction.[17] This theory has different names: KISS (keep it simple, stupid), don't assume a burden of persuasion that you do not have, everybody on the other side is not a damn liar, and so on.

Remember that the jurors come into court with a set of intuitions, sensibilities, and points of view. We might call these prejudices, and if any juror possesses them to an unacceptable degree we challenge for cause or peremptorily. We are fortunate to have *voir dire* and challenges, for these tools give us far more control over who decides the case than a speaker before a public assembly in ancient Greece or Rome—or even a candidate for office or member of a deliberative assembly.

For the jurors who are selected and sworn, we dignify their presuppositions by calling them common sense, or we work to identify them and show how they cannot properly be applied in our case. Thus, the first canon of minimal contradiction is that our story should be one that jurors are ready to accept. Ideally, you will not challenge their basic assumptions—or not all of them. In the major's case, we had to accept that the jurors assumed sodomy to be a crime and that some of them thought it an abomination against God. The military judge would instruct on the first of these principles, and *voir dire* revealed the second. We might have put the issue directly and asked for a nullifying verdict. This is an honorable tradition in criminal cases, but it takes a jury convinced that a certain stance is so morally right that one ought properly to defy the judge's interpretation of strict law. We decided not to pursue this strategy—it would have been foredoomed.

But the legal rules of conduct were not the only principles in play. There was also the idea of reasonable doubt—of the prosecution's burden. The principal witness was a civilian, accusing an officer with a distinguished career. So rather than confront the prosecution's and jurors' principles head on, we counterpoised them to another set of equally compelling ones. Jurors are mindful of their oath. And they understand that they do represent a particular community— in this case, a military one.

A second form of contradiction is with the story being put forth by our adversary. Both sides are working with almost the same body of data—allowing for whatever secrets remain in these days of open civil discovery. Why and how must our story differ from the adversary's? When you read Edward Bennett Williams's opening statement in Chapter Three, note how most of it relates evidence that will not be contradicted. He has chosen to emphasize different items of evidence than has the government and has put them in a different context, but he has narrowed the scope of dispute to what is really important, and that is the credibility of just one witness.

As we work toward a theme, we must first examine all of the adversary's evidence, and all the witnesses on their side, for material favorable to us. "Even their witnesses tell us," "even their documents say"—these are refrains we begin to develop. Perhaps my desire to mine the other side's ore has its basis in criminal defense practice, where the "reasonable doubt" standard and conventional wisdom often make the defense presentation of "its own" witnesses truncated or absent. But I am convinced that it has more general application. You are looking for the minimum perceptual shift that brings the entire story in line with your viewpoint.

For those who study martial arts, even the less violent ones, there is a helpful image. Suppose an assailant aims a blow at you. To maximize your own power, use his energy to increase your own. Take the arm that is delivering the blow and pull it through and beyond its intended target. Continue the motion until you have upended the assailant and he is flat on his back.

In harmony with this teaching, do not label as liars all the opposing witnesses. It may be that some of them have forgotten or are misunderstood or did not have as good a chance to observe as your witnesses. All the documents on the other side may be authentic, relevant, original, and either nonhearsay or covered by a hearsay exception. Yet the essential meaning of those documents may support your side, as can be seen by looking at other documents or having a perceptive witness provide needed context.

To illustrate, let us take an ordinary breach of contract case.[18] The plaintiff, Brendan Newton, sent a story idea to World Film Enterprises and had one meeting with a WFE vice president, Wilson Turner. The story was in the form of a "treatment," a standard format in the industry for pitching a film idea. Turner made notes of the meeting, which included the words *half a point of BO*—presumably box office—*screen credit,* and *memorialize a deal.* WFE is about to release a film that resembles Newton's idea. WFE says that it never acted on Newton's proposal because it already had a similar idea in the works and that it never made a deal with Newton for screen credit, one-half of 1 percent of the gross proceeds, or anything else.

Newton claims that WFE stole his idea and that Turner agreed to pay him the 1/2 percent and give him a screen credit if his idea was used.

Newton's story is straightforward—a contract was formed, and he wants its benefit. A deal is a deal. No formality, no writing is required to make a contract.

The defense to this cannot simply be that it didn't happen the way Newton says. That is an important thing to say, but it makes the case into a collision of memory and veracity between Newton and the executives of WFE. No, WFE wants to say not only that Newton did not have a deal, but also that neither he nor anybody with an ounce of knowledge about the film industry would think that he did.

The defense will look for documents—letters, memoranda—by Newton that cast doubt on his version. More important, the defense has a story to tell—a story about stories. Many people would like to think that if they had a good idea and told it to somebody, an obligation would be created. The hearer, in this version, must account to the teller for any profit made from the idea. The WFE folks had better show that everybody in their industry—and that would have to include Newton—knows that ideas are protectable property only if steps are taken to protect them. Not only must they tell a story about their industry; they must do so without arrogance and in a way that makes it fair to stick Newton with the consequences of that story.

In the telling of such a story, one can accept most of the strictly factual assertions the plaintiff is making. One is looking at those facts from a different point of view. And point of view is the initial and very important decision that every storyteller makes.

When you have worked on the story, and when you finally have the evidence and legal rules in hand, you have a trial plan. Do not lightly depart from your trial plan. "That's my story, and I'm stickin' to it," as the saying goes. Too often I have seen trial lawyers buffeted by the opponent's evidence, who respond by starting to make hurried changes to their trial plan. They compound the hurt by looking fearful.

DEMONIZATION

John Brown demonized slavery. Prosecutors seeking a death penalty must demonize the defendant—make him or her something other than, less than, human, so that jurors will feel comfortable ordering somebody to take the defendant from a cell one day and pump poison into the veins until death.

We are all prone to demonize. We might call it by the more polite term *stereotyping*. Ben Stein's book *The View from Sunset Boulevard* deals with the stereotypes perpetuated by television—the sleazy lawyer, the underhanded banker, and so on. We have our own lists—computer geeks, greedy plaintiffs, insurance defense lawyers, corrupt corporations, corrupt labor officials, and so on.

Jurors have their lists. One purpose of *voir dire* is to find out what's on everybody's list.

Your opponent wants to say, "This is just another instance of ___" and then fill in the blank. Be candid: you would like to do the same thing. Research shows, for example, that a local corporation with a good reputation, whose advertisements and delivery vehicles are all over town, starts off with an advantage in the jurors' eyes. In a society saturated by media, image counts as the relevant reality.

You have two options, depending on your case. You can go with the current, or you can swim someplace else. If you are trying the case of an injured worker in a working-class community, favorable images are already in the minds of many jurors. You are going to talk about what this case means in "our" community.

But if your case presents an unattractive client, somebody the jurors will "love to hate," then you must shift the argument. Jurors care about the facts and the law. They care about their oaths to be fair. From *voir dire* onward, you must make a virtue of your client's unpopularity. There is a long tradition of such contrarian advocacy. It begins, in our culture, with four key Bible verses:

- Exodus 22:21: Thou shalt neither vex a stranger, nor oppress him: for ye were strangers in the land of Egypt.
- Exodus 23:9: Also thou shalt not oppress a stranger: for ye know the heart of a stranger, seeing ye were strangers in the land of Egypt.

- Leviticus 19:34: But the stranger that dwelleth with you shall be unto you as one born among you, and thou shalt love him as thyself; for ye were strangers in the land of Egypt.
- Deuteronomy 10:19: Love ye therefore the stranger: for ye were strangers in the land of Egypt.

Your story, your claim for justice, for such a client, is based on a set of transcendent and shared values. If you represent the "other," you must make the "other" into "us."

The advocate who seeks to demonize the opposition runs a great risk. As the trial goes on—and longer trials make it harder for the tactic to succeed—the jurors become caught up in the process of rational inquiry. They begin to see all the players in the courtroom drama in human terms. And with time, the words of Alexander Pope become apt:

> Vice is a monster of so frightful mien,
> As to be hated needs but to be seen;
> Yet seen too oft, familiar with her face,
> We first endure, then pity, then embrace.[19]

NOTES

1. MICHAEL E. TIGAR, EXAMINING WITNESSES ch. 1 (1992) (hereinafter EXAMINING WITNESSES).

2. See JOHN HOLLANDER, LEGAL RHETORIC, in LAW'S STORIES 176 (Peter Brooks & Paul Gewirtz, eds. 1996) (hereinafter LAW'S STORIES).

3. As discussed in EXAMINING WITNESSES, making your presentation memorable includes the use of prologues, loops, and transitions in direct examination. EXAMINING WITNESSES ch 2.

4. J. M. BALKIN, A NIGHT IN THE TOPICS: THE REASON OF LEGAL RHETORIC AND THE RHETORIC OF LEGAL REASON, in LAW'S STORIES 211, at 214–15.

5. For a discussion of the semiotics of sedition trials in historical context, see Michael E. Tigar, *Crime-Talk, Rights-Talk and Doubletalk*, 65 TEX. L. REV. 101 (1986). See also Michael E. Tigar, The Trial of John Peter Zenger (1986) (a dramatization).

6. On the John Brown trial and its semiotic/historical significance, see Robert Ferguson, *Story and Transcription in the Trial of John*

Brown, 6 YALE J. L. & THE HUMANITIES 37 (1994), discussed in ROBERT WEISBERG, PROCLAIMING TRIALS AS NARRATIVES, in LAW'S STORIES 61, at 79–82.

7. ROBERT FERGUSON, UNTOLD STORIES IN THE LAW, in LAW'S STORIES 84, at 87. This essay by Professor Ferguson tells the story of slaves on trial in Virginia in 1800 for rebelling. The story chillingly captures the slave leaders' grasp of the social, political, and cultural significance of their trial.

8. *Id.* at 87.

9. *Id.* at 88.

10. The jury convicted of conspiracy and of involuntary manslaughter of federal agents. It acquitted of use of a weapon of mass destruction, arson of a federal building, first-degree murder of federal agents, and second-degree murder of federal agents.

11. In the French original, it is *"Par ma foi! Il y a plus de quarante ans que je dis de la prose sans que j'en susse rien."* Molière, *Le Bourgeois Gentilhomme, acte 1, scène 4.*

12. Or perhaps earlier, if one credits the accounts of one Corax, who is said to have taught rhetoric in Siracusa. See source notes in EXAMINING WITNESSES, at 303, and works there cited.

13. See JOHN HOLLANDER, LEGAL RHETORIC, in LAW'S STORIES 176, at 181.

14. *See also* J. M. BALKIN, *supra,* in LAW'S STORIES, at 273 (notes). In this restatement of principles, I credit the essay by John Hollander cited above in LAW'S STORIES at 181.

15. EXAMINING WITNESSES ch. 9.

16. EXAMINING WITNESSES ch. 5.

17. EXAMINING WITNESSES ch. 8.

18. I wrote up this idea as a short story, under the pseudonym Edward Michaels: *The Lawyer Who Broke the Retaining Wall,* 18 LITIGATION 27 (Fall 1991).

19. AN ESSAY ON MAN, Epistle II, l. 217.

Chapter Two

Beyond Invention: The Speaker and the Hearer

I agree with those who say that communication is context.[1] To convince jurors, we must take a certain position toward them and understand how they regard us and what we are saying. We must, in short, define the speaker and hearer in a particular context of time and place. To understand how to do this, we will have to toss some intellectual baggage overboard. In a trial, the lawyer must be a narrator, not quite omniscient, but in command of the evidence and aware at all times of the impact the evidence should be having on the jurors. We say "should be having" because we cannot actually know.

As lawyers, we fool ourselves into believing that words have some fixed meaning that does not depend on the time, place, speaker, hearer, and system of social organization. We sometimes argue that a document "speaks for itself" or that a contract is "clear on its face." If such expressions have any meaning, it must be:

1. the document contains enough clues to its author, its circumstances, and its intended audience that we can upon reading it put ourselves into the place of its author; or
2. the contract was made between people who understood all of its terms, and we can know enough of its context to tell what they must have understood.

Of course neither of these assertions holds true, save in the rarest of cases. Most "integrated" contracts that contain clauses saying that the contract's written words constitute the whole bargain are not negotiated at all. They are standard forms drafted by lawyers and signed by people who don't understand the meaning or purpose of many of the terms. Saying that a contract is clear on its face does not say anything about communication, but rather expresses a rule of law—founded on the objective theory of contract. And even an integrated instrument must be construed in light of its context.

When we say that a document "speaks for itself," we are also expressing a rule of law, in this case of evidence. This is the "best evidence," or "original writings" rule. The writing is the preferred evidence of its contents. We take secondary evidence of contents only if the original—or its duplicate— is missing through no fault of the proponent.

Of course, we do not really let the document "speak for itself"—not if we are trial lawyers with a grain of sense. We prove the circumstances of its making with all the detail permitted by the rules on hearsay and personal knowledge. We want the jurors to know how to hear the document when it "speaks for itself."

And we don't let the document just lie there and tell its story. We "publish" the document in the way we think is most effective: reading it aloud; having a witness read it aloud; choosing portions of it, subject to Federal Rule of Evidence 106 (the rule of completeness); putting it up on a screen; passing out copies to the jurors.

The point of all this analysis is that the advocate does not let "orphaned communications" loose in the courtroom. Every communication must have a recognizable voice or source and must be seen to have been made at a certain time and place. We know that the meaning of words is vitally determined by who said them, to whom, and in what context.

Stanley Fish has written brilliantly on this theme. In one of his essays, he describes a slip of paper in a book he received, carrying the inscription "with the compliment of the author." Fish imagines all the different ways in which such a sentiment might have caused the book to be sent his way—from the author's genuine desire that he have the book to the publisher's commercially motivated desire to have the book in Fish's hands, perhaps to gain it favorable mention.[2]

We know this principle to hold true in at least some important trial contexts. The hearsay rule tells us that out-of-court declarations cannot generally be trusted to "speak for themselves." We think it is not just unseemly but dangerous—the "hearsay dangers"—to let these utterances in without some guarantee that they will not do mischief. The notion is that the jurors should, by preference, hear only statements of fact made by witnesses who are there before them. Such witnesses show us their demeanor, and their meaning, memory, perception, and veracity can be tested by cross-examination.[3]

Indeed, when a hearsay declaration comes in, the opponent can cross-examine the witness to provide as much context as possible and can even introduce extrinsic evidence about the declarant to the same extent as if the declarant were on the stand.[4]

Indeed, no document comes in for its truth unless it meets one of the hearsay exceptions. So the law recognizes some limits on this "speak for itself" concept. The document must be (A) authentic, (R) relevant, an (O) original writing, and (H) either not admitted for its truth or covered by a hearsay exception. AROH does not make an acronym, but the initials may help. You could rearrange them as HOAR, which has the virtue of suggesting the dull grayness of this area of law, but the order of initials makes some difference in thinking about the issue.

I explore this theme at greater length later in this chapter. For now, one can generalize from documents—which are evidence of past communication—to the structure of the case. Just as there is no abstract communication, there is no abstract justice. You will win your case because you tell a story that convinces a discrete group of people—the jurors—who have a discrete group of preconceptions, ideals, and preoccupations. These people are united by some shared values about the justice system—perhaps fewer and different ones than you think. They are united by respect for the symbols they see in the courtroom and by the oath they take to listen to the evidence and heed the judge's instructions on the law. By similar token, each of these individuals brings something different to the process, and the expanded access to jury service makes those "somethings" increasingly diverse.[5]

Once we understand that context is paramount, we organize our work in a certain way. We view the client's version from an imaginary viewpoint of a potential jury. We develop and test themes for those who will have that viewpoint.

In Chapter One, I noted that you usually have some choice of forum in litigation. If you are stuck in a forum where the odds are against you, there are two rules to follow:

First, be realistic and courageous. Edward Bennett Williams told the story of Bernard Goldfine, accused in the media of having paid off President Eisenhower's administrative assistant, Sherman Adams. Goldfine summoned the young Williams to a meeting, with an eye to retaining him. At the meeting were Goldfine's secretary and a young in-house lawyer named Slobodkin. Goldfine mercilessly ordered Slobodkin about, setting him the most menial tasks, such as getting coffee or fetching the newspaper. After Goldfine outlined his activities, including failure to file tax returns, Williams gave him a candid assessment: "Mr. Goldfine, you don't have a defense."

"Defense! Defense! Of course I don't have a defense. If I had a defense, I'd get Slobodkin to represent me."

On the other hand, enough cases that looked impossible at the outset have yet yielded a victory. Enough, that is, to understand that "realistic" requires judgment and sometimes patience. After you have understood the case, trying to settle it may be the best course. We know that more than 90 percent of cases—civil and criminal—are settled.

Sometimes you cannot settle the difficult case. This happens a lot on the criminal side. The prosecution wants too much, maybe the death penalty. That was surely the situation that faced John Brown. Or maybe settling involves giving up some important principle; maybe that was why John Peter Zenger went to trial, or maybe he and his allies feared that his case was the beginning of a planned campaign to silence the governor's opponents. Sometimes a civil litigant cannot afford to settle—the stakes are too high or the consequences somehow too great. So, be realistic.

Second, try your case *in* and *beyond* the courtroom at the same time. So many great advocates have faced the hostile court or jury that the lesson can be drawn by example. Fidel Castro, speaking to the tribunal that condemned him for the assault on the Moncada Barracks, said, "History will absolve me." John Brown made his trial, the conclusion of which he knew, into an indictment of slavery. That was also the road chosen by the rebel slaves in a famous Virginia trial.[6] They were speaking as well to a world outside and to hearers even into the next generations.

Few of us will find ourselves in trials with such high stakes or with an influence reaching to so far a horizon. Many of us will, however, try cases seeking to change the law in some way. We will try these cases *in* courtrooms but also *beyond* them; only our definition of *beyond* will be chosen to fit the occasion. We may be trying to speak to the community about a problem. Like the civil rights litigants of the 1960s in the American South, we may be using the litigation to help organize a disenfranchised group. We may be thinking that our case will attract the legislature's attention. More prosaically, the trial court may be a way station to the court of appeals— a necessary stop that, had we a choice, we would not make.

Talking about *beyond* in this way reminds me of the old saw, "The lawyer who tries the case with an eye on the court of appeals will surely have to go there." There is little necessary truth in this assertion and much implicit false-hood. You had better have an eye on the court of appeals—in the sense of making proper objections to "preserve the record"—or you will quickly learn the meaning of *waiver, deliberate bypass* and that most weasel-like of phrases, *plain error.* The nugget of truth is this: jurors are often a lot more open to ideas about justice than you may suppose. Imagine John Peter Zenger's surprise when he was actually acquitted.

By thinking of your case as in and beyond the courtroom, you may get more from the jury than you thought possible. For the jurors, this courtroom symbolism with all its legal rules is strange and somewhat alienating. Usually you want to remind the jurors of the limits that law puts on all of us in the process. Sometimes, however, you wish to pose them a challenge to think of the case as an opportunity to do justice and in so thinking to approach interpretation of legal rules in a new way. Jurors have the power to do this, particularly by acquitting in criminal cases. Power aside, we know that when jurors deliberate they think in terms of a just result, usually before pondering how to find a result that fits the legal formula they have been given. For this reason alone, the study of cases where lawyers speak in and beyond the courtroom is worth the effort.

In sum, this jury in this courtroom forms only one part of the context of speaker and hearer in which your case will be tried.

This observation is, however, only the beginning. Despite the variations among speakers and hearers, there are certain universal principles of persuasion that can be learned and applied. These principles are not a recipe or a bunch of answers. Rather, they present the advocate with a series of choices that must be faced and made in every case. Granted, we would all prefer to remember than to think. No such lux-ury is afforded the advocate. Having seen the primacy of story, let us examine some of these choices.

ROUND CHARACTERS AND
FLAT CHARACTERS[7]

Any story is peopled with protagonists and observers. There will also be incidental characters who will have something more or less important to contribute. An incidental character may simply identify a document or may play an important role as, for example, an expert witness.

As you think of retelling the story in summation, you cannot expect the jurors to remember and care about every detail of every witness's life. Nor would you wish them to do so, for you would risk cluttering the story with unnecessary detail. Like the dramatist, you will spend time and energy making only a few characters "round," in the sense of deeply exploring their motivations, background, needs, strengths, and weaknesses. These are the characters with whom you wish the jurors to identify, either to embrace and sponsor them or to reject them. You want the jurors to recall the flat characters, but only as connected to some event, trait, or object.

To illustrate, consider this case—Mary Johnson, an African-American, has long worked for Barkis Industries. She is in charge of purchasing. She is thirty-five years old, divorced and the mother of two children: a daughter, seven, and a son, five. Ms. Johnson retains you to sue Barkis and her immediate superior, Thomas Copperfield, for racial discrimination in promotional and pay policies. In our first look at this situation, assume you have rejected the idea of a class action—you will try this case on the theory that Ms. Johnson was denied raises and promotions due to the racial bias of Copperfield, acquiesced in by upper-level management.

The trial will feature dozens of witnesses. You must decide how to present these witnesses—yours and the opponents'—memorably and persuasively. Ms. Johnson must be a round character. You must present all the details of her qualifications, her preparation for this job, her aspirations, and the unjust events at work. You have no choice in this regard, because the defense will also present her as a round character, though possessing different characteristics. They will wish to show her as unprepared, unqualified, ill motivated. Unless the other side is stupid, some of the negative aspects will be supported by evidence; were this not so, the case would settle short of trial.

By the same token, Mr. Copperfield must also be a round character. The other side will present him as thoughtful, reasonable, careful. The evidence may offer you choices about how to present him. Is he the architect of these wrongful acts, harboring an active racial bias? Or is he going along with a policy—tacit or expressed—from those in the hierarchy above him, willing to advance himself at the expense of others? If you make the latter choice, and the evidence is there, you may want to introduce another "round" character: one of Copperfield's superiors, who directs events while staying in the background.

The point is that you must—early on—choose your major characters and identify their motivations. This is why you must start work on each case by thinking about your summation. Every day, or every week, pick up the file and "say your case."

Speaking at a law firm luncheon, I was shown rhe firm's state-of-the-art moot courtroom. A partner was preparing to use the courtroom to work on opening and closing argument. Trial was only weeks away. I wanted to know whether the lawyers had used the courtroom when the case first came to the office, to test out whether their story fit the known facts and to see if their characters fit together. They had not.

Maybe one doesn't need to get a moot courtroom early in the case; there may be simpler alternatives. I was appointed to a criminal case, and I began to sift through the initial police reports and talk to the defendant and his family. I took a long walk with a good friend and sketched a full, round picture of the defendant and his relationship to the events. My friend—a wise lawyer and colleague—wrinkled his nose. He reminded me that my point of view did not do the defendant justice. Focusing on his lack of success in life, relationships, and career would help to reinforce an image of "loser" and indeed might for some people play into a motive for desperate acts. Rather, my friend said, we needed to show the qualities of self-reliance, dignity, compassion, and decisiveness that also lurked in the defendant's character and were reflected in his actions.

Reflected is a key word, for it leads to the next step. All moviegoers since the release of *Citizen Kane* have seen the dolly shots in which the camera circles the action, round and round. We are given an illusion of omniscience—that we can see what any witness can, or could. Imagine the round characters as standing at the center of a room and ask how we would understand everything important about them. Some of our understanding comes from the characters themselves— when and if they testify. But no one sees, or appreciates, every relevant thing about himself or herself. Thus we must seek the views of others, who see the character and the key events from different perspectives. We will add tangible objects—paper and other things—that complete the picture. In our trial, our witnesses and the opponent's will present different perspectives of our client as each side seeks to project its preferred image. The lawyer wins who convinces the jury that his or her side gives jurors the best vantage points from which to claim omniscience as to the relevant events.

We cannot, and would not want to, tell the complete story of every witness who will provide this kind of perspective. Rather, we want to extract from these witnesses' stories just the relevant, important material and present it memorably. So we will make these witnesses into flat characters, possessing only one or a few characteristics that matter. We will introduce these flat characters and give them titles, to help us identify and remember their functions.

Tony Axam and Robert Altman[8] have called this process part of the "picture theory of trial advocacy." They tell us of a witness named Maria, who saw significant things. Maria was a maid. So the trial lawyer called her "Maria the maid" every time her name came up. Her profession gave her access to the events at issue, and the phrase conjured an image of her witnessing the events.

In our case, we might have "Micawber the personnel director." Or maybe, for our case, we would call him "Micawber the personnel *man*." If Copperfield's assistant supports the defense, we call her "Copperfield's assistant Ms. Smith." On our side, we might have "Ms. Johnson's friend Sara Ball," "the next-office man Mr. Wilson," "the damages expert Dr. Overby."

Usually you will identify and be able to name all the flat characters before trial begins. Sometimes a flat character can pick up a picturesque nickname as the case goes along—the doctor who helped out, the executive who couldn't remember, the accountant who made a mistake.

We care for these characters only as they shed light on the people who are central to our story. In tragic and comic drama, in opera, in films, in novels and stories, there are round and flat characters. The flat characters must be there to move the action along, and the author wants us to remember them well enough to know who they are if they disappear somewhere in Act One but come in again for the denouement.

ECONOMY OF EXPRESSION

To derogate the old adage, you will notice how few words it takes to make a picture. Thomas Sullivan is a man. "Policeman Tom Sullivan," the witness, is an image in jurors' minds. If Mr. Sullivan lied, then sometime in argument he may become policeman Tom Sullivan who lied. To call him "liar" may be permissible, but only if you are sure that the evidence supports you. To drape adverbs and adjectives over your descriptions avails you nothing. They simply get in the way of the facts. They add nothing to the image you are trying to evoke. A single descriptive word might be all right— "the young sandwich maker," "the gray-haired landlady." But be careful.

Words evoke states of being. They tell the listener something important, and then the listener can, to paraphrase C. S. Lewis, be left to feel and interpret them for herself. Speech is of course linear, in the sense that one word must follow another and that meaning depends on context.

Lewis has written about imaginative writing, but his observations are as true of courtroom speech:[9]

> One of the first things we have to say to a beginner who has brought us his MS is "Avoid all epithets which are merely emotional. It is no use telling us that something was 'mysterious' or 'loathsome' or 'awe-inspiring' or 'voluptuous.' Do you think your readers will believe you just because you say so? You must go quite a different way to work. By direct description, by metaphor and simile, by secretly evoking powerful associations, by offering the right stimuli to our nerves (in the right degree and the right order), and by the very beat and vowel-melody and length and brevity of your sentences, you must bring it about that we, we readers, not you, exclaim 'how mysterious!' or 'loathsome' or whatever it is. Let me taste for myself, and you'll have no need to *tell* me how I should react to the flavour."
>
> In Donne's couplet
>
>> Your gown going off, such beautious state reveals
>> As when from flow'ry meads th' hills shadow steals
>
> beautious is the only word of the whole seventeen which is doing no work.

In a jury trial, we want the quiet force of facts to do the work. Let the jurors supply the adjectives and adverbs. In *Examining Witnesses,* I quoted apt words of the great Irish barrister Dan O'Connell:

We can't drag the jurors along with us. Make them imagine that their movements are directed by themselves. Pay their capacities the compliment of not making things too clear. Rather than elaborate reasonings, throw off mere fragments, or seeds of thought. These will take root and shoot up into precisely the conclusions we want.

Mark Twain, in a devastating critique of James Fenimore Cooper, set out rules for developing and telling a story, all of which he said were ignored in *The Deerslayer.* Twain was writing about techniques for an author of fiction, but the same canons of style and construction apply to telling any tale.[10]

- A tale shall accomplish something and arrive somewhere.
- The episodes of a tale shall be necessary parts of the tale, and shall help to develop it.
- The personages in a tale shall be alive, except in the case of corpses, and always the reader shall be able to tell the corpses from the others.
- The personages in a tale, both dead and alive, shall exhibit a sufficient excuse for being there.
- When the personages of a tale deal in conversation, the talk shall sound like human talk, and be talk such as human beings would be likely to talk in the given circumstances, and have a discoverable meaning, also a discoverable purpose, and a show of relevancy, and remain in the neighborhood of the subject in hand, and be interesting to the reader, and help out the tale, and stop when the people cannot think of anything more to say.
- When the author describes the character of a personage in his tale, the conduct and conversation of that personage shall justify said description.
- When a personage talks like an illustrated, gilt-edged, tree-calf, hand-tooled, seven-dollar Friendship's

Offering in the beginning of a paragraph, he shall not talk like a [vaudeville caricature] in the end of it.

- Crass stupidities shall not be played upon the reader as "the craft of the woodsman, the delicate art of the forest," by either the author or the people in the tale.
- The personages of a tale shall confine themselves to possibilities and let miracles alone; or, if they venture a miracle, the author must so plausibly set it forth as to make it look possible and reasonable.
- The author shall make the reader feel a deep interest in the personages of his tale and in their fate; and that he shall make the reader love the good people in the tale and hate the bad ones.
- The characters in a tale shall be so clearly defined that the reader can tell beforehand what each will do in a given emergency.

In addition to these large rules there are some little ones. These require that the author shall:

- Say what he is proposing to say, not merely come near it.
- Use the right word, not its second cousin.
- Eschew surplusage.
- Not omit necessary details.
- Avoid slovenliness of form.
- Use good grammar.
- Employ a simple and straightforward style.

The message here is part of the same theme—give the jurors a simple, clear structure for decision and not a rococo room.

PERSONIFYING THE FICTITIOUS PERSON

If you represent a corporation or other entity at trial, you face a special challenge. Your opponent will put a human face on that entity, and you need to do likewise. Usually it will not be the physical face. That is, the usual suit against a corporation involves *respondeat superior* liability based on the conduct of an employee not part of management. *Fictitious person* refers to any entity—it can be a corporation, but also a voluntary association, a labor union, a public agency, or even a class of persons "represented" in litigation and at trial under Federal Rule of Civil Procedure 23 or its state counterpart.

There are exceptions, where senior executives themselves made or ratified the decisions that form the basis for suit.

A corporation at trial must be represented by someone— it is entitled to have its "representative" present. Carefully choose someone whose demeanor reflects confidence in the case. Remember, however, that in a civil case the opponent may call corporate representatives as adverse witnesses in its case. I know of a case where the corporate representative was chosen carefully, and counsel told him everything except to be ready to be called to testify. Plaintiffs called him as their first witness. It was a disaster. So your representative must look nearly as good after being subjected to hostile examination early in the case.

Your corporate representative is exempt from the "rule on witnesses"[11] and thus can testify in your case and sit there throughout the trial. This can be important. In many kinds of cases, some issue of corporate operation or policy must be explained to the jury. Sometimes you will have an expert to do the "background" explaining. But you need somebody on the "inside" to tell how the body of knowledge the expert describes was really put to work.

This gives you a good combination of characteristics for your representative, for the insider who has useful experience will often enjoy talking about that experience and will be persuasive in doing so.

For example, in an antitrust case, one issue was the cost to our corporate client of processing crude oil into products. We had an economist to describe the industry's cost and price patterns. But we wanted to talk about how a refinery operator makes economic decisions. We were lucky to find somebody in the company who was a graduate petroleum engineer who had moved into management—including time spent in the very refinery that was important to the case. He was used to talking to professional groups and also to making presentations inside the company. He was somebody who showed up every day for work and made useful products out of crude oil. The decisions he faced on a daily basis were ones that people could understand and sympathize with.

In another case, we had to defend a company policy. The company's most senior executives did not seem to be good witnesses for us. We had a choice of two senior people directly involved with the company decisions that concerned us. One was a superb numbers person, who also knew the law and regulations. The other had a broader view of the process and did not know the regulatory details.

We chose the second candidate. The first one had that terrible tendency to think several questions ahead and seemed to lack flexibility and compassion. What we lost by not having his expertise we could make up by using a hired expert on the subject who could put things in context.

To make this kind of presentation, you need to have a relationship with your corporate client that permits you to tell them hard truths, such as who will be a good witness and who will not. If necessary, use your trial consultant to watch a witness preparation session and provide criticism. The consultant can say things that you could not without harming your own relationship with the client.

For you and your client, the corporation is just folks. For the jurors, it may be different unless you take care to point out the ways in which the corporation makes a solid contribution.

If you are suing the corporation, you need to personalize its decisions. To be sure, if nobody remembers who did something, or if documents have gone missing without explanation, the anonymous "it" may become your target for those purposes.

In most cases, however, it was an individual or group of individuals who made the decisions you are attacking. When you identify them, you will probably take their depositions and consider using some or all of them as adverse witnesses in your case.

Often the issue in corporate cases is management's deliberate indifference, or failure to act in the face of mounting evidence that something is wrong. This theme plays out in many contexts, from negligence to intentional misconduct. I once summed up in a case where each management person claimed not to have heard the bad news or not to have a duty to do anything about reports that something needed attention. So I used a Mr. Potato Head to illustrate that the corporation was not a brownish anonymous lump. It had eyes (Mr. X), ears (Ms. Y), a nose (Mr. Z), and a mouth (X, Y, and Z) to tell somebody to make a different decision. The individuals who did something should not be able to hide behind the anonymity of the entity. Later in this chapter is an excerpt from the summation.

Of course, no entity is truly monolithic. If you represent an entity, you may be confronted with documents from its files that you wish had not been written. In these days of e-mail, the creation and saving of writings that in past days would have just been idle comments in the air has become pandemic. Buddy Low, the great lawyer of East Texas, has an approach to this problem. "You know, we are not a dictatorship over there. We have all sorts of people working at our company, and not all of them agree with what the company management is doing. We think that letting people speak their minds makes for better decisions. So of course you are going to find dissent and disagreement. That doesn't mean that the dissenters are automatically right, any more than it means they are automatically wrong. You know, it is a little like a family. In my family, we have Uncle Jack—he is outspoken and opinionated, and a lot of the time he doesn't make any sense. But he is part of the family, and sometimes he does actually have a good idea."

In your case, or your part of the country, you may not be able to use precisely this approach. And few of us match the storytelling ability of Buddy Low. But making your entity client come alive as a group of people all working toward a goal is always important.

ARRANGEMENT: TRIAL MATERIALS

In my talks on trial preparation, I stress arrangement of trial materials as the most important organizational task of lead counsel. From such organization flows the best arrangement of your presentation to the jury.

From the simplest case to the most complex, the biggest challenge is to organize information. Given the penchant to overdiscover, the documents and depositions pile up faster than any one lawyer can absorb their contents.

Yet, unless the jury believes that you are in complete command of the facts and the law, you and your client suffer. That is the paradox. You cannot resolve it by delegating tasks to junior lawyers and paralegals and expecting to be "briefed" just before trial. You must take charge early and stay that way.

We do it with three basic documents that we insist be created early in the litigation and updated regularly. In a small case, we can do it ourselves with a paralegal/secretary. In a more complex case, these are the case control documents that a team of junior lawyers, paralegals, and investigators works on.

Yes, investigators. A trained investigator can and should do the work that many law firms assign to paralegals. The investigator can interview witnesses, handle documents, and even be in charge of these case control documents. In every major city, there are investigators who are computer literate and have plenty of experience in helping to manage litigation. If your firm litigates regularly, start and maintain a working relationship with somebody like that.

The three documents are:

- chronology
- who's who
- exhibit list

The chronology is printed in landscape format—that is, across the eleven-inch expanse of the page. It provides document control and witness control. It gives you an up-to-date overview of your case. It looks like this:

CHRONOLOGY OF [CASE NAME AND IDENTIFIER], DRAFT OF [DATE], PAGE [X] OF [Y] PAGES ATTORNEY-CLIENT PRIVILEGED—ATTORNEY WORK PRODUCT				
DATE	PLACE	EVENT	SOURCE	EVIDENCE

By using landscape format for printing, and ten-point type, you can get a lot of information into these cells. The heading should carry over from page to page. The date and place columns are self-explanatory. For each "event," you need a short description. How you break down events by date and time will depend on your evidence and on the importance of the event to your case. For example, on a key day, you might have fifty or more entries. If you are establishing a background fact, the date entry might cover several months, and the "event" be something like "James Johnson employed at XYZ Corp. as vice-president for Human Resources." The "source" tells you how you know the facts given under "Event," for example, by interview with a witness, by an identified document, or even by a newspaper report. The "Source" column tells you at a glance how "good" or "solid" is your information. Near the beginning of trial preparation, the "Evidence" column will mostly be blank. Your case preparation is designed to get admissible evidence of the "events" listed.

Let's use an example to see how this works: One allegation in your sexual harassment case is that company president John Jones called Mary Smith at home during the evening and made sexual advances. In the early stages of the case, the chronology for a portion of the day might look like this:

DATE	PLACE	EVENT	SOURCE	EVIDENCE
7/10/96, 5:10 P.M.	Darrow, Ohio	MS leaves XYZ offices	MS interview; XYZ time records	XYZ time records; MS testimony
7/10/96, 5:40 P.M.	Darrow, Ohio	MS arrives home	MS interview; interview with Joyce Wilson	MS testimony; Joyce Wilson testimony
7/10/96, 6:17 P.M.	Darrow, Ohio Altgeld, Ohio	JJ calls MS and talks for ten minutes, tells MS that it would "help her to advance at XYZ if we could meet for drinks tonight"	MS interview; MS caller-ID printout	MS testimony; caller ID printout

At the time this version is prepared, we have interviewed our client and her friend Ms. Wilson. We have not yet deposed Jones. Our document requests are not yet answered. The chronology provides us a quick study of what evidence we need to prove the key facts about the call. We need documents from the phone company, Jones's calendars, and a deposition from Jones. When we get the documents, the "Source" column will contain our internal document control identifications.

As trial draws nearer, the "Evidence" column will have actual exhibit numbers. Until then, it will include deposition exhibits. The rule is that anything in the "Evidence" column is available and admissible. The fifth column forces you to get serious about what can be proved at trial—as opposed to being something that you "know" happened.

The second organizational keystone is the "who's who." In one case, my who's who ran to hundreds of pages. We really needed it, because we would look at the chronology and draw a blank on who was talking or who the witness was.

The who's who is a list of witnesses by name. Every witness, even those whose names you got from the newspaper, is on the list, each with a short (one-sentence) description of who this is.

The chronology and who's who are made on a word processing program. They are therefore usable by people with minimal computer skills. They are searchable by word or phrase. In a huge case, when the chronology may run to hundreds of pages, put it on a CD-ROM. At regular intervals, collect the CD-ROMs and replace them. The CD-ROM can also be used to hold other information of your choice, such as key documents, depositions, and memoranda.

Because the chronology may contain sensitive information about the case, and because the risks of inadvertent disclosure are high, we sometimes make two versions. One version has asterisks to note omitted information (such as privileged information that is not subject to discovery and will not be in evidence). A master copy containing all the information is kept in a safe place. As discovery rulings or tactical decisions expand the scope of producible or admissible material, information may move from the "complete" copy to the version in regular use. This might happen if you decided to use an advice-of-counsel defense in a case, which would open up previously privileged material to discovery production and to use in evidence at trial.

The third organizational item is an exhibit list. This will be in two forms. One is the form you are building for trial, and that will be turned over at pretrial. You want your list and your opponent's list. A second form, which may be required by the local rules but which you should in any event make for yourself, lists exhibits by witness. There may be some duplication in this version, because a sponsoring witness may authenticate the exhibit, but a fact witness may make better use of it.

For example, suppose you get a toll record that shows Jones's number calling Smith's number. A phone company employee may authenticate it. But you will publish it during Smith's testimony, as part of her story of the call—this helps your direct examination and corroborates her as she is testifying. You may publish a given exhibit several times during a trial, each time with a different witness. You would do this with a chart, a memorandum addressed to several people, or a record of an event that several people participated in.

The exhibit list is also a reality check, particularly in a document-intensive case. Making an exhibit list helps you test items of evidence. It helps you see which items are admissible, useful, and efficient storytelling aids.

In an antitrust case a few years ago, my opponent wanted to wire the courtroom with all kinds of devices to present exhibits on video monitors. The exhibits would mostly be documents that had been scanned onto CD-ROMs. They said this was necessary because they had 20,000 exhibits to introduce.

I responded, "They're not telling you the truth, judge. Nobody can keep a jury interested in a trial with 20,000 exhibits. Most of the material on their exhibit list, which they have just served, is not admissible anyway. I suggest we defer technology until counsel can confer on these exhibits and get a realistic designation." And so we started the next day figuring out what would really be in evidence.

I am not a Luddite when it comes to organizing your exhibit materials while preparing for trial. You may want to scan your documents in so that they are searchable with a program like ZyImage and then add your pleadings to that database. You can use a CD-ROM for the fruits of such activity and make an updated disk every once in a while. That way, all team members can have instant access to key documents on desktop or laptop computers.

Once your case materials are organized, you can arrange your case, and everything about it. Your opening statement, each cross-examination, the order of presentation of your witnesses, your closing argument—each fits an overall pattern, and each has its own internal structure.

ARRANGEMENT: THE STORY ITSELF

We learn to think in triplets—arguments in threes—to make our story memorable and as a guide to arrangement. From ancient times, rhetoricians have known that ideas expressed in triplets are more easily grasped and remembered. In a typical plaintiff's case, the overall structure will be (1) who this person, our client is; (2) what happened to this person and what the other side did or failed to do that brought us to court to get justice; and (3) what the jury can do to set things right. The typical defense case organizes the elements differently—as 2, 1, 3 and not as 1, 2, 3. This gives us (2) what "really happened," (1) who our client is and why this lawsuit is being brought, and (3) why neither damages nor other relief is proper.

The defense tends to organize differently because from opening statement onward, defense counsel must acknowledge that something happened that brings the case to court. Making this concession early and frankly is thus vital to maintaining credibility.

For example, in the Terry Nichols case, the prosecution opening was more or less in the typical order—what happened, what Terry Lynn Nichols was alleged to have done to make that happen, and what the jury should do about it.

Here we had 168 people dead and great devastation. Somebody was criminally responsible for this act. Our situation was not unlike that of anyone defending a case with obvious damage but questionable liability. In many cases, from product liability to negligence to toxic torts, it is clear that something very bad has happened. If you are defending, you had better confront and acknowledge that reality from the beginning. Put more generally, every arrangement of a case must include a prompt and thorough identification of what is not in dispute.

So in *Nichols* I began by telling the jury that Timothy McVeigh parked the Ryder truck in front of the Murrah Federal Building in Oklahoma City, and set the bomb to go off and that he was not alone. Our three-part opening—which in that complex capital case Ronald G. Woods and I shared—told the jurors (2) who bombed the building, how they planned it, and how they did it—a plausible alternative to the government's theory; (1) who Terry Nichols was, his background, his actions before and after the day of the bombing; and (3) how the government's investigation impeded the search for truth and what the jurors could do about that.

Your arrangement must carry forward from the opening to your entire case—your order of witnesses and then your closing argument. Arrangement serves story by being faithful to it. The focus on arrangement reminds you to stick to your trial plan except for the most compelling reason.

STYLE

Style is the embodiment of presentation—its form in words. Later we get to the actual delivery. As I said in Chapter Fifteen of *Examining Witnesses,* whatever style and delivery you use must be your own. You cannot buy or borrow them. As in *The Wizard of Oz,* you cannot long tell the jurors to pay no attention to what is going on behind the curtain. They will pull it aside and reveal the true you. They will have had this epiphany sometime during the case and will act on it in the jury room.

Jurors resent phoniness, innuendo, and grandstanding. They expect lawyers to be vigorous advocates for their side and will understand that sometimes an overstatement or dramatic gesture is well meant and therefore forgivable. However, it is always wise to apologize for any overstatement that may have offended the jurors.

At the same time, figures of speech, expressions of emotion, and verbal images are vital elements of argument. Some of these images move your argument along. Some help to mark a key event, exhibit, or bit of testimony as unforgettably as a graphic exhibit. Sometimes a figure of speech may embody the entire idea of your story and therefore become the theme around which jurors will rally to your support during deliberations.

The best style may not be a metaphor, simile, or analogy at all. It may be simply an unvarnished statement of an event—letting the quiet force of facts do the work. For example, in the case of Terry Lynn Nichols, I began like this:

> May it please the Court, Counsel, Mr. Nichols, members of the jury, on the 19th morning of April at 9:02 in the morning, or actually just a few minutes before, Timothy McVeigh parked in front of the Murrah Building in Oklahoma City. He was in a Ford F-700 truck from Ryder rentals with a 20-foot box. And Timothy McVeigh was not alone. With him in the cab of that truck were one or two other people. The driver parked the truck and set the bomb to go off. Yes, Terry Nichols was not there and did not know about the bombing until the next day. He was at home in Herington, Kansas, at 109 South 2nd Street in a house he'd bought and moved into one month and six days before. He was at home. With him there were his pregnant wife, Marife; their infant daughter, Nicole; Marife Torres Nichols, born in the Philippines, who came to the United States as Terry Nichols's wife. Terry Nichols was building a life, not a bomb.

This "opening of the opening" marched with declarative sentences, all in the active voice. Somebody did something, not "something happened." In a negligence case, it would be "Peter Smith ran the red light and crashed his Ford truck into Bill Johnson's small car." It would not be "Bill Johnson was injured." It would be that somebody did something to Bill Johnson that injured him. In short, the most vivid verbal image is often drawn in the simplest strokes.

There may, however, be room for figures of speech in the classical sense. Be more sparing in their use in opening statement than in closing argument, for the opening is not supposed to be argumentative. You can pack a lot of power into an opening statement, without sustainable objection, if you are describing. If you begin to use metaphor, however mild, you seem to many judges to stray into forbidden territory.

Here is another excerpt from the *Nichols* opening:

> And on the 19th morning of April, in Oklahoma City, a half-dozen witnesses, each of whom will be called to testify before you, spotted Timothy McVeigh and his accomplice. And Terry Nichols wasn't there at 9:02 A.M. Actually, a few minutes before, Timothy McVeigh and his accomplice got out of the Ryder truck. An explosion as quick as a heartbeat and sadness as long as life. McVeigh was arrested less than 90 minutes later.

Notice some repetition to make the transition: "the 19th morning of April," and "actually, just a few minutes before." The first of these is designed to emphasize that Terry Nichols was not there and the second to help create the sense that something is about to happen. That is, we can usually tell when an airplane crashed or two cars collided or somebody fired somebody. But all such events have preludes that form the basis of our proof. During the prelude somebody commits acts that make them responsible for "the event." Thus we may use a verbal cue to designate that prelude time: "in the nighttime hours before he took the wheel, drunk, and drove his car," or "in the months of summer, as he plotted and planned." When you have chosen a verbal cue of this kind, stick with it.

Then there is the simile, "an explosion as quick as a heartbeat and sadness as long as life." This, too, was a theme. We did not contest the devastation and destruction, nor the criminality of those who actually did the bombing. The simile was designed to point to and to embody this idea.

Expand your vision of imagery. You can use symbols as stylistic elements. In a contract case, you can have the actual contract on counsel table, constantly referred to and often used in examining witnesses.

In the corporate contract case discussed above, the corporation said that the person who took the messages was not the proper person to process orders, and hence the corporation did not deliver the goods my client ordered. How should I convey that this is not some anonymous set of decisions, a kind of pattern of unfortunate events for which the corporation cannot be held responsible? This is often the problem in cases involving entities. Whether the entity is your client or your opponent, you must personalize its decisions—bring real people to the fore who actually heard, saw, and said the things that make the case.

So in argument, I said:

> These defendants want to say that BMI did no wrong, that BMI never hurt anybody. It is just a neutral thing, harmless, maybe like this potato. [Holding up a good-size russet of a regular shape.] But you heard the evidence. That is just not so. The corporation acts through people. Ms. Smith, the secretary, she is supposed to hear what customers are saying. [I put Mr. Potato Head ears on the potato.] Mr. Johnson, the vice-president, he is supposed to look at his messages, supposed to—what did he say was his job—"oversee" things. To see, or to oversee, he is BMI's eyes. [I put Mr. Potato Head eyes on the potato.] If things are not going right, if they

don't smell too good, that odor is supposed to reach the noses of Mr. Jones and Ms. Smith. [The nose went on the potato.] And together, when they see and hear and smell, Ms. Smith and Mr. Johnson are supposed to tell somebody what to do, so that these orders are handled the way they should be. [I put the Mr. Potato Head mouth on the potato.]

This example suggests the use of objects to illustrate an opening or closing. I sound a caution here. The jurors want to know your case so they can decide it. They are less impressed with fancy argumentative charts than with the exhibits themselves. They will have the exhibits in the jury room. They need an introduction to those exhibits so that they can find their way through to a verdict. We pick up this theme in later chapters.

However, be careful with imagery. When you have planned your argument, go through your notes and identify every figure of speech you are using. List these, on paper or mentally. Then decide which ones you really want. Have your colleagues challenge you on each one, as the "metaphor police." Look for inconsistent images—clashing depictions that destroy and do not support one another.

MEMORY

Memory refers to how you store your discourse so that you can pronounce it when it is time. A part of memory is having your exhibit lists and chronology ready at hand. You may on a given trial day have a key exhibit or pleading at your table. Another part of memory is the notes you take during trial, to refer back and jog recollection. Yet another may be the transcript or transcript index. Mainly, however, we are talking about preparing to give your argument or examine your witness.

There are points of view about memorizing. Here is mine. Never write out what you are going to say and then read it.

This goes for opening statement, closing argument, direct examination, and cross-examination. Some lawyers disagree. They write out their arguments, word for word. Some say that they have memorized the argument and the written version is just insurance. I have observed lawyers with their scripts for thirty years. The scripted argument is flatter than a more spontaneous one. A scripted interrogation is not only flat, but the lawyer's concentration on the written word makes him miss what the witness is saying; thus he ignores gifts the witness may be giving in the form of explanations or concessions.

I can remember cases in which the other side approached the lectern for each witness—on direct and on cross—with a notebook. On the notebook cover was the case title and number and the witness's name. Some of the opposition lawyers had a separate page for each question; some would have several questions on a page. But most of them had written out the questions and (for direct examination) the expected answers. Worse yet, some of them would have a pen and visibly check off each question as it was answered. Watching an examination conducted in this way is like watching two people balance their checkbook. The jurors could not feel a part of what was going on, for the process visually and structurally excluded them from it.

Similarly, when a lawyer makes an argument that visibly comes from a notebook, it appears staged. Jurors want to have what they need to decide the case. They want to hear what the lawyers say and evaluate it. They feel shut out—some report feeling cheated—by an argument that appears staged.

You want what you say to be memorable. How can it be memorable if you can't remember it yourself? If you need to read it aloud? I have in a very complex case written out a proposed opening statement, because I wanted to test it on my colleagues and I did not want to overlook anything. My written version was, however, without ornament or exhibit. It was designed simply to see how the material could be organized. I then jettisoned the written version and made notes with key ideas. I started a fresh page for every transition, to signal myself that I needed to introduce the jurors to a new topic. Some lawyers use index cards in the same fashion.

How should you use memory? Some lawyers can call to mind every witness and every document, without notes. This is easier in a short trial. Most lawyers need some help: they use notes and other reminders. What kind of notes and reminders? To answer this question, consider its other and most important side. How will the jurors remember what you have said? In most trials they cannot take notes. They will therefore expect your presentation to contain clues to the relative importance of ideas and events, and they will retain your vision of the case if you illustrate it.

In most trials, jurors come to court with no idea of what your case is about. In celebrated trials, they come to court with a good idea of what they think the case is about; this is often worse for you than having a clean page to write on. We are all subject to the temptation to tell stories as though our listeners were there for a significant part of the action.

Whatever device you use, the connection between memory and memorable is key. In opening statement, you may not be able to use exhibits. You will be able to use them in closing argument. Using exhibits to punctuate an opening or closing helps your and the jurors' memory, for the exhibits help to recall the explanation that went with them. When you hold up an object or a document and explain it, you create that mental link.

As discussed in the preceding section, figures of speech punctuate an opening or closing, helping to make it memorable. But the best memory tool is organization around themes so that the argument marches from one point to the next. By being clear about your themes, you help put what you are going to say into memory. By making sure those themes derive from the basic story of the case, you serve your overall goal.

DELIVERY

In delivering, whether in argument or examination, the rule remains the same: you must be you. If style is how you form your thoughts, delivery is how you communicate them.

When law students arrive for their first year, some of them are good writers and speakers, and some have trouble with one or the other. Almost all of them then read a few appellate opinions in the casebooks and begin to adopt the stilted style and jargon they find there. When they become lawyers, they have a lot to unlearn. In most law schools, nothing in the first-year curriculum prepares you to listen or to care.

Too, styles of argument change over time. We read lawyer speeches from one hundred years ago, in trial and appellate courts, that go on for hours or even days. Today, in the usual case, a half hour may be allowed for opening statement and an hour for closing argument. In complex cases particularly, wise judges will let advocates go on longer, but this is not the norm. In appeals courts, a half hour on a side for argument is a long time—the norm is more like twenty minutes.

Even if you could talk for several hours, it is usually not a good idea to do so. Juror habit of mind is fixed by reading, listening, and viewing habits. Most jurors get their information from television and radio, which means in small bites. Your job is to talk. Theirs is to listen. It is not good if they finish before you do. Brevity is good, although in a long trial a summation that lasts a day is not out of order.

One hundred years ago, an effulgent tub-thumping style of argument was in vogue. We have already seen that today's style is rather shorn of ornament. Bombast turns off jurors because it is not how they are used to being addressed and persuaded and it looks like an effort to ride over the difficult issues. Jurors use words like *innuendo* and *misleading* and *inappropriate* to describe it.

What is the proper mode of delivery? In most courts, you must use the lectern to argue. So step up to it. Acknowledge the court, counsel, the parties, the jurors. Look at the jurors. Speak to the jurors as though you were convincing yourself in the mirror—yes, the mirror—or telling yourself a story.

Do not practice this in your office, for if you are known to have a mirror in your desk drawer in which you look at yourself, you will be thought vain. Stand in front of a bathroom mirror, about two or three feet away. Yes, I know this is closer than the jurors will be from you, but remember that you will probably have a microphone. Now start saying your argument. Watch your expression. Modulate your voice. Run over some main points of your argument. Does this seem strange to you? Remember Demosthenes, one of Athens's greatest orators, who conquered his speech defect by filling his mouth with pebbles and arguing at the waves. If you have ever been in a Greek amphitheater, you have a sense of what Demosthenes had to contend with. He had to address all of those people without a microphone. You are doing what he did, but with a very different forum in mind.

Now work on doing this for a wider audience—a roomful of people. If you don't have a roomful of people, use just a room. Notice how your voice carries in that space. Do not overwhelm the space. Fill it.

Little-known fact: Clarence Darrow's co-counsel in the *Scopes* trial was Dudley Field Malone of New York. Malone delivered an impassioned opening. As he took his seat, Darrow looked at him and said, "Dudley, of all the opening statements I ever heard . . ." Malone leaned forward. "Yes, Clarence." And Darrow concluded, ". . . that was the loudest."

Delivery includes tone. You are telling a story in which you believe—not the ethics-forbidden personal belief in the justice of the cause, but a belief that the evidence will compel the conclusion that you want. Arrogance has no place in your recital. Your emotional tone must be driven by the evidence you are relating, and when in doubt, understate.

VOIR DIRE: YOU AS HEARER, JURORS AS HEARERS

We lawyers are ill prepared by our training to listen and to care. In law school, we do not come in daily contact with those who are going to decide our jury trials. Our job as lawyers is not to talk but to communicate. To communicate, as the word's etymology suggests, we must commune with or become connected to the jurors. Only then will they hear us.

In *voir dire,* we are speakers. But we must also be hearers. We are having the only two-way communication that the trial process permits. That process is somewhat off putting to jurors. Because effective *voir dire* takes time, many judges limit it severely, choosing to ask the questions themselves. Asking that the judge use a questionnaire to be completed by prospective jurors, and making lists of proposed *voir dire* questions can help to bridge this gap, but these are imperfect substitutes.[12]

If you get lawyer *voir dire,* however, you need to think about yourself as hearer. How long has it been since you spoke to somebody else and really listened in an interested way to his or her story?

From the jury questionnaire you get subjects about which to talk with the jurors. Be interested in what the jurors want. You cannot feign this interest. You have to practice listening to people. In a particular case, you might want to do a little research at night to prepare for *voir dire* the next day. In one trial, we got on the Internet to find out about the different meanings of *bioenergetics.* We needed to talk to a juror about his interest in this subject to probe whether he was really a serious researcher with a scientific bent or had a more superficial knowledge and interest. Our research led to questions that led us to believe he would be an excellent juror, a challenge for cause by the other side was denied, and the other side had to use a peremptory challenge.

Here are portions of a newspaper article that captures the flavor of our version of voir dire. It is from the October 19,

1997 *Daily Oklahoman*. This is the paper of record in Oklahoma City. It was not favorable to the defense in the Oklahoma City bombing cases. It ran editorials denouncing defense tactics such as having moved for change of venue. The article is critical of some of my questions, but it illustrates an approach to prospective jurors. I have annotated it with commentaries:[13]

In the three weeks of jury selection, [Tigar has] quoted Latin to the Latin teacher, talked landmarks in Paris with a woman who went to college there and asked fans of the novel *The Horse Whisperer* if they support that gentle approach to breaking horses.

COMMENTARY

This is not "making conversation"—it is a way to find out how these folks approach difficult issues. If you can find out what books jurors have read recently, you know that a given juror reads books, and you will find that a lot of them have read popular books about the legal system such as those by John Grisham or Scott Turow. *The Horse Whisperer* was a popular book at the time of this *voir dire*. It said something about an approach to people and issues.

He sits next to Nichols at the defense table—which he had scooted over to get a better view of the candidates. He often puts his large right hand on Nichols's shoulder, as if to comfort his client.

COMMENTARY

See Chapter Four on courtroom control theories. Your client gets credibility from you. You must have a visible relationship of trust and confidence. To communicate with me, the client has a yellow pad and pen or pencil, to prevent interruptions of my concentration.

Jury candidates are questioned one at a time, and U.S. District Judge Richard Matsch lets prosecutors go first.

So Tigar, waiting his turn, makes listening an interactive exchange. Leaning toward the candidate with shoulders slumped, he holds a firm grin and bobs his head in response to certain answers.

COMMENTARY

Don't make a big show of this, but you are maintaining eye contact with the jurors as they answer your opponent's questions. No big gestures, but one theory of *voir dire* is to give positive reinforcement for good answers.

When his time comes, he carries his imposing figure to the podium, where his baritone voice commands the room.

"My name is Michael Tigar," he tells the candidate. "And Ron Woods, sitting right there, and I are lawyers. We were appointed . . . shortly after the bombing to help out Terry Nichols."

"And I'd like to follow up on some of the things that were asked and spend a little time with you."

Tigar's folksy manner often gets results—candidates respond more candidly.

They are engaged by his knowledge as he sprinkles in references to bioenergetics, farming, birthing methods—whatever applies.

He also is a master of the oddball question.

"You milk the goat?" he asked one juror candidate, whose family raised a few animals as pets outside Denver.

"No. No," she said.

Tigar wants to know whether candidates choose spanking or time-outs with their children.

COMMENTARY

In a criminal case, this is a key question, particularly when the jury will decide punishment. I think it also illuminates juror attitudes in any case where punitive damages or a theory of deterrence may be in issue.

He asked a study hall supervisor how he decides who is right when there is a classroom fight.

──────────── COMMENTARY ────────────

The study hall supervisor decides "cases" all the time, such as when there is a fight in school. How does he do it? Does he listen to both sides? Does he find it hard to set aside some preconceived idea based on who is involved?

He asked a school bus driver how students would describe her.

──────────── COMMENTARY ────────────

Tough but fair? Caring? Safe driver? How?

From No. 52, a nursing assistant who thought death was too easy for a criminal, Tigar wanted to know what she thought a crook should contemplate while in prison.

"That they would regret what they've done and that they would know that they have committed a crime that is wrong," she replied.

He sometimes goes out of his way to not seem overbearing when he is getting unsatisfactory answers and has to ask more questions.

"Well, I hear you say, 'I think I would,'" he said softly to one candidate. "It's like if my wife said, 'Do you love me?' and I said, 'I think I do,' she'd want to ask another question."

──────────── COMMENTARY ────────────

This approach, like many others in our *voir dire*, was suggested by Robert Hirschhorn. If a juror doesn't answer your questions directly, you need to keep on asking. Then, when you get a candid answer, you need to say, "Thank you. I know this is difficult territory." The most important element of *voir dire* is the open-ended question. Don't be afraid of the "bad" answer, even if you are doing *voir dire* to the entire panel. If you get such an answer, thank the juror: "I appreciate your point of view." Then ask, "Does anybody have a different idea about this that you would like to share with us?" You are not only getting answers; you are watching people participate in something like a deliberative process.

Tigar impressed a Teamsters member by describing the logo on his union handbook.

"You still get a little booklet there with the two pictures of the horses in front looking at each other?" Tigar asked him.

"Right," he said.

COMMENTARY

We knew from the questionnaire that this juror was a loyal union member. He had been on strike with his union. Under his contract, he is paid his full wage during jury service. He had read his contract and knew his rights in this respect. He is therefore the kind of thoughtful intelligent juror one might want. It is important to show respect for somebody who goes to that trouble to prepare to meet you. As for knowing what is on the Teamster contract—the logo—that is old knowledge we happened to have, but if you need to understand how union contracts provide for jury service, you should study that before you talk to this juror.

Tigar even spoke the language of No. 763, a psychic and energy reading enthusiast who believed her karma would catch up with her if she sentenced someone to death.

"Now, much of your reading is about the energy in the human body. Is that right?" Tigar began.

"Right," she said.

"I mean, chakras are—well, how would you define a chakra?"

"I would say the chakras are points in the body, in the energy body that interact with the physical body; and they're data centers and energy centers where we're receiving and energy is leaving our bodies," she said.

"And in your view, do they occur along meridians?" Tigar asked.

"Yes."

"So that there are meridians of energy that run in the body and along these are the chakras that are centers; is that—" he said.

"That's correct."

"And is that based on a study of Eastern medicine?" Tigar said.

"That's an ancient knowledge, yes," she replied.

COMMENTARY

We wanted to know just how serious this juror was. The other side wanted to portray her as a flake. She wasn't.

When No. 657 turned out to be a Latin teacher, prosecutors and reporters knew what to expect as Tigar approached the podium.

He didn't disappoint.

"Have you ever heard the expression, 'Ubi societas ibi jus'" he said, then gave the translation. "'Wherever there is society, there is this idea of justice.' . . . My pronunciation is wrong, please don't grade my paper; but there's this social structure within which we all live that defines . . . what the rules are?"

"Uh-huh," No. 657 said.

COMMENTARY

The Cicero quote is a potent observation on the rule of law and can get the discussion started on that issue in a high-visibility trial. The aphorism is usually contrasted with another, *inter arma silent leges,* which means "in time of war the laws are silent."

Tigar sometimes slips in a point during his questioning—kind of to get potential jurors thinking ahead to his defense.

Jurors are expected to hear testimony that Nichols set off small explosives with his son in Kansas and a brother in Michigan. The defense will contend they were just having fun.

So, Tigar took special notice when a school bus driver wrote on her questionnaire that she had a friend with a homemade cannon.

"Made a big noise?" he asked.

"Yeah," she answered.

"Did everybody enjoy that?"

"Yeah," she said. "I guess so. Sometimes it was pretty loud."

"Well, you wouldn't jump to the conclusion that some fellow that wanted to set off things that made a noise on the Fourth of July was a bomber, would you?" the defense attorney said.

"No," she said.

"Wouldn't be logical?" he asked.

"No," she said again.

Point made.

COMMENTARY

Voir dire is not the place to get commitments on the facts. But you can ask generic questions along the line of "Just because somebody says X is true doesn't make it so." If you are doing *voir dire* to the panel, you must begin with a general statement of what the case is about. You must "say your case," tell your story in just a few words—no more than five minutes. At the end of your five minutes, the jurors should know what the case is about, who is involved, and—most important—what you will ask them to do.

It doesn't always work.

Tigar tried to use a construction superintendent's work experience to turn him around from his belief that someone who intentionally kills many people deserves the death penalty.

"Did you ever have a situation where you had a worker out on a job and you looked at him and you thought, 'Gee, you know, that's probably not going to be a very good worker,' and it turns out they just really do a great job?" Tigar asked.

"Yes," the candidate answered.

"You know, the situation (where) somebody kind of doesn't look like they're too coordinated and you put them in a house and you tell them, 'Go tape and float that drywall,' and you come back and, whew, they've got a lot of square feet done?"

"Uh-huh."

"So in your life, . . . you have been able to withhold judgment until you've seen how it worked out?" Tigar said.

"Sure. As the old saying goes, you can't judge a book by the cover. I don't know how anybody can judge from the outside what's on the inside."

Still, No. 667 was adamant about imposing the death penalty.

A few jury candidates have been put off by Tigar's manner—and said so.

A Fort Collins scientist said he had seen that manipulative behavior from attorneys when he was on previous juries. He complained of how Tigar smiled and nodded as the judge spoke to candidates September 17.

"It appeared to me that he was smiling and nodding not necessarily because he was in agreement with the judge but because he was signaling to the rest of us his agreement with the judge," the scientist said.

COMMENTARY

> The journalist is being a little unfair. This "scientist" is the same one who was interested in Eastern medicine. When she said on her questionnaire that she had formed some impression of the lawyers, the quoted response was her explanation of that. You must treasure these bursts of candor. Most jurors at one level or another distrust the lawyers, and here is somebody who is admitting it. Your follow-up must establish that this is a thoughtful person and then get a commitment that the facts as proven will determine the result—not lawyer posturing.

Another candidate, No. 848, complained, "I felt very uncomfortable with the defense. I would not want to be in a dark alley, a light alley, day or night with them."

---- COMMENTARY ----

> This juror will be off for cause, so don't worry. But you need to make sure that she has not spread her ideas around the other panel members. Jurors wait together to be questioned, and if there is any strong negative impression, ask if the juror has shared it with others. If you are doing *voir dire* with an entire panel, and get a response that slaps you in the face—about you or your legal theory or your client—immediately take advantage of it. Say "Thank you for letting me know your feelings. There are no right or wrong answers here, just honest answers, and I appreciate your being honest with me. Now, does anybody else on the panel have a different view that they might like to share with us?"

Tigar at first had no questions, but jumped to his feet as the candidate got ready to leave.

"Excuse me, your honor. May I just put one question?" he asked.

"Yes, you may," the judge said, then joked, "In self defense? Is that name-clearing?"

But Tigar was serious.

"Ma'am," he asked, "Have you shared your views—to which you are entitled—with any of the other jurors riding in the van or in any other context?"

"No, sir," she replied.

The judge turned serious, too, telling Tigar he appreciated that question "because I didn't think of it."

Victories come in small doses.

The judge is trying to find 64 acceptable potential jurors, weeding out those who could never vote for the death penalty and those who automatically would.

Then he will let prosecutors and defense attorneys make cuts, until 12 jurors and six alternates are left. Each side gets to knock off 23.

Defense attorneys try to save their cuts for the most objectionable candidates and try to force prosecutors to waste the government's strikes.

So, defense attorneys end up trying to persuade opponents of the death penalty to consider voting for the punishment. If that happens, the judge will accept the candidate and frustrated prosecutors will have to use a strike they might have saved for someone worse.

Tigar has won admirers for his skill in swaying potential jurors to be open-minded.

It happened most dramatically with No. 474, who said, "I think that's something that should be left up to God and not for me."

Prosecutors didn't ask any questions—certain the judge would remove No. 474.

But Tigar switched the business manager's opinion by first asking if she would defend herself if foreign troops invaded American soil. By the time he was finished, she agreed to consider both life and death sentences.

Tigar has not been reluctant to take on Matsch, despite the judge's reputation for keeping tight control of his courtroom and having little patience with presumptuous attorneys.

He asked the judge to stop telling potential jurors it was OK to change in court any answers they had given under oath on written questionnaires Sept. 17. Jurors might get the impression it is permissible for government witnesses to give testimony that conflicts with previous statements, Tigar complained.

The judge agreed to change his remarks.

Tigar also complained about the "tone and content" of the judge's questioning of a computer software consultant, who thought computers might be better jurors than humans.

"Your honor raised his voice, put him on the spot . . . we think . . . that it would be better to reward him for his honesty," Tigar said.

COMMENTARY

After a recess, the judge apologized. It is important to make sure your position is clear, and this sometimes requires you to confront the judge. Your manner need not, probably should not, be confrontational, but a soft-spoken statement that makes the point and preserves the record may be in order.

In doing *voir dire,* we remember that all jurors come to court with prejudices. We all have them. We dignify them by calling them intuition or common sense. So be clear with the jurors.

> "We all have some prejudices. I know I do. It is our God-given right to have prejudices. Maybe you are prejudiced against lawyers who look and talk and act like I do. Or maybe you think that cases like this don't belong in court. Whatever. The point of all these questions is that maybe you have some ideas that you brought to court that mean you should sit on some other case and not on this one."

American lawyers are often reproached for our concern with jury selection. In England, we are told, juries are almost never available in civil trials, and in criminal cases *voir dire* is perfunctory and devoted mostly to the jurors' statutory qualifications. Federal judges curtail jury selection time and often keep advocates from participation in the process. Yet nothing is clearer to a student of history than that important public decisions are the product of predominant social sentiments and ideologies. Putting aside prejudice is a rare quality.

We know, however, that communication involves both the speaker and the hearer. If John Brown's sole audience was those inside his courtroom, his rhetorical ability was irrelevant. For us, as advocates, there is a vital interest in preserving our client's right to speak to the potential deciders and to play a role in selecting them.

NOTES

1. A most delightful and eloquent spokesperson for this view is Stanley Fish. *See* Doing What Comes Naturally: Change, Rhetoric, and the Practice of Theory in Literary and Legal Studies (1989).

2. With the Compliments of the Author: Reflections on Austin and Derrida, in Doing What Comes Naturally 37.

3. See Examining Witnesses ch. 8.

4. FED. R. EVID. 806 expressly permits this evidence and is a powerful weapon against potentially hurtful hearsay.

5. Batson v. Kentucky, 476 U.S. 79 (1986), and its progeny ensure that the jury in both civil and criminal cases will be more diverse than before. In a society itself containing so many currents of thought, the challenge of presenting themes and images that address all the jurors is great.

6. ROBERT A. FERGUSON, UNTOLD STORIES IN THE LAW, in LAW'S STORIES 84.

7. This distinction was first suggested to me by reading E. M. Forster's discussion in JAMES BOYD WHITE, THE LEGAL IMAGINATION 145 (abridged ed. 1985). I have expanded and changed Forster's and White's concept, however.

8. *The Picture Theory of Trial Advocacy,* 12 LITIGATION 8 (Winter 1986), available on WESTLAW.

9. C. S. LEWIS, STUDIES IN WORDS 317–18 (2d ed. 1967).

10. MARK TWAIN, JAMES FENIMORE COOPER'S LITERARY OFFENSES. I have taken the text from the CD-ROM edition of Twain's works. I have edited Twain's indictment of Cooper, without always using ellipses.

11. FED. R. EVID. 615.

12. Good books on jury selection include ROBERT HIRSCHHORN, BENNETT'S GUIDE TO JURY SELECTION AND TRIAL DYNAMICS IN CIVIL AND CRIMINAL LITIGATION (1995).

13. You can read the transcript of *voir dire,* indeed of the entire trial, on the Internet.

Chapter Three, Part I

Elements of the Opening

ADVOCATE DUTIES, JUROR DUTIES

You know everything about your case. The jurors know nothing, except what little gleanings they have from the judge's initial comments and *voir dire*. If the case has generated media attention, the jurors may think they know something about it, but almost certainly they do not. Even if the case has been covered in the media, and the jurors do know a lot about it, they are supposed to start with a clean slate. This is a fiction, and we will discuss it in the pages to come.

The point is that your opening statement is your opportunity to "say your case." If you represent a defendant, you will not put on evidence for a while except through cross-examination. Even if you are the plaintiff, the evidence will not come in as a "story." The jurors need a place to "put" each item of evidence as they hear or see it.

It is easy to forget this lesson. We see lawyers who jump right into the middle of their facts in opening statement. We see this error repeated when they do direct examination and don't give enough background. We see it also on cross-examination, when they give no hint of why these questions are being asked.

If the jurors have not begun with a clean slate, you must address that in opening statement. And if you have been the beneficiary of favorable media coverage, do not bask in this glory; you must all the more insist that the case be decided on the evidence presented in court. So you may say: "You know from *voir dire* that this case has attracted some attention from the media. All of you who saw or heard any of that coverage were right out front in telling us about what you saw and heard. And then as we talked [or, as you talked with the judge], two things became very clear. First, nobody thinks the media gets it right all the time, or maybe even most of the time. And second, we all are here under the oaths we took to try this case based on what can be proved right here in this courtroom. And we are prepared for that."

Or perhaps your case involves issues on which there are deeply held beliefs or even community prejudices. Your opening may indicate: "We are grateful to you for talking to us in *voir dire* about this issue of sex discrimination in the workplace. This is a case that involves those issues, and we can see how easy it can be to let our emotions get into it. But this is not a case about whether there should be laws that prohibit sex discrimination. There are those laws. The judge here is going to tell you exactly what those laws say and how you should apply them when you go to deliberate on your verdict. So that is not the issue. The issue is the old, plain and simple one of who you are going to believe, who had the best opportunity to know what was going on, and, yes, who is telling the truth. I say old, plain and simple. Well, it is not really simple. It takes judgment, it takes evidence, to make those kinds of decisions. That's why you are here—to make those decisions. Let's talk about the evidence."

In the *Nichols* case, we knew there would be two dozen or more witnesses who would tell heart-rending stories of personal loss and of witnessing devastation, injury, and death. So I warned the jurors and reminded them of their role:

And just as in life, the last bit of evidence about an important thing may light up the whole picture, so we beg you to have open minds. We'll present evidence to you, beginning with our cross-examination of the very first witnesses that take that witness stand; but for the first few weeks of the trial, the Government has the choice of what witnesses to bring, what evidence to bring. He that pleadeth his cause first seemeth just, but the defendant cometh and searcheth it out. Over and over again, you're going to hear about the presumption of innocence. That means we start with a clean page. That means that suspicion, prejudice, prejudgment, speculation have no place.

You might express the same theme in a more matter-of-fact way: "Sometimes when you are making an important decision—to buy a car, for example—you get a lot of information. You see a lot of cars. You compare prices. And then the last thing you read or hear or find out might be the one that makes the decision. Maybe it is an article you read about the safety or lack of safety of a car you have been considering. Or maybe it is a detail about the car that you notice. The same thing can happen in a lawsuit—the last piece of evidence can be the one that has the most importance to you in deciding."

A little farther on in the *Nichols* opening, I did what you must do every time. You must tell the jurors what you do not dispute, tell them the bad facts, and tell them how the evidence will put those facts into context. You can often do that while discussing the elements of the claims and defenses, and this is so whether it is a criminal or a civil case:

Now, the first charge is that Timothy McVeigh, Terry Nichols, and others used—conspired to use a weapon of mass destruction against the Murrah Federal Building and the people in it. We do not contest that Timothy McVeigh did indeed conspire with several other people to blow up that building. We agree and understand and stipulate and concede that at least 168 people died from that crime, that the crime visited enormous harm on hundreds of others. There's no dispute about that. The dispute is can they overcome the presumption in law that Terry Nichols had nothing whatever to do with it.

But I want to warn you: The prosecutors may choose not to accept the reality that we accept. They may choose to put before you graphic, emotional, tragic evidence of the devastation on April 19. This evidence— these events, I repeat, are—they're not in dispute. We understand that there's not a joy the world can give like that it takes away.[1] The prosecutors may replay these terrible images over and over as if to say that somebody has to be punished for these things. That, of course, is not the question. The question for you at the end of the evidence will be who; and that is a question to be answered, we trust, in the light shed by the evidence and the law and not in flashes of anger. If the prosecutors present this evidence, our concern will be to show how it fits the picture that we have drawn and not theirs. We will cross-examine all the witnesses who come here, even those who have lost so much. By doing that, we mean them no disrespect. To the living, we owe respect. To the dead, we owe the truth.[2]

DIVIDING INTO PARTS

The opening statement is—as you may tell the jurors—a map, a guide, a sketch, a plan, an introduction. Of course, building your case is like making a mosaic: You cannot put all the pieces in at once. You are not even in charge of putting a lot of the pieces in, for your opponent has a significant role to play; I acknowledged that by telling the *Nichols* jury that the last bit of evidence may prove decisive. However, you will organize your evidence as much as possible, to make it easier to follow and remember. You will organize each cross-examination.

The opening statement is, however, your chance to show where these disparate pieces fit. To do that, the opening must be in parts, with transitions between parts.

Opening statement begins with your looking at the jury. Then you say "May it please the court, counsel, Ms. Smith [your client], members of the jury." I prefer "members of the jury" to "ladies and gentlemen."

Then you tell the jury what this case is about, in one or two sentences. You say your story: "This case is about Mary Smith [indicating], who is a qualified legal secretary and who needed her job. And it is about John Jones, who made her life at work unbearable by making crude and unwanted sexual advances. And we are here to present our evidence and, based on that evidence and the law, to ask you for a verdict of substantial money damages."

Next you introduce yourself and your team. "My name is Paula Winston, and with the other members of our team we are going to present the evidence that proves what I just said. The other people on our team, whom you will see here in court working on the case, are. . . ."

Next acknowledge your burden of proof. "We brought this case. We have the burden of proving to you what we say. We accept [or embrace] that burden." Notice you do not say that "this opening statement is not evidence" or any such self-deprecating thing. Rather, you state: "In this opening statement, I am going to outline the facts we are going to prove."

Having told the jurors of the burden, tell them how your opening will go. "After I tell you the legal 'elements' of our case, my discussion falls into the three main areas that the proof will reveal." These are the three parts—the triplets—discussed in Chapter Two. Here your triplets might be "First, I want to talk about Mary Smith, who she is and how she qualified for a job with John Jones. Second, I want to talk about what happened to Mary Smith when she began work with John Jones, how she was mistreated, and how these people violated the law of the land." Notice we are calling people by their first and last names. You know her as Mary, but in court she has a last name and she is Mary Smith or Ms. Smith. "Third, I will tell you all the ways in which Mary Smith was harmed, for as we said in *voir dire,* when we prove our case it becomes necessary to figure what sum of money in damages will put Mary Smith back where she would have been without this wrongful conduct, and if you make the findings we contend the evidence requires, what these defendants should have to pay in exemplary damages." If liability and damages are bifurcated, or more likely if the punitive damages aspect is bifurcated, you obviously don't introduce it in that way.

Now tell the jury the elements of the case—the items that must be proved to have a verdict in your favor. This is an "outline" of the case, based on the pretrial order. It is also a chance for you to say, as you list these things, what is and is not disputed.

Once you have done these introductory parts, you will tell the facts as you intend to prove them, using the triplets with which you began. Tell them as a story. Introduce the witnesses, letting the jurors know why they will be here. No need to introduce all the witnesses—too much detail bogs the story down. For example, "You are going to hear about the kinds of comments that John Jones made to Mary Smith starting the first week she was on the job. One witness will be Anthony Parsons, the secretary who sits at the desk closest to where Mary Smith was sitting. He was able to see and hear better than anybody. And he will tell you. . . ."

If there are problems with your evidence, tell the jury about them. "Now I want to be fair about this. Mary Smith is not perfect. You are going to hear that when she gets frightened or upset, she. . . ."

If you represent the defendant, the same basic principles apply, except that you must do and say things to capture the jurors' attention, to open their minds to your version. If your opponent's opening is lackluster, this is not much of a challenge. But in a high-profile case, where jurors have come to court with some impression of the facts, getting their attention in your opening is critical. The same caution will apply if your opponent's opening is dramatic and effective.

Some cautions for defendants: First, never assume a burden of proof you don't have. Talk about why the evidence will not support these claims that are being made. This is a difficult rule to follow, and I am often asked by lawyers whether it contradicts the basic idea that your opening must tell a story. That is, how can you tell a story without, expressly or tacitly, offering to prove the story true?

I accept the relevance of this question, but I say it can be done. I think jurors understand and appreciate the burden of proof. By the end of *voir dire* they should—if you have done your job. Let's look at some examples. First, get the jurors' attention with an image about open-mindedness. For example, I often begin as defendant in a civil or criminal case by holding up my hand: "Members of the jury. Can you see my hand? You cannot see my hand. Not until I've turned it over and shown you both sides can you say that you have seen my hand."

Now, in introducing the elements of your opponent's case, repeat the idea, as I did in the *Nichols* case:

> So let's begin by asking: What are those prosecutors charging that Terry Nichols did? What are they going to try to prove beyond a reasonable doubt? Well, you know there's an indictment, and there are 11 separate charges. When the case is all over, Judge Matsch will tell you what the formal, legal elements of each of these charges are; and he'll say to you, in effect, that if the government fails to prove any element of a charge beyond a reasonable doubt, then it becomes your duty to acquit on that charge and to say not guilty.

You may return to the theme again:

> In saying what the evidence will show—by the way— we don't assume a burden we don't have. Terry Nichols is innocent. He's presumed innocent. If they want to change that, they've got to bring you evidence, to satisfy you beyond a reasonable doubt. We don't have any burden of proof here. And our job is simply to show the

reasonable doubts; and to do that, we'll show you the hard evidence, the truthful alternatives to their theory. And from the first witnesses they present, we'll do that when we rise to cross-examine.

Another useful caution: Do not use opening statement to get into a fight with your opponent. Never say, "It is not like what she said," or any words like that. Set out your story as a freestanding and independent structure. Surely you will talk about your opponent's "theory" or "what they must prove," but avoid personal references.

STATING YOUR THEME

I have repeated the importance of story so many times that this reminder may be unnecessary. But I have heard too many opening statements to be confident that the message has come through. Perhaps one way to view the issue is to say what "stating your theme" is not.

An opening statement may contain an attack on the other side's evidence, but it is not such an attack. That is, you can say in opening that the jury will hear witnesses who bear a grudge, have changed their story, or could not possibly have seen what they will relate. But these things are not themes—they are predictions of the evidence that will or will not support a theme.

A theme is not what you want. It is why you are entitled to what you want. That is, you cannot decently ask the jurors to give you a money judgment, to give you a verdict of no liability, or to acquit your client unless they have a reason to do it. And that reason is your theme.

A theme is not an attack on the other side's lawyers. In many cases, you will have to explain why your adversaries are wrong. Sometimes you will show that they behaved with stupidity or even cupidity. Such a conclusion must flow from the evidence. It is not your story. At most it supports your story.

USING EXHIBITS

Many judges will not permit you to use exhibits in opening statement. If exhibits are allowed, they must be ones that have been admitted in the pretrial order. As I said in the previous chapter, and in *Examining Witnesses,*[3] you must use exhibits to empower the jurors as well as to persuade them. Jurors are empowered if they can see the actual exhibits they will have in the jury room. In opening statement, you begin to show how those exhibits might be useful in deliberations.

If you want to "dress up" an exhibit, you might have a portion of it enlarged for use in opening statement, perhaps with some graphic representation of where the excerpt is found in the original.

You may also be able to use charts and other items of "demonstrative evidence." I do not think such things are helpful. You might write key words on a white board, on a transparency for an overhead projector, or on a piece of paper on the ELMO. The ELMO is a display mechanism that picks up the image of an object, paper, or photograph and transmits it to video monitors in the courtroom. I have seen fancy charts that cost a great deal and take up a lot of courtroom space. They get in the way of lawyer communication with the jurors, and they have a very short life in memory, for they do not reappear in evidence.

In some cases you may have videotape or audiotape evidence. If you have a staged video—such as a view of a relevant place or a "day in the life" of a plaintiff, or the story of a corporation's activities, you might play a portion of it in opening statement. You might play portions of video depositions. If you have an audiotape, have the text displayed on an overhead, on the ELMO, or on large white poster boards while you are playing the tape.

I have a decided preference against using large poster-type materials, whether as summary evidence, as demonstrative evidence, or to illustrate an argument. I prefer to use eight-and-a-half-by-eleven-inch materials—charts, documents, pictures—and display them on an overhead projector or with an ELMO device. That way I can keep the actual material close at hand to use whenever I wish during trial.

Remember also that juror concentration on such passive evidence as audiotapes and videotapes is short. I am not sure why this is so, but at about three minutes juror attention significantly drops off.

If you are to use exhibits—in evidence or demonstrative—in opening, they become a means to organize your presentation. They become markers that you can put out to guide the jurors' consideration of the evidence.

> May it please the court, counsel, members of the jury. This is a case about how enterprising companies get crude oil out of the ground, and spend hundreds of millions of dollars on equipment and talent to turn that crude oil into useful products—gasoline and oil for our cars and trucks, heating oil for homes, and even plastics that are used in our homes, our cars, and our places of work. This is a case about crude oil from a particular place—the Wilmington basin—under the sea just off the City of Long Beach.
>
> Now, when we think of oil, maybe we think of what we put in our cars at the service station, or even the light oil that we use around the house or in the shop. But that oil is not what comes out of the ground, especially in Long Beach.
>
> This is what comes out of the ground. [Here the lawyer holds up a quart jug of heavy crude oil. He pours some of it into a beaker. It hardly will pour. He sniffs it and wrinkles his nose.]
>
> This stuff is no good to anybody, except maybe to spray on dirt roads to keep the dust down. To get it out of the ground without spilling it into the ocean, my client had to spend [a dollar figure].

The opening continues. The lawyer has a diagram of the recovery operation—showing how the oil is extracted and then put in a pipeline to the refinery. Another diagram shows the refinery itself. The refinery costs a certain amount to build and run. With this investment, the company can get 75 percent gasoline from this heavy crude oil. And gasoline is what we need for our cars.

The case is about a contract. Here is a copy of the contract, signed by the same plaintiffs who want to redo the entire deal after they have received the benefit of it.

In this hypothetical situation, the lawyer is putting before the jury two kinds of "marker" exhibits. Charts are one kind of evidence, but these charts summarize real evidence and will be available to the jurors in deliberation. In this group we also include tabular material. These are not big "blow-up" charts. The second type of evidence consists of actual documents and pictures that will be in evidence. If any of these items is key to the case, it can remain at counsel table throughout the trial, as a constant reminder.

Often you have exhibits that you got from the other side. If so, let the jury know where they came from:

> In this case, we will show you that the plaintiff's own employees wrote memos saying that our client was living up to the contract and that a lawsuit would simply lead to embarrassment. Those people were overruled and somebody decided to bring this case. Here is one of the memos these employees wrote. These are people responsible for managing things on a day-to-day basis, and they know what they are talking about. [Display the memo and read the relevant part.] Now you may ask, How in world did we find this? Well, when anybody gets sued, they have the right to demand that the other side produce any relevant memoranda and other papers, and make their employees available for examination under oath in depositions. You will see a lot of evidence in this case that we got in just that way—by using our right to make them produce the relevant material.

KEEPING ALIVE THE SENSE OF JUSTICE

Trials are about justice. Hamlet declaimed:

> The time is out of joint; O cursed spite,
> That ever I was born to set it right![4]

In case after case, jurors report that their deliberations ended with a strong sense that they were not simply "solving the case" or "finding the facts" but doing justice between the parties. Jurors want to know the right thing to do. Your arguments to them must always focus on why it is just that you prevail.

NOTES

1. The words are from Byron's *Stanzas for Music*.
2. The words are from Voltaire: *"On doit les ègards aux vivants; aux mortes, on ne doit que la verité."*
3. EXAMINING WITNESSSES ch. 6.
4. See Conclusion for more on this theme.

Chapter Three, Part II

The Opening Statement—An Example

It was 1975. John Connally, former Secretary of the Treasury, had been charged[1] with accepting an unlawful gratuity "for himself" and "for or because of official duty performed by him."[2] The prosecution's theory was that Jake Jacobsen, a Texas lawyer who worked as a lobbyist for the Associated Milk Producers, Inc. (AMPI), had paid Connally $10,000 in two equal installments as a "thank you" for Connally's support of high milk price supports.[3] The case was tried before Chief Judge George Hart in the District of Columbia.

Connally had also been charged with lying to a federal grand jury about whether he had taken money from Jacobsen, but those counts were severed for trial. After the acquittal, those charges were dismissed on the government's motion.

Edward Bennett Williams delivered the opening statement immediately after the prosecutor's opening. I have left in some of the interruptions of the court and opposing counsel and eliminated others. As you read, remember that the prosecutor had already outlined the case the government expected to prove. The jury had already "met" Jacobsen, AMPI, and price supports. Mr. Williams is not starting with an entirely new picture. He is shifting viewpoint just enough to show the case in a different light.

* * * * * * *

May it please the court, ladies and gentlemen of the jury:

What Mr. Sale said to you this morning is the opening statement made on behalf of the prosecution. It is a statement of what they hope to prove during the course of this trial, it is not evidence in the case.

Likewise, what I say to you now, members of the jury, is not evidence in the case.

COMMENTARY

I disagree with this characterization as unnecessarily deprecating one's opening. Instead you can say that the prosecutor has presented a theory and you will present facts. Indeed, Williams does this in the next couple of sentences.

Rather, it is a statement of what we confidently expect to demonstrate to you through the testimony of witnesses whom we will call to the stand, through documents and written materials that we will offer in evidence for your inspection.

COMMENTARY

The process of empowering the jury begins. The defense will offer these "for your inspection." You could use other forms of words, but you must let the jury know that you know they are the ones who will decide. This is all being done so that they have a fair chance to decide.

Now under the rules of this court, as in every court in the land, the prosecution gets the opportunity to offer its case first, to call its witnesses and put in such documents and written materials as it chooses to offer which are receivable in evidence.

COMMENTARY

The prosecution not only goes first, it gets to choose which part of the story to tell. The defense will complete the story. This is a cue to open-mindedness.

Not until all of the prosecution's evidence has been laid before you does the opportunity come to the defense to give you its side of this case, and for that reason, right at the outset, I ask you ladies and gentlemen of the jury to keep an open mind during the course of this trial, bearing in mind that not until you have heard all of the prosecution's side does the defense have the chance to come forth with its side of the case.

As the mountaineer said about his pancakes, "no matter how thin I makes them, there is always two sides to them."

And so it is with every contested case that is ever tried in this courthouse or any other courthouse in the land, there are two sides. In the ordinary process the prosecution goes first and we come second.

There is one other thing that I would like to say to you right at the outset about opening statements in general made in a Court of law. An opening statement by a trial lawyer to a jury is not like a politician's speech. When a politician is seeking office and he makes a speech to people whose votes he is soliciting, he can promise the moon because he doesn't have to deliver on his promises until after the votes are cast, until after the election is over.

But what I say to you this afternoon, members of the jury, in this opening statement, made on behalf of the defendant John Connally in this case, I must deliver on. I must deliver on before you go to your jury room, before you begin your deliberations, before you cast your ballot, because you will hold me responsible for everything I say to you this afternoon when I say that I will prove certain things to you, and well you should.

I welcome that responsibility, because what I say to you this afternoon, members of the jury, in this opening statement made on behalf of the defendant, we shall prove to you through the testimony of witnesses who will take the stand, through documents, and through other written materials that will be offered here before you.

COMMENTARY

Williams is telling the jury that the defense will prove certain things. I would not be so categorical. I would introduce reasonable doubt early. There is plenty of room to disagree. In fact, the deliberating jurors did focus on the concept of reasonable doubt, based on final argument and the judge's instructions.

One last word. His Honor said to you this morning, and I want to underscore this so that there will be no misunderstanding on the subject. This, ladies and gentlemen of the jury, is not a Watergate case. Although the prosecution staff is attached to the Watergate prosecution staff, as His Honor said to you this morning, it is not a Watergate case, and my friends at the other table will readily agree with this.

COMMENTARY

The *Connally* case was brought by the Watergate Special Prosecutor's office, which had not lost any cases before District of Columbia juries. By the time of Connally's trial, Richard Nixon had resigned. Washington political air was still redolent of scandal. So it was important to distance this case from Watergate. In any given case, you may have a key misimpression to dispel, in the same way that Williams did. Note that he includes opposing counsel in the disclaimer, challenging them to object if they disagree.

John Connally was out of the government: he had finished as Secretary of the Treasury before the episode known as the Watergate episode took place, and before the so-called cover-up took place.

COMMENTARY

Williams is doing several things here. He is telling us what the case is "not about" and trying to avoid spillover prejudice from the other Watergate cases. We did this in the case of Terry Nichols, by stressing how different was the case against him from that against Timothy McVeigh. The trial judge had told prospective jurors in *voir dire* that he had granted a severance in the cases because the evidence was different as to the two men. Whether the trial judge does it or not, one must pursue such matters in *voir dire* and by juror questionnaire. Williams also knows that the most lethal allegation against a party is that he or she "covered up" the truth—lied, destroyed documents, and so on. There were, to be sure, charges that Connally had lied to a grand jury about the matters being litigated, but those charges had been severed.

This is not a Watergate case, and I want to lay that to rest right at the outset.

Now, a word, members of the jury about the defendant—just a word

COMMENTARY

He does not mean "just a word," as the next few paragraphs show.

about the defendant himself who is on trial here before you, the defendant John Connally.

He is 58 years old, he was born in Floresville, Texas on February 27, 1917, one of eight children. His father was a bus driver. Floresville is a little town of about—

THE COURT: Mr. Williams, I think you are getting into your closing argument. Let's get to what you expect the evidence to prove.

MR. WILLIAMS: I want to identify the defendant, Your Honor, as part of—

THE COURT: Well, all right, but with discretion. Go ahead.

MR. WILLIAMS: Yes, sir.

COMMENTARY

The judge's interruption is probably not well taken. From the opening as a whole, it is clear that Connally will testify. Williams therefore puts Connally's background in issue at least to the extent that such evidence bears on credibility and intent. So it is proper to have this sort of summary. Chief Judge Hart is probably exercising some anticipatory control, knowing that in

Williams he has a voluble, persuasive, and dynamic advocate. Note that Williams chooses to explain his position to the court and gets some reprieve. You have to know the judge before seeming to argue an adverse ruling. Some judges will prefer that you ask leave to approach and state your position. The judge's interruptions can be lethal to your case, and you must object early—but politely—as soon as the tendency appears. Williams might have forestalled the objection—and this is a good tactic in opening statement—by saying that Connally would take the stand and that the evidence would show such-and-such. The prefatory remark "the evidence will show" has shielded many an otherwise argumentative statement from objection in opening statement.

He, members of the jury, while a student at the University of Texas entered politics, campaigning in 1937, as far back as 1937 for the late President Johnson when he sought office, and he remained in political life all the rest of his days.

He was married in 1940 to Mrs. Connally, they have three children all of whom are grown. That's 35 years ago.

And in 1949 he came to Washington, he came to Washington in public service as the administrative assistant to President Johnson.

COMMENTARY

He means then-senator Lyndon Johnson. But see the pattern here. Williams is distancing Connally still more from the Republican Party of Richard Nixon. He is also providing important information about Connally's family and his public service. During *voir dire,* several jurors spontaneously said they remembered the day President Kennedy was killed and then-governor Connally wounded. When they remembered this, they looked at Connally differently than they had before.

All of this description "dedemonizes" the defendant.

He came back again, members of the jury, in 1961 as the Secretary of the Navy under President Kennedy.

And he came back still again as the evidence will show in this case, and in 1971, as the Secretary of the Treasury, as the first Democrat in the Nixon administration. He began service on February 5, 1971.

And it is the period during which he served as Secretary of the Treasury which is relevant and germane to this case. It is the period during which he was the Secretary of the Treasury when the acts with which he is charged took place. He served as Secretary from February of 1971 until June of 1972.

Now, what are the charges that have been leveled against him in the Information that was filed in this case?

COMMENTARY

Note the locution—"charges that have been leveled against him in the Information." With a gesture and these words, Williams says that the government's case is simply a theory.

The charges were felonies, which came to be prosecuted by information. In federal court, under the Fifth Amendment and FED. R. CRIM. P. 7, all felonies must be prosecuted by the indictment of a grand jury. Initially Connally was indicted, but our pretrial motion revealed a fatal flaw in the grand jury's indictment in that it omitted an element of the offense. We chose to consent to the government filing an information, which is simply a formal charge signed by the prosecutor, rather than have the publicity attendant upon a reindictment. This would not necessarily be one's tactical position in every case. At the time, I was not sure that it was wise to consent to the information. Reading the opening statement, it seems to me now that *information* is a softer word than *indictment*.

As you were told this morning, there are two charges. First, is that on May 14, 1971, he received $5000.00 in cash because of official acts performed by him, namely his recommendation in his official capacity concerning an increase in federal milk price supports to be fixed by the Secretary of Agriculture.

The second charge in this two-count Information is in all respects the same except that the date is different, he is charged with precisely the same act on September 24, of 1971, some few months later.

Now, as you were told this morning, he is not charged, members of the jury, with the crime of bribery, it is not charged by the Government that his opinion or judgment or action or conduct as the Secretary of the Treasury was in any way improperly or corruptly influenced by the receipt of any money or anything of value.

COMMENTARY

Williams is repeating a caution that the prosecutors gave. This is not a bribery case. Notice that he does not speak directly of the prosecutors. It is the passive voice—"as you were told." But when the defense speaks, Williams uses active language. When he tells the jury what the evidence shows, he tells them who did what.

It is rather charged that he received a gratuity or a contribution, if you will, from one Jake Jacobsen, a lawyer for the Associated Milk Producers, Incorporated.

Now, I want to say to you at the very outset that our position is, of course, we agree with the prosecution that if he received anything of value as charged in the Information which I just read to you, if he took anything whatsoever as charged in the two-count Information, it would be a violation of law, but we will show you members of the jury that those charges that have been leveled against him in this two-count Information are without any basis, and that the proof will show that he did not, while he was serving as Secretary of the Treasury, receive anything from the milk producers or Mr. Jake Jacobsen, or anyone else.

COMMENTARY

Here Williams is combining two tasks. He is denying and he is putting the denial in the form of "without any basis." This phrase, coupled with "charges leveled," is the key defense position. The defense will say that Jacobsen is not to be believed and that Jacobsen and Connally are the sole witnesses. To be sure, Williams couples this with "the proof will show that he did not," which might be construed as accepting some burden of persuasion that the defense does not have.

Some advocates spend more time than does Williams talking about the burden of proof beyond a reasonable doubt. In some cases, one must. In this case, it is a credibility contest, and Williams has used enough imagery for his purposes. In another case, you might wish to say that the prosecutors have a great burden to bring evidence in support of their theory. It is as though they have a big rock on their table, called "beyond a reasonable doubt," and they can't just chip away at it—they must break it all up and carry all of it away.

Now what will the evidence show with respect to who the Associated Milk Producers, Incorporated were, and what their interests were, and who Jake Jacobsen was, and what his problems were?

────────────── COMMENTARY ──────────────

This sentence is elegant. The Associated Milk Producers, Inc. [AMPI] has "interests." Jacobsen has "problems." This is picture advocacy. AMPI is an interest group. Jacobsen is a man with problems.

The Associated Milk Producers, members of the jury, were and are a national cooperative of dairy farmers covering some 22 states and having a membership of approximately 40,000. They are based in San Antonio, Texas.

In short, the evidence will show that the Associated Milk Producers are an association of dairy farmers joined together with common economic interest, seeking common economic betterment through collective action. They are to the dairy farmers, the Associated Milk Producers, Inc. is to the dairy farmers what a labor union would be to the wage earner.

────────────── COMMENTARY ──────────────

Now we understand what AMPI is. For this jury, the idea that they are like a labor union is a favorable image. For the defense theory of this case, this is a good characterization. If the theory were that AMPI had attempted to corrupt Secretary Connally, then they would be "a lobbying group," or "seekers of influence." You will see, however, that Secretary Connally had a legitimate interest in AMPI's (and the dairy farmers') well-being. AMPI is not the adversary in this case; Jacobsen is.

Now, you will hear in this case a great deal about parity, and about price supports. And I want to take just a few moments to tell you what the evidence will show with respect to these subjects, because they play such a crucial part in this case and in the issues to be resolved by you.

COMMENTARY

"The issues to be resolved by you"—this is the jurors' case. Now we are going to get some background that is essential to seeing what the case is about. On the simplest level, this case is about whether Jake Jacobsen gave John Connally $10,000. The evidence will be that Jacobsen and Connally met. There is evidence that Connally spoke up on behalf of milk producers. Thus, context is all-important. The jurors do not know the context; this is always the case and requires that the advocate not assume that they know based on his or her own familiarity with the case. In addition, the jurors may think they know something about the case from the media. Whatever they know is probably wrong from the advocate's perspective, so that is another reason to start fresh.

What follows is an outline of milk price supports. One might think it dull, but it is crucial to juror understanding of the issues in the case. When Connally took the stand, he spoke persuasively and knowingly about these issues—remember that he had had a career in politics and this was one of "his" issues. There had to be a reason in the evidence why he would meet with Jacobsen (representing AMPI), why he would speak up for the milk producers' interests, and why Jacobsen would be able to get $10,000 from AMPI saying that he would give it to Connally but in fact never doing so.

Of course, it is an element of the offense that the defendant had committed an "official act," and it will be an issue whether Connally's position as Secretary of the Treasury made milk price advocacy such an act. But this is not an issue that will be argued to the jury.

Some 40 years ago, during the great depression of the thirties, the idea of agricultural equality was introduced to our economic system, and an act was passed designed to give the farmers a fair share of the national income.

This was in the Agricultural Adjustment Act of 1933. And as a measure of determining whether the farmer was getting a fair share of the national income the idea of parity came into our economic vocabulary.

This was at a time when farms were being foreclosed and the farmer was in a desperate financial strait. Parity, members of the jury, is simply this: The evidence will show that the parity price for a farm product, in this case milk, is that price which gives the farmer the same purchasing power that he would have, that he had during a specified period of time known as the base period, when all agree that he had a fair share of the national income.

Now, the base period that was used was 1910 to 1914, when all agreed that he had a fair share of the national income.

The idea is that if a farmer could buy a pair of overalls for what he could sell 100 pounds of milk for in 1914, he ought to be able to buy a pair of overalls for what he can sell 100 pounds of milk for in 1975. If he could buy a pair of overalls for $2.00 in 1914, and he was selling 100 pounds of milk for $2.00 in 1914, and if today it costs him $8.00 for a pair of overalls then he ought to get $8.00 for 100 pounds of milk.

Now, that is a terrible oversimplification of the idea.

First of all, you will hear milk referred to throughout this case by the 100 pound weight because that is the way dairy farmers sell it, not by the quarts, there are 46 and 1/2 quarts in 100 pounds of milk, and the base period is not 1910 to 1914 any longer, it is a ten-year period during which the farmer had a fair share of the national income.

And, of course, the price is not pegged just to overalls, but to all those things that the farmer needs to make a living and to produce milk, to buy his feed, to buy his grain, to buy his food, pay his interest on his mortgage, and so in an ideal society, if the farmer were to get a fair share of the national income, he would always be getting the parity price for his product.

The dairy farmer would be getting the parity price, the same price he got 20 or 30 years ago, translated into an inflated dollar of today.

Now, in order to give the farmer a fair share of the national income, the idea of price supports was born. Price supports are not a new idea, members of the jury. Price supports are 42 years old in our economy, they came in in the Roosevelt administration, and every administration, Roosevelt, Truman, Eisenhower, Johnson, Kennedy, Nixon, and Ford have followed the concept of price supports for the farmer.

COMMENTARY

This part of the opening is carefully researched and carefully crafted. First, we researched the history of price supports. We documented all these facts. Then we talked the matter over with our client, who turned out to have a good grasp of this information. Then Williams and the team worked it into a form that could not only be understood but also seen sympathetically. The idea of parity comes through, not as a government giveaway program but as ensuring fairness to farmers—a "fair share" of national income as Williams repeats several times.

Now, price supports are designed, members of the jury, to hold the price in the case of milk up to a certain level so that they will not fall, the price will not fall to such a low that the dairy farmer will not have a fair share of the national income.

So if the price of milk is set at $4.66 per hundredweight, that means that the Government will buy all the milk that the farmer cannot sell at that price. Meaning that the price will always be held at that point during that year.

Now, the evidence will show that the Secretary of Agriculture by law fixes the price supports on milk. And the law says he may fix it at any point between 75 percent and 90 percent of parity. For example, if the proper parity price of milk should be $5 per hundred weight, the Secretary of Agriculture is empowered by law to fix the price support at 90 percent, which would be $4.50, or at 80 percent which is $4, or at 75 percent which is $3.75.

He can fix it wherever he chooses, and he does that each year just about April 1st, just did it the other day, he fixed it at $7.24, the new Secretary of Agriculture. That was fixed at 80 percent parity.

Now, in 1971 price supports on milk were at $4.66 per hundredweight. That is where they were fixed. That is where they had been. This is about ten cents per quart to the farmer, and the farmers were very unhappy about it, and the Associated Milk Producers, the representative of the dairy farmers, were very unhappy about it, and they were in Washington beseeching the Secretary of Agriculture, Mr. Clifford Hardin, to raise price supports for the year 1971–72.

They came in February of 1971, and they were urging that price supports be raised. They wanted price supports to be up at $5.05, so that they could survive, as they put it. But they would have settled at $4.93.

They would like to have had 90 percent parity, but it was well known that they would settle at 85 percent parity.

And they were making their case, they were making their case to the Secretary of Agriculture through their representatives. They were deeply concerned that if he did not increase supports that their members would face economic disaster.

Now, in addition to making their case to the Secretary of Agriculture, the evidence will show that they had gone to the Congress and they had asked the Congress to act in the event that Mr. Hardin didn't act. They were asking for legislation to be passed, they were looking for a law to be passed to raise price supports to 85 percent.

They had, as the evidence will show, 136 members of the House who were willing to put their names on a bill to raise price supports to 85 percent, or $4.93 per hundredweight. They had 35 members of the Senate who were willing to put their names on a bill to raise price supports on milk from $4.66 to $4.93, or 85 percent of parity.

Now, John Connally came to Washington and began as Secretary of the Treasury in February 1971, at a time, members of the jury, when this issue was before the Department of Agriculture, before the Secretary of Agriculture. But the representatives of AMPI were visiting all the members of the government trying to enlist the support of those members of government for an increase in price supports.

COMMENTARY

Here the opening details evidence that Williams will bring out in cross-examining the AMPI representatives. They will be called as government witnesses simply to say they gave Jacobsen money to give to Connally. But on cross-examination, they can be made into defense witnesses and all this information brought out as within the "subject matter" of direct examination. Once again, the context is important because it shows that there was nothing unusual about approaching Connally for his support on this issue and nothing unusual in the Washington of those days about that support being given.

John Connally had had a long record in public service, a long record for fair price support for the farmer, and for the dairy farmer, they knew his record. They knew that he was sympathetic to their position because his record was a public record that had gone back for years on this issue. There had been no question about the fact that his public record had been 100 percent in favor of the farmer throughout his long political career.

On March 12th of 1971, on March 12th Secretary Hardin announced his decision. He announced that price supports would stay where they were. They were frozen at 80 percent of parity or $4.66 per hundred pounds.

This came as a shock and disappointment to the representatives of the dairy farmers who were here in Washington. It came as a grave disappointment to AMPI and its lawyers, and to the dairy farmers themselves. They felt, as the evidence will show, that they had been done in.

COMMENTARY

In this paragraph, Williams repeats the same message in three slightly different forms, building to the somewhat argumentative "done in," which is softened by "as the evidence will show." But this is a good example of triplets in rhetoric.

Now, AMPI took its case to Congress. Now, I have explained to you who AMPI was, the Associated Milk Producers, and what their interests were, and how they were working for the economic betterment of their constituents.

COMMENTARY

A transition paragraph that ends the discussion of AMPI to lead to a consideration of Jacobsen. And again, Williams uses triplets.

Now, what will the evidence show about Jacobsen? You heard a lot about Jacobsen this morning. The evidence will show, members of the jury, that Jacobsen was a lawyer for the Associated Milk Producers, Incorporated. His testimony will be offered, as you heard this morning, in support of charges against John Connally.

What will the evidence show on Jake Jacobsen? The evidence will show the following: that Jake Jacobsen, during the relevant time in this case was twice indicted by federal grand juries for perjury, for testifying falsely before a federal grand jury in Texas, and for testifying falsely before a federal grand jury here in this very courthouse on the sixth floor.

COMMENTARY

A word picture. The grand jury is in "this very courthouse," and—eyes directed upwards—was on "the sixth floor."

The evidence will show that Jake Jacobsen was indicted at the very time with which we are concerned, at the very time relevant to this case, and the charges which are before you, by a federal grand jury in San Angelo, Texas, for fraud, crooked loans, crooked deals, on the depositors and shareholders of the First Savings and Loan Association of San Angelo, Texas.

COMMENTARY

As I pointed out in *Examining Witnesses*, a witness who makes a plea bargain will not necessarily be disbelieved. Jurors often understand that the way to catch one wrongdoer is to give some leniency to a confederate. Williams knows this. He is setting up two "extra" reasons to doubt Jacobsen: first, he was charged with lying under oath, and second, he bargained to avoid prosecution for bank fraud in cases unrelated to this one. Note that Williams begins consideration of Jacobsen by recounting his deal. The prosecutors have told the jury about it and about what Jacobsen will say. But they have not done so in the detail Williams now uses.

He was indicted in Texas for seven felonies, each of which was punishable with a possible term of imprisonment for five years. He was indicted by a federal grand jury sitting in this courthouse for perjury punishable by a possible term of imprisonment for five years.

We will show that the testimony that he has given before a grand jury against John Connally and which we are told he will give in this case has been and will be given in consideration for the prosecution's agreement to drop those charges against him, possible imprisonment of 40 years, and allow him to plead to a one-count indictment for which his possible imprisonment is two years.

We will show, members of the jury, that this is the bargain which he has made for himself.

Now, who else, what else, is there in the way of evidence on Jake Jacobsen? Jake Jacobsen, members of the jury, is a lawyer. He began practicing in Austin, Texas. He served for a time as assistant to the Attorney General of Texas, and as assistant to the Governor, Price Daniel, and he was one of Price Daniel's supporters when Governor Connally ran against Price Daniel for Governor of Texas and defeated him.

COMMENTARY

Jacobsen is thus identified as a political opponent of John Connally.

We will show you that the defendant John Connally knew Mr. Jacobsen, and knew him well. He knew him from politics in Texas, he knew him as an opponent when he ran for Governor of Texas from 1963 to 1968, and he knew him when he was Secretary of the Treasury.

Jacobsen besides being a lawyer, had many interests which are relevant to this case. Jacobsen had large shareholdings at various points in a number of banks and savings and loan institutions.

There was mention this morning of the Citizens National Bank of Austin, Texas. He was the chairman of the board of that bank and the controlling shareholder, the bank which lent Bob Lilly $10,000 so that in turn could be handed over to Jacobsen on April 28th of 1971.

COMMENTARY

It is important in this opening to have every detail of the financial relationship between Jacobsen and AMPI. Now Jacobsen's banking connections are being used for this purpose.

We will show that he was on the board and a large shareholder in the First Savings and Loan of San Angelo, the Lubbock Savings and Loan of Lubbock, Texas, the Community Savings and Loan of Fredericksburg, Texas, the Community National Bank in Austin, the First State Bank in Bowie, the Galleria Bank in Houston, the Parland National Bank in Houston, the Travis Bank and Trust Company in Austin, and the City Bank and Trust Company in Dallas.

His practice, members of the jury, was in the field of banking, savings and loans. He had relationships to a number of savings and loans, and banks in Texas during the relevant period in this case. In addition to this, he was a member of the law firm of Jacobsen and Long in Austin, Texas, and a member of the law firm of Semer, White and Jacobsen in Washington, D.C., both firms representing the Associated Milk Producers, Incorporated, on a very substantial retainer.

Now in addition to representing AMPI as a lawyer, Jacobsen traversed the length and breadth of the central part of the United States during the relevant periods in this case urging the dairy farmers to become politically involved, to support candidates for Congress, to support candidates for the Senate, to support presidential candidates, to work for them so that in the event that they had economic problems in Washington, they would get a friendly ear in the halls of Congress.

COMMENTARY

We are getting a picture of Jacobsen. He is of course a round character in this drama. The prosecutors have described his relationship with Connally and the alleged payments. They have not given this degree of detail. Williams's use of detail is telling the jury that the defense knows all the relevant facts and can be counted on to put them in evidence. This sort of promise does not undercut the presumption of innocence because these are collateral facts. They provide background. Nothing Williams is saying will be disputed.

In 1969 he was instrumental in forming an organization known as TAPE, T-A-P-E. TAPE stands for Trust for Agricultural Political Education.

It was the political arm of AMPI. Under the law, corporations and labor unions are not permitted to contribute to political campaigns, federal political campaigns, and so labor unions frequently create trusts so that their members may make voluntary contributions to those trusts, and the trusts in turn can act as a political arm for the labor union and contribute to campaigns of candidates favorable to their positions.

That's what was done in 1969 by AMPI. They created TAPE so that they could become very active politically, and in 1969 contributed to many congressmen and many senators, in 1971 contributed to 20 senators and 50 congressmen; hundreds of thousands of dollars so that they would have a receptive ear in the halls of Congress, that they would have congressmen who would be friendly to agriculture, be friendly to the dairy unions, and be friendly to their position.

The evidence will show, members of the jury, that they had made contributions to the most powerful members of the Senate in both parties, political contributions. They had contributed to every candidate, every one in the Democratic Party who aspired to the presidency in 1972. They had contributed in 1969 $100,000 to the President of the United States.

They had made hundreds of thousands of dollars in political contributions in a three-year period. They did that in 1969, '70, '71 and into '72, so that their voice would be heard when there was a problem that they wished to take to Congress.

And as the evidence will show, members of the jury, the time came in 1971 when they had a problem which they took to Congress looking for a receptive ear, and favorable action.

Now, let us see what the facts are in this case. That is what the evidence will show as to who Mr. Jacobsen is, as to what AMPI was and is, and as to what TAPE was and is. That is what the evidence will show with respect to the cast of characters in this case.

Now, let us see what the evidence will show with respect to what each of them did when and how and where.

As I said to you earlier, the evidence is going to show you members of the jury that John Connally had a long record of being favorable to the farmers, to the farmers' problems, to the dairy farmers in particular. And they were well aware of it.

AMPI was based in San Antonio, Texas, not far from his home, and they knew what his record was with respect to agricultural problems and with respect to dairy problems.

When he came to Washington in 1971, it was right at the time that AMPI and its representatives were here trying to persuade Secretary of Agriculture Hardin to raise milk price supports. He came in February, the price support level had to be fixed in March for the coming marketing year, the marketing year begins April 1 and runs through March 31 each year.

And so there were a number of members of AMPI here present. During the first two months that John Connally served as the Secretary of the Treasury, he spent most of his time, as the evidence will show, on Capitol Hill testifying before various committees of Congress, the Senate Banking and Currency Committee, the Senate Finance Committee, the Senate Foreign Relations Committee, and the comparable committees in the House.

Both houses of Congress were controlled by the Democrats and Secretary Connally was a Democrat. The evidence will show that he knew better than anyone in the Nixon administration what the temper of Congress was with respect to price supports. That many leaders of Congress spoke to him on the subject of price supports and spoke to him about the legislation that had been put together preparatory to enactment of raising price supports to 85 percent or $4.93 per hundredweight.

COMMENTARY

Count up the facts in this portion calculated to impress this jury. Connally is a Democrat. He testifies before Congress about important issues. He knows congressional concerns. Also, we have a context. We have a busy public servant. We have AMPI representatives all over town. An approach by Jacobsen to help AMPI is not out of place in this scenario.

At the time that he was testifying on Capitol Hill before these various committees, Mr. Harold Nelson, the general manager of AMPI, was here. Mr. Bob Lilly whose name you heard this morning was here. Mr. Jacobsen was here, and Mr. David Paarlberg, another lawyer for AMPI, was here, all pleading the case of the milk producers before Secretary Hardin, and before any other members of the government who would hear their pleas.

They had asked for a meeting with the President. They wanted to articulate their problems. They were telling everybody who would listen in the halls of Congress and in the Department of Agriculture that they were in a bad way, that prices had gone out of sight for feed, and that dairy prices had been forced, and that they couldn't make it any longer, that they were going under and that there would be a shortage of dairy farmers because they couldn't survive economically.

During this period Jacobsen visited John Connally at the Treasury Department and he asked for his help for the dairy farmers.

COMMENTARY

There will be no question that Jacobsen visited Connally at the Treasury Department. Every visitor is logged in and out of the Secretary's office. Thus, it is essential that the opening statement not only acknowledge this fact but also, if possible, embrace it and turn it into a positive element of the case.

Connally quickly said that he would do whatever he could to urge the raising of price supports because of the economic plight which the dairy farmers were facing. Many leaders of Congress spoke to him about it. He was the only Democrat in the administration to whom they could turn. And as the evidence will show, the dairy farmers thought and believed he was the one man in the administration who understood their problem.

Notwithstanding all the efforts being made by the dairy farmers and their representatives in March of 1971, the Secretary of Agriculture acted. He acted on March 12th. Secretary Hardin froze price supports at $4.66 per hundred pounds, keeping it right where it was the year before, and in the eyes of the dairy farmers doing them a grave injustice.

The moment that that decision was announced, the representatives of the dairy industry turned to Congress. They went to the halls of Congress, they went to all those candidates who had come to them when they were running, they went to all the senators and congressmen from dairy states, and within a matter of a few days they had 28 separate bills introduced lifting price supports to $4.93 per hundred pounds.

They had the leadership of the Senate and the House. They had some of the leadership of both parties ready to act, and override the Secretary of Agriculture's decision, and lift price supports. Over 100 congressmen put their names on these bills that I have just spoken about, and over 30 senators put their names on the bills, they not only announced that they would support them, but they put their names on them.

Senators Bayh and Bentsen, Cook and Cranston, Eagleton, Fulbright, Gravel, Harris, Hart, Hollings, Hughes, McGovern, Mondale, Muskie, Proxmire, Stevenson, Symington, Tunney, Kennedy, Allen, Nelson, all supported the increase in price supports.

--- COMMENTARY ---

This list of names will make an impact on this jury and put Connally in a large group of like-minded political figures who did

> not—so far as the evidence shows—get money in connection
> with their support of dairy farmers.

Now, John Connally gave advice to the President of the United States.

————— COMMENTARY —————

The President is in this story many times, but rarely is he "President Nixon." The Nixon association is being muted.

He told the President of the United States in March of 1971 that he believed the fair, the just, and the right thing to do in an economy that was rising was to raise price supports to 85 percent and at the same time that he gave that advice to the President of the United States, he told him that it was his opinion from his many conversations in the Congress of the United States, both the Senate and the House, that if the Secretary of Agriculture didn't act and reverse his decision of March 12th, that it was inevitable that the Congress was going to pass a law and raise price supports to $4.93 or 85 percent of parity.

Now, on March 23rd of 1971 the President of the United States met in the White House, he met in the White House with the leaders of the dairy industry.

————— COMMENTARY —————

Williams is now leading up to a controversial White House tape of a political meeting. The prosecutors were to claim that Connally said on the tape that there were political contributions to be had if Nixon supported AMPI's demands. The tape, in the opinion of the trial judge, contained no such audible statement. It was played for Connally at trial during his cross-examination, and he was asked about it. But Williams in opening cannot know what use the prosecution will make of the tape, nor whether they will be able to claim that its controversial portion will be argued to support an inference of some *quid pro quo*. The controversial part was a conversation involving only Connally and

Nixon. The rest of the tape is innocuous. At least some of this tape is clearly admissible. John Connally was at a meeting with President Nixon and others at which price supports were discussed. Williams therefore embraces the potentially adverse fact and promises that the jury will hear the disputed tape.

This meeting was not scheduled hurriedly in March. It had been scheduled for many weeks beforehand. It was scheduled for 10:30, members of the jury, on March 23rd.

It began actually at 10:35 A.M., and it lasted until 11:25 A.M.

And in that meeting the dairy farmers told Mr. Nixon and they told the Secretary of Agriculture and his assistants the problems that they had. They said that they couldn't make it unless they had a raise in price supports, they pointed out the rising costs of their feed for their animals and said that they could not survive economically without it, and they stated a very powerful case directly to the President.

That afternoon, that very afternoon, the President had a meeting in his office at 5:05 P.M., a meeting that lasted until 5:35 P.M.

Members of the jury, as was indicated to you, that meeting was taped, and if the Government does not offer that tape the defense will, because at that meeting there were present the President of the United States; the Secretary of Agriculture, Mr. Hardin; his first assistant, Mr. Campbell; the director of the Office of Management and Budget, Mr. Schultz; his first assistant, Mr. Rice; Mr. Whittaker, Mr. John Whittaker, who was a White House assistant concerned with matters of this kind; Mr. Ehrlichman, and Secretary of the Treasury John Connally was invited to be present.

COMMENTARY

Connally did not seek to attend. He was asked. Not a word is wasted in Williams's opening, and every word is made to count.

And at that meeting, as the evidence will show, the taped conversation which you will hear in this case Secretary Connally stated very forcefully what the facts were. He told that group that unless price supports were raised, that it was inevitable that the Congress was going to act, that the Congress seemed united on this subject, and that they would act to raise price supports to $4.93 from $4.66.

He pointed out that the leadership of the Senate and the leadership of the House was for it, and that if the bills passed as inevitably they would, one of them, that the President would have the situation before him of either signing or vetoing the bill and that if he vetoed it, that it would be very damaging to him across that part of the country where the dairy farmers lived.

He suggested to that group, as the tape will show, it will be better if you strike a bargain with the dairy farmers and give them an increase at this point to $4.93, or 85 percent of parity, and get them to agree not to come back next year for another increase, get a two-year deal because in the long haul it will be better for the government, and better for the dairy farmer.

And everyone in that room, everyone in that room agreed that that was the proper, fair thing to do. The Secretary pointed out what the inevitable facts were, and he pointed out to the President what the political costs were in this problem.

— COMMENTARY —

This introduction to the tape hints at, but of course does not capture, its real character. Connally was not the only person in the room with significant farming experience, but was the most articulate on the problems of farmers. He also described in some detail the kind of lobbying effort that AMPI was making.

And an agreement was reached at that meeting, as you will hear when you hear the tape recording of the 30-minute meeting that took place on March 23.

He left that meeting, he did not know nor did anyone else at the conclusion of that meeting whether the dairy farmers would agree not to come back the next year because no one could quite read what their position would be about taking a two-year deal. No one could predict what the economy would be the next year, whether prices would continue to spiral as indeed they did. But that was what was planned, and that plan was executed on.

And on March 25th of 1971, Secretary Hardin, the Secretary of Agriculture, who was the only one empowered to make this decision under law,

--- COMMENTARY ---

This is in part a technical grace note, saying again that Secretary Connally had no real authority to set milk price supports. In part, however, it will form part of the "illogic" argument about these charges.

reversed himself and changed the price supports on milk from $4.66 per hundred weight to $4.93 per hundred weight, raising the price from 80 percent of parity to 85 percent of parity.

And as the evidence will show throughout most of the history of the price supports on milk and price supports on all agricultural products, the supports have been upped to 85 percent because assume, as the evidence will show, when the experts take the stand, that that is the maximum price that the farmer can get for his product; he still isn't getting a fair share of the national income because only if he got 100 percent of parity by the very definition of the term would he be getting his fair share of the national income in relation to all the rest of the economy.

Now, would Your Honor take a break here?

--- COMMENTARY ---

Most judges understand that jurors cannot sit and listen to lawyers for more than an hour at a time. They can hear testimony perhaps for a longer period, because there is more "going on." It is important to watch your jurors and ask for a break at intervals.

THE COURT: If you wish. Do you wish?

MR. WILLIAMS: Yes, sir.

THE COURT: We will take a ten minute recess.

AFTER RECESS

THE COURT: All right, Mr. Williams.

MR. WILLIAMS: Thank you, Your Honor.

Ladies and gentleman of the jury, before the recess that I asked for, I said to you that the evidence would show that, through the political arm of AMPI, large amounts of contributions had been made to Congress, to members of the Senate, members of Congress during various political campaigns.

The evidence will show, ladies and gentlemen of the jury, that indeed the chances were very high that, if the Congress had acted in 1971, the price support would have been raised not to $4.93 per hundredweight but to $5.05, to 99 percent of parity.

A sampling of the evidence will show with respect to the contributions that TAPE made, that during the years that are relevant to this case, they have contributed large sums to Senator Bentsen, Senator Hubert Humphrey,

---

COMMENTARY

At the time of this opening, Williams still hoped that Senator Hubert Humphrey of Minnesota, who had been vice president under Lyndon Johnson, would agree to be a character witness for Connally. Humphrey eventually declined.

Senator Muskie, Senator Proxmire, Senator Adlai Stevenson, Senator John Tunney, Senator Harold Hughes, Senator Aiken, Senator Barry Goldwater, Senator Henry Jackson, Senator Mondale, Senator Taft, Senator Pell, Speaker Carl Albert and the then-Congressman Gerald Ford.

Now, I said to you that on March the 25th, the decision of Secretary Hardin was changed, that he reversed himself—and a settlement was made at $4.66 per hundred-

weight, the idea being advanced by Secretary Connally
that they should make a two-year deal at that price.

COMMENTARY

Williams is telling the jury that Connally's intervention—getting
the support at 85 percent of parity and for two years—actually
saved the taxpayers money because Congress would have set it
higher. He also gets a chance to list the people to whom AMPI
made political contributions. There is a risk here—that the jury
will think that AMPI is just a money machine and all the politicians who took from it are potential wrongdoers. The risk is min-
imized by the defense theory that Connally did not take any
money and that Jacobsen in fact pocketed the funds that he said
were to go to Connally.

On April 28th of 1971 Jacobsen went to Lilly, Lilly being
an employee of AMPI, and he said to him: "Secretary Connally has been very helpful to us in our fight for higher
supports. I think we should make $10,000 available to him
to give to various candidates in Congress and to campaign
committees.

Lilly said, "I have got to get an okay from Nelson and I
will be back to you."

Several days later Lilly said, "I have the okay," and then
he came to Austin, Texas, and Lilly went to Jacobsen's
bank, to Citizens National Bank of Austin, Texas—that's
Jacobsen's bank—and Lilly borrowed $10,000 from that
bank and gave it to Jacobsen in cash.

Jacobsen put it in his, Jacobsen's, safe-deposit box, one
of the several safe-deposit boxes.

Now members of the jury, months later, in a conversation that [Jacobsen] had with Secretary Connally, in a casu-
al manner, he said, "Mr. Secretary, you are very helpful to
us and we have $10,000 available for you to make any
contributions you wish to make to campaign committees
or congressional campaigns that you choose," confident,
ladies and gentlemen of the jury, that Secretary Connally
would turn that down, as we shall show.

The evidence will show you, members of the jury, that Secretary Connally said, "No, Jake"—without hesitation—"I am a Democrat and this is a Republican administration. As a member of a Republican Administration I will not contribute to Democrats, and, as a Democrat, I will not contribute to the Republicans, so I don't want it."

We will show you, members of the jury, that Jacobsen—confident that Connally would not accept it, had it made.

He never told anyone in the world, Lilly, Nelson or anyone else at AMPI that Connally had turned the money down. He kept it and it worked so well, ladies and gentlemen, that in October of 1971 he went back to Mr. Lilly and he asked Mr. Lilly for another $5,000 for Secretary Connally.

Mr. Lilly once again handed him $5,000 for Secretary Connally and, not only did [Jacobsen] keep this, but he didn't even mention this $5,000 to Secretary Connally—he put it in his box.

COMMENTARY

The information charges that Connally got $10,000, in two payments of $5,000 each. These alleged payments coincide with provable Jacobsen visits to the Secretary of the Treasury office. However, Jacobsen undeniably got $15,000 from AMPI to give to Connally, and even he never claimed he gave Connally the last $5,000. It also emerged at trial that at about the time Jacobsen got the first $10,000 from Lilly, he made a $10,000 payment on his debts. This was proved by Jacobsen's bankruptcy petition.

He told no one about it and he used it. He converted it to his own use.

During the following months, as he converted the $10,000 to his own use, he embezzled the money.

That is what the evidence will show you, members of the jury.

Now, in June of 1972, specifically on June 5, 1972, John Connally, before there was any Watergate episode,

---
COMMENTARY

That is, before the Watergate break-in.

---

resigned from the government, he resigned as Secretary of the Treasury to resume his law practice in Houston, Texas.

Later that summer he was asked to be chairman of a group called "Democrats for Nixon" since he had served in the Nixon Administration and he accepted.

During the fall of 1972, in the fall of '72, Jacobsen once again mentioned that he had $10,000 available for contributions to Democrats for Nixon, and once again, spontaneously without hesitation, John Connally turned the contribution down. He turned that down, saying to Jacobsen, as the evidence will show, "No, Jake, there has been too much publicity about AMPI and its political contributions."

And there had been a long series both in The Wall Street Journal and in the Washington Post about AMPI and its multiple contributions.

"I don't want to take any AMPI money for Democrats for Nixon, and I don't want any large cash contributions any longer—there has been too much focus on that kind of thing."

And he turned that down. That is what the evidence will show, ladies and gentlemen of the jury, happened in 1972.

COMMENTARY

Why is Williams going into so much detail about Connally's words to Jacobsen? Why is he being so precise about dates? In the usual case, the opening statement should allow some flexibility. Granted, detail makes the opening more credible and lets

---

the jury know that the lawyer is in command of the facts. Beware, however, of predicting the unpredictable, and setting yourself up for a loss of credibility when things don't turn out just as you said they would. In this case, Connally had appeared before a federal grand jury and given his version of events. Williams is using, word for word, what Connally told the grand jurors he said. He therefore accomplishes two tasks at once. First, he tells the story. Second, he reinforces the credibility of the grand jury testimony, which has been and will be challenged by the government.

As you will see later, Jacobsen also used these words in his grand jury and Senate committee appearances, quoting Connally as spurning the money. One theory of this defense is not only to confront Jacobsen with his prior testimony but also to say that the prior version was true—changed only when Jacobsen needed to bargain his way out of unrelated criminal difficulty.

Now we will show you that these charges—one of which refers to $5,000 in May of 1971 and one of which refers to $5,000 in September of 1971, and neither of which mention the third $5,000—were false, and that the monies that were obtained by Jacobsen from Lilly, both in April of 1971 and again in October of 1971, were kept by Jacobsen and never disclosed by him, that he had retained those funds and indeed had used them for his own purposes.

Now in 1973 the Watergate grand jury sitting in this courthouse, began to look at the so-called Watergate episode and the so-called cover-up about which all of you indicated that you heard and read, and the Ervin Committee, the Senate Committee on Presidential Campaign Activities, began to function and to hear witnesses and to hold hearings which were televised across the nation during that year.

They began to fan out in their areas and not to focus just on the Watergate and its cover-up, but to look at other activities,

---

COMMENTARY

This is not a Watergate case, as Williams told the jury at the beginning. He repeats the point for emphasis. He must, however, get into the investigative phase of this case. Jacobsen's story was that he called Connally in a panic and that Connally summoned him to Houston. At that Houston meeting, according to Jacobsen, Connally gave him $15,000 to put back into his safe-deposit box. That way, as the story goes, Connally and Jacobsen could deny that any money had ever changed hands and Jacobsen could hand over the $15,000 to the Watergate prosecutor and say that he had it all along.

During the Connally trial, the government would call a couple of dozen witnesses to say that all the bills that Jacobsen said he got from Connally were in fact in circulation on the date Jacobsen said he got them. The defense refused to stipulate that this was so. So labored an effort at corroboration was therefore required, the prosecutors thought. Of course, the time it took far outweighed its importance, and the idea of doing it at all was a backhanded way of telling the jury not to believe Jacobsen unless a dozen witnesses corroborated him. At trial, the proof failed, as it turned out that some of the bills could not have been in existence at the time Jacobsen and Connally met.

But the government is charging an effort to obstruct justice. The formal charge had been severed from this trial, but evidence of such an effort can doom the defense. Williams therefore anticipates the proof and provides the answer.

---

and specifically, they began to look at the activities, as the evidence will show, of AMPI and TAPE and Jacobsen and Nelson and Parr and Lilly, and they began to look at the activities of the lawyers and the officers of those organizations.

And in October—specifically October 26th of 1973—Jacobsen told Connally that he had been subpoenaed to testify before the grand jury.

They wanted, the grand jury wanted, to ask Jacobsen about all of his activities, and they wanted to ask him about all the things that he had been doing for AMPI and all the thing that others had been doing for AMPI, and he said to Mr. Connally, "I am going to have to testify and it may be that your name will come up because Lilly knows that I got $10,000."

At that time, ladies and gentlemen of the jury, John Connally, as former Secretary of the Navy and as former Governor of Texas, and as former Secretary of the Treasury, had a high political profile and Jacobsen said to him, "If I mention your name it may hurt you politically because you have never been mentioned at all in any of this, and I am prepared not to mention your name."

John Connally said, "No, don't do that. You just tell it like it is. You tell it precisely the way it was. You did nothing wrong and I did nothing wrong."

COMMENTARY

Again, this version tracks that given by Connally to the grand jury. Connally denies having told Jacobsen to make up a story and adds that Jacobsen offered to lie without any urging from Connally.

Because at that time John Connally did not know that Jacobsen had converted that money to his own use.

"You just go in there and you tell the truth about it and let the chips fall where they may and whatever will be will be. If there is any unfortunate publicity, so be it."

That was the conversation, and on November the 2nd, ladies and gentlemen of the jury, Jacobsen came into this building—November 2nd, 1973—into this building in which we are sitting today and he went to the grand jury upstairs and he testified under oath about many things and he was asked as to whether or not Lilly gave him any money.

And he testified, under oath, that he had asked Lilly for $10,000 to make available that money to John Connally so that John Connally could make contributions to members of Congress and congressional campaign committees, that he had offered it to John Connally in the spring of 1971 and that John Connally had refused it and told him, "I cannot make any contributions as a Democrat in a Republican administration, not to a Democrat because I am in a Republican administration and not to a Republican because I am a Democrat."

That is what Jacobsen told the grand jury.

The next day the evidence will show that he went up to the Ervin Committee and he was asked—by the way, before this grand jury sitting on the sixth floor of this courthouse on November 2nd, 1972, whether he had in fact gotten another $5,000 and he denied it—he testified falsely to that. He denied it because he feared an embezzlement charge.

COMMENTARY

This criminality is of course unrelated to any charge that he gave money to Connally.

He went the next day to the Ervin Committee and he was interviewed there by the lawyers for the Ervin Committee on these particular subjects, in depth, these very subjects.

And what did he say? He said, "Yes, I got $10,000 from Lilly so that I could make it available to John Connally to make contributions to members of Congress and campaign committees and I offered that to him and he turned it down."

He said, "He turned it down saying, I can't, I can't make contributions—I am in a strange position. I am the only Democrat in the Nixon administration and I can't contribute to Democrats being a member of the Nixon administration and I can't contribute to Republicans being a Democrat."

And he said he made another gesture when Connally headed the Democrats for Nixon, and this is the testimony of Jacobsen before the Ervin Committee on November the 3rd of 1973, ladies and gentlemen, that he said Connally again said, "No, I won't take it."

Four days later, four days later, asked in Texas—in the Westgate Building—he testified again, under oath, in a suit brought by Ralph Nader called *Nader v. Butz,* when he was called by Ralph Nader's lawyers as a witness.

He was placed under oath and he was asked by Mr. Nader's lawyers: "Did you ever give any money to John Connally when he was Secretary of the Treasury?"

And he said, "No, sir."

"Do you know of any money, AMPI money, ever going to John Connally while he was Secretary of the Treasury?"

And he testified, under oath, "No, sir."

On December 15th of 1973, once again he was put under oath on Capitol Hill, just a few blocks from here, before Senator Ervin's Committee, he raised his hand and he swore to testify the truth, and they asked him many, many questions about many, many subjects.

Once again they asked him whether or not he had ever given any money to John Connally as the Secretary of the Treasury, and, once again, he testified under oath, "No," he had not, and he told the Ervin Committee the circumstances under which he had asked for money from Lilly to make it available to John Connally for contributions to members of Congress and to members of the Senate who were running for office and that John Connally refused saying, "I can't make contributions while I am in the position of being a Democrat in a Republican administration."

He told how he had offered it to him when he was chairing the Democrats for Nixon and how he had once again turned it down.

─────────── COMMENTARY ───────────

The defense strategy in the case will reflect this opening. The majority of time Williams spent in cross-examining Jacobsen was spent reading his prior statements to him and getting him to admit he had made them. The press corps, looking on, became restive at this tactic, calling it boring and pointless. They were wrong. Over and over, Williams drilled home Jacobsen's detailed denials that he gave money to Connally and each time recalled the reasons Connally had given for refusing to take money. Often a turncoat witness has given only the sketchiest prior statement. Where, as here, the witness has a litany of prior statements, and they are admissible substantively because given under oath in a prior proceeding, you should use these statements early and fully.

In the Terry Nichols case, some journalists criticized my colleague Ron Woods as boring. "As cuddly as a hypodermic needle," one smart-aleck press person reported. But Ron was always factual, prepared, and unflappable. The jurors came to trust him implicitly, and when he had made his points, and he put it all together dramatically in closing argument, his overall effectiveness was proved.

On January the 21st of 1974, once again, right here in this courthouse, upstairs, he was hailed before the grand jury to testify again, under oath, and he came in and he was sworn, and he was asked some more questions.

Once again, he said that the money he had gotten from Lilly he had put in a safe-deposit box and he had left it untouched.

That, as the evidence will show, was false because he did not leave it untouched, ladies and gentlemen. He did use it. He did use it for his own purposes.

Once again he denied that he had ever given any money to John Connally.

Now, on February 6th of 1972, members of the jury, the evidence will show you that a federal grand jury, sitting in San Angelo, Texas, returned a seven-count indictment against Jake Jacobsen on matters wholly unrelated to this case, for frauds that he had perpetrated in his relationship with the San Angelo Savings and Loan Association, for stealing money down there from his depositors and from his shareholders.

That particular indictment in seven counts against him on February 6th also charged him with perjury before the grand jury down there about those thefts and that embez- zlement and that fraud.

The next day—the next day, on February 7th, Jake Jacobsen was interviewed. He was interviewed by two lawyers—two lawyers who had been retained by AMPI to investigate the activities of the officers and lawyers of AMPI in relationship to the money in AMPI.

AMPI retained a distinguished American lawyer who had been a past-president of the American Bar Associa- tion, Mr. Edward Wright of Little Rock, Arkansas, and he went to Austin, Texas, to interview Jacobsen with one of his junior associates, Mr. Isaac Scott, and they asked Mr. Jacobsen myriad questions about all of his activities and the evidence will show, ladies and gentlemen of the jury, that Mr. Jacobsen told the lawyers for his own clients, AMPI, the lawyers who were looking into this matter for his own client:

"I was never a party to giving any money whatever to John Connally and I have no knowledge of milk money going to him."

"I will return the money to AMPI when I get clearance from my attorney, Arthur Mitchell, of Austin, Texas."

The evidence will show you, members of the jury, that this was the sixth time, the sixth time that Jacobsen had given evidence before various bodies, that he had never given a penny to John Connally and that whatever money he had gotten from Lilly he had kept.

Also the sixth time that he had falsified as to receiving the other $5,000 that he had gotten in October and which he had also kept four times—the evidence will show— under oath, and two times not under oath, once in an informal interview at the Ervin Committee and once before Mr. Edward L. Wright, the attorney for AMPI.

COMMENTARY

The statements not under oath will clearly be admissible for impeachment, though not substantively under FED. R. EVID. 801.

Now two weeks went by and he was now under indictment for fraud against the shareholders and his depositors
in San Angelo, Texas—a federal indictment—and two
weeks later a grand jury sitting in this building, a federal
grand jury, indicted him for perjury, for lying to them on
January 25th of 1974 when he testified that he had not
touched the money from the day that Lilly gave it to him
and when he put it in his box.

Now he stood indicted in Texas and he stood indicted
in the District of Columbia. He stood indicted for eight
felonies, the possible punishment for which was 40 years
in the penitentiary and, indeed, the evidence will show for
the first time he began to scheme as to how he could
extricate himself from this trouble—

MR. SALE: Your Honor, may we approach the bench for
a moment, please.

THE COURT: Well, come on up.

(At the bench)

MR. SALE: Your Honor, I have been very hesitant, but I
think that this has gone so far now. Mr. Williams's last
comment was that the evidence will show that he began
to scheme at this point, and this is inflammatory and it is
summation.

MR. WILLIAMS: No, it isn't. I am going to prove this. I
told the jury, your Honor, I would prove it and I am going
to prove that he did begin to scheme as to how he could
extricate himself from this trouble by making a deal with
these people.

MR. SALE: Well, that is all—

THE COURT: Well, I think he can say that. However, we
don't need to characterize lawyers as former presidents of
the American Bar Association and that type of thing. Of
course, we allow a little more leeway to the defendant that
[sic] we do to the Government, but I think you have been
taking full advantage, Mr. Williams, and let's see if we
can't simmer it down a little bit.

MR. WILLIAMS: All right, Your Honor.

(End of bench conference)

```
─────────────── COMMENTARY ───────────────
```

"I am going to prove this"—the first and best answer to such an objection. By this time, Williams is steamed up and the flow of his accusations is steady and strong. Would the "average" judge sustain an objection? After all, Williams did use the magic words "*the evidence will show* for the first time he began to scheme as to how he could extricate himself." In my experience, most judges will allow a loaded word like *scheme*. By the time you make your opening you should know your judge's attitude. You will have been in her court, and watched some opening statements, or had some sparring about openings. If you use a loaded word, and get called out for being argumentative, have another word ready. For *scheme,* say, "the evidence will show that he planned." Note that Chief Judge Hart is not really concerned with *scheme* but with the characterization of Edward Wright as former ABA president. The judge's objection is better grounded than the prosecutor's. Wright's former position adds nothing to his credibility as a witness; it will be in evidence, if at all, only if Wright testifies and then by way of brief introduction.

MR. WILLIAMS: Now in March of 1974 the evidence will show that Mr. Jacobsen began to negotiate with the Watergate prosecutor's office, to get the charges that were pending against him in Texas and the charges that were pending against him in the District of Columbia dropped.

We will show you, members of the jury, that on May 21, 1974, he entered into an arrangement with the prosecutors that all charges pending against him brought by a federal grand jury in San Angelo, Texas, arising out of the San Angelo Savings and Loan Association fraud would be dropped and the perjury charges against him in the District of Columbia would not be pressed, that there would be no charges brought arising out of these transactions, in return for his giving testimony. The testimony that he has given before the grand jury and the testimony that the prosecutor says he will give in this court.

Testimony which we will show you, ladies and gentlemen of the jury, is totally contradictory of testimony that he gave four times under oath before the grand jury, in deposition and before the Ervin Committee and totally contradictory of the testimony that he gave in the interviews with the Ervin Committee and in interviews with Mr. Wright and Mr. Scott representing AMPI.

The arrangement that he entered into was that he would be allowed to enter a plea to one count which had a maximum punishment of two years in the penitentiary.

COMMENTARY

Note how Williams is dealing with the plea bargain. Dropping the unrelated charges comes first, then he discusses the plea bargain in the case on trial. Jacobsen cannot be portrayed as a co-felon who made his peace. Jacobsen did plead guilty to giving Connally the unlawful gratuities that Connally was charged with receiving. Williams used this plea bargain to Connally's advantage in closing argument.

We will show you, members of the jury, that his testimony against the defendant John Connally which brought about the charges in this case is false testimony. We will show you, members of the jury, that from the time that the investigation was launched into the defendant John Connally by the Watergate prosecution staff and by the Ervin Committee, by the FBI, by the Treasury agents, that John Connally has cooperated fully, that he has turned over in the course of a 15-month investigation every single appointment diary, every log, every telephone call record, every bank record, every business deal, every financial record that he has in the world dealing with the relevant period.

We will show you that he has testified before the grand jury, he has testified on two occasions for several hours. He has submitted himself to interviews by the Watergate prosecutors and he has submitted to interrogation under oath by the grand jury on two occasions and before the Ervin Committee for several hours.

He testified truthfully and we will show you that he has not stonewalled it. He has never refused to give them anything that they have asked for. He has cooperated fully from the moment this investigation was launched.

We will show you that he has made all of his records available and that the investigation into him was massive, in an effort to find some evidence supportive of the charges leveled against him.

COMMENTARY

The defendant's attitude toward the government during the investigation can be a powerful argument for innocence. In any case where discovery has been extensive, having cooperated in the process can be a mark of good faith.

I have spoken to you at great length. I hope I have not tried your patience or overtaxed you.

As his Honor indicated to you earlier, there was no requirement that I make an opening statement and lay out everything before you at this point in the trial but I wanted to lay out all the proof and lay out every piece of evidence for you. I could have lain back and listened to what evidence they had and what they would offer, but I did not choose to do that.

COMMENTARY

I can hardly imagine a case in which I would reserve opening statement. In some criminal cases, one must do so because the course of proof is uncertain and the defense wants the benefit of surprise. In one recent complex bank fraud case, Robert Hirschhorn advised counsel for a marginal defendant not to make an opening statement at all. The idea was that this defendant should simply disappear into the wallpaper. The strategy worked; the defendant was acquitted. But for most cases, you will make an opening statement. If you do so, why not give yourself credit for having done it.

And you will see that that is not our style in this matter. We want all of the evidence before you and, when all the evidence is before you, it will support everything that I have told you here this afternoon, and when that evidence is before you ladies and gentlemen, and I assure you that it will be before the expiration of this trial, I will ask at your hands a verdict of acquittal for John Connally on both charges which have been brought against him.

Thank you very much.

NOTES

1. Initially Connally was indicted, but the indictment failed to allege an essential element of the offense. Rather than send the case back to the grand jury, the defense consented to the filing of an information containing the same charges.

2. 18 U.S.C. §201.

3. An unlawful gratuity differs from the more serious offense of bribery because the former offense does not require proof of a specific *quid pro quo* for the unlawful payment. A bribe is a payment made with the understanding that the political figure will do an official act in the future in exchange for the payment. Bribery may be committed by giving or receiving money for the official or for any person or entity designated by the official. A gratuity must be paid to the official personally. This is a way of limiting criminal liability so that payments to campaign committees made because the giver supports positions taken by the official are not criminalized.

Chapter Four

Persuasion During Trial

Invention, arrangement, style, memory, delivery: the five elements of persuasion. Many people believe that they are
important only in argument—to a judge or jurors. They are
wrong. At every moment of the trial you must pay attention
to how you are persuading the jury, whether you are examining a witness, making an objection, or just listening to testimony being offered by the other side.

JUST SITTING THERE

All lawyers know—or should know—that the jury may be
watching at every moment. That is, while a witness is talking, one or more jurors may be looking at your counsel table
to see how you are reacting. They may be watching the
judge or court clerk for clues to understanding—or simply
from curiosity or boredom. They may watch your co-counsel or paralegals or people such as family members of parties they know to be connected to the case.

You may know all of this and do it naturally. More likely,
however, you do not naturally concentrate on the case
before you at every moment, conscious always of how you
and all the other members of your team appear to the jurors.
This is a skill, a habit, and it comes with practice.

The jurors are trying to get clues about how to behave. You
may cast an eye in their direction from time to time and be
noticed doing it. Of course, your contact with the jurors will

begin during *voir dire.* At that time you will be focused on their answers. You will have watched them file in, watched how they sit, observed their conversations with other jurors and their reactions to what is going on. You will have talked with them about the case, if you get a chance at lawyer *voir dire,* and showed genuine interest in their beliefs and feelings.

I like to sit at one end of the counsel table, preferably the end farthest from the bench and with the best view of everything. If I can't see everything from that spot, there is something wrong with the way the counsel tables are arranged. Of course, if it is a multiparty case and you represent a minor player, you may want to fade into the wall and have a spot that is not so visible.

At any time, a juror may be watching anybody on your team or anybody associated with your cause. Therefore, all must be schooled in the art of being polite to one another and of watching the case with interest. It is not right to react to testimony, particularly negative events, with gestures or expressions. It is especially not right to doodle or do anything else that trivializes what is going on. You may think it unnecessary to say all of this, but you would be surprised by how many lawyer teams fail to play by these rules.

Your voice and manner should say that you know the facts and law and are ready for this case. If it is not your turn, you are waiting for your turn. You are watching the case, listening to its every nuance, and registering your reactions within a very narrow compass. When Casadesus and Francescatti played violin-piano duets, neither one used the other's solo as a chance to trim his nails. In tennis doubles, it may not be your ball, but you are watching every stroke.

When you stand or move, you are using the courtroom space deliberately, as part of your persuasive process. This has to do with style and delivery. For example, if your opponent is presenting charts, or has a witness off the witness chair demonstrating or showing something to the jury, you are entitled to watch from a vantage point that lets you see it and object to anything improper. So get the court's permission and go stand someplace where the jury can see you as well as what the opponent is presenting. Become part of the tableau of presentation.

OBJECTING

Many judges bar speaking objections in the jury's presence. Others limit your trips to the bench or sidebar. Your objection style is to some extent dictated by these judicial preferences. There are some general rules. You know your adversary. You know the kinds of objectionable things he or she is likely to do. You know also that not every objectionable question or tactic should be objected to. Jurors may resent too much objecting, because it may seem to block their consideration of the case.

For example, say your opponent has put on a witness who saw relevant events but who also heard a lot of what other people said about those events. Some of what the witness heard is admissible as a present sense impression of the declarant, but much of it is objectionable. If all the people overheard are going to testify, or if this witness's version will be contradicted, you may want the hearsay to portray this witness as one who does not hear or remember very well. If, however, you are determined to object, you must know your purpose in doing so. Assume the witness to a car crash heard another bystander say, "Gosh, he was going fast." You hear the question that will elicit this:

Q: Your friend Bill Olson, was standing next to you when this happened?
A: Yes.
Q: What did he say?

You [rising with dignity from your chair]: Object to the hearsay, Your Honor. And if speaking objections are permitted, add "Mr. Olson will be here, so the jurors can hear him for themselves." And add in any case, "Also object to opinion testimony on this, Your Honor, and we'd like to approach."

If you don't have warning, you can't add the last part. If the hearsay objection is overruled, and the testimony comes in, you will have to move to strike the testimony.

Let's look at what is happening here. You will tell the jurors in *voir dire* and perhaps in opening statement that there will be objections. The judge will tell them that this is the lawyer's duty and not to punish you for it. None of this excuses you from using even the nonspeaking objection as a means to inform the jury and carry your case forward.

Thus we say, "Object to the hearsay," "Object because this is not the best evidence," "Object because the letter really speaks for itself" (which is another formulation of best evidence). You say, "They haven't proven it is authentic—no chain of custody." You say that the record was not "kept in the ordinary course of business" or that "it wasn't in the ordinary course of business to keep these records."

In these formulations you are of course invoking code words that preserve your record and refer to the rules of evidence. True, you are saying "best evidence" instead of "original writings," although you could say "it is not the original or a proper duplicate of the original." You are also choosing words that let the jury know why you object. These words carry a message—you don't want hearsay because you want the jurors to see the witness. You want the jury to have authentic evidence, which means one thing under the rules of evidence but something slightly different in ordinary speech. You don't want a business record that wasn't kept in the "ordinary" or "usual" way.

DIRECT EXAMINATION TECHNIQUES

I have spoken of the case as a journey. You have taken the journey over and over in your mind's eye and in any mock trials you may have done. The jurors are new to it. With every direct examination, we rediscover the principle that jurors must be introduced to the witness and to what the witness will say. This does not mean that with every witness we repeat details that others have given. It means that we introduce each witness and establish why he or she is here. Direct examination is a conversation with a witness, done for the benefit of others who may be listening. If you think of it like this, your manner and your technique will be real and persuasive. Jurors will know you think this conversation is interesting and are more likely to find it so themselves.

Q: Good morning. Tell us your name, please.
Q: What do you do for work?
Q: You worked at the offices of XYZ corporation during 1995, didn't you?
Q: And you had a desk next to Ms. Smith's desk?
Q: Let me show you a diagram of those offices that the jurors already know about because it is in evidence as Plaintiff's 25.

Now you have introduced the witness and the subject matter. You have used two leading questions—permissible because this is preliminary matter—and you are going to use a diagram to get things started. You let the jurors know that you care about not wasting their time. You are using this witness to "fill in" the story. You have already used someone else to set out the main details of the office, where people sat, and what jobs they had. So you use a leading question to set the stage and a diagram to put this witness in the picture. Then you get right to the matters on which this witness has a unique perspective.

In doing direct examination, presenting your client poses special problems. You become most acutely aware of this issue when preparing your client for deposition or trial testimony. He or she is filled with a sense of righteous indignation—at being harmed if a plaintiff, at being sued if a defendant. There have been costs to pay, delays to endure, tactics by the other side that lawyers may take in stride but clients do not. These signs of impatience and anger can undo your case.

Client anger can translate into client lying or client obstruction of justice. If the system seems stacked against your client, or the process too long and expensive, moral relativism creeps in. The client may not level with you about the documents. The client may shade the truth. From the very first moment of your representation, you must explain the ethical, legal, and strategic pitfalls that await the litigant who is other than candid. You know these. Tell the client. People who lie or cheat get prosecuted. When liars and cheaters are exposed—and the adversary system makes the likelihood high—they lose their cases and get sanctioned by the court or subjected to civil liability for their misdeeds, including punitive damages. Punitive damages and sanctions for willful misconduct may not be covered by whatever insurance the client may have.

Client anger can make the client an unbelievable witness. This is the most cogent use of the concept of "journey." Something happened that led to this lawsuit. There was an accident, an injury, an employment decision. The client is testifying about it today, months or years after it happened. Time has of course altered memory, knocking off the hard edges. With time, the client has learned to translate the event into a claim for justice—now the client wants something from the system. The client may be angry about the way the system has handled the claim, but even without anger the client is suffused with a sense of entitlement. The jurors do not share that sense of entitlement—at least not yet. We have to bring the jury with us to share that sense with us.

We have seen it over and over. We start to prepare the client to testify. Direct examination goes fine, considering it is our first time through the material. Then we start a mock cross-examination. Now we begin to see the anger, the impatience, perhaps even arrogance. The client is here, now, caught up in the process. The client needs to be back when it all started, ready to help the jurors "catch up."

This arrogance is particularly marked when your client is a defendant, or the "representative" of an entity, charged with doing something wrong. For such a witness, anger and arrogance translate into looking guilty.

Some clients can hear and understand this message. Some need to be taken through a mock cross-examination, perhaps even see themselves on video. You must develop a conversational direct examination that moves through the facts, using exhibits as much as possible to illustrate. Not only do exhibits help to "mark" the story as it is told, they help to bolster the credibility of the witness who has the most to gain or lose by the jury's decision.

For cross-examination, the client must be prepared. Listen to each question. Take a moment to think about it and the answer. This gives time for an objection if one is necessary. Look at the examiner and answer just that question. Do not embroider. Do not anticipate the next question. Remember that your own counsel can do redirect. If you don't remember, say so. If you don't understand the question, say so. Above all, keep the same even temper as on direct examination. Do not argue with the questioner.

There may be exceptions to this rule. In many cases there will be one question that calls for some indignation. If you can anticipate that question, and your client can hold back until and unless it is asked, there may be room for a spirited answer back. But such opportunities come far less often than advocates seem to imagine. And jurors, to repeat, resent somebody trying to play unfairly on their emotions.

CROSS-EXAMINATION TECHNIQUES

Cross-examination tests four attributes of the witness's testimony: meaning, perception, memory, and veracity. Not every opposing witness is a liar. The testimony of some will, when clarified, be neutral or supportive; this is meaning. Some did not see the events from the same perspective as your witnesses; this is perception. Some have gaps in their memory. And some, but only some, have an implied bias that might lead them to stretch the truth or can be proven to be giving contradictory or false testimony.

When you rise to cross-examine, you must know which categories you think the witness fits, for this will let you assume the appropriate mien. In general, cross-examination serves two purposes—it keeps your promises as to what the evidence will show, and it repels attack from the other side. Keeping promises is most important for the defense, for you will have told the jury in opening that your case begins when you cross-examine the first witness tendered by the other side. For plaintiffs, by contrast, the purpose is to repel attack. For the defense in a civil case, sometimes that first witness is your client, who has been called and examined with leading questions—so you have the added task of teaching your adversary why that bit of hubris was a mistake.

Much has been written and said about how to cross-examine, but very little about how to appear when you cross-examine.[1] The jurors watch you when you get ready to begin. We would say "when you rise," except that in some jurisdictions you must do this while seated. If that is your lot, you must develop a series of gestures that are effective from a chair, punctuated by trips to the witness chair to show a document.

Jurors tell us that they get clues from the way a lawyer approaches the witness. Is there a smile? Does the lawyer have a lot of notebooks, files, or papers? I like to outline a cross-examination in advance and then try to add the matters raised on direct to that outline. I want the witness to see that I am ready, so I have all the prior statements in notebooks, with tape flags marking key passages. My notes will contain references to these materials. For a complex cross, you can use more than one color tape flag.

The typical outline does not include the greeting, which is "Good morning" or "Good afternoon," with a smile. As an example, in the trial of Terry Nichols, a key witness was Michael Fortier, who said that Timothy McVeigh told him that McVeigh and Nichols would bomb the Oklahoma City federal building and enlisted Fortier's help in planning the bombing. The outline topics were:

- Prior statements: For a month, Fortier told the world that he knew nothing.
- How he knows it: Fortier never heard Nichols say he would bomb anything or kill anybody, so we have to make clear that to believe Michael Fortier, we must rely not only on his credibility but also on McVeigh's as the hearsay declarant.[2]
- Fortier, the dope-dealing loser: With tapes from bugs and taps of his house, and material from his press interviews, and the names of his suppliers and customers, I take him over the months before the bombing, including statements about how much money he thinks he will make by selling his story.
- What happens when he makes his deal: What does he bargain for; even when he agrees to "tell all," he does not say that Nichols was to have a role.
- Contradictions.
- Other lies.

In the *Connally* case, Williams's tactic was to make Jacobsen acknowledge the many prior statements he had made exonerating Connally, then talk about Jacobsen's deal with the government, then finish with a letter Jacobsen had written to Connally thanking him for his many kindnesses.

In a cross-examination based on perception, your entire focus may be on putting the witness into a scene, with a lot of detail about where objects and people were located.

Your outline lets you move from topic to topic while appearing in command. If there are areas where you don't really know what the witness will say, but can take a chance, you can tuck those in the middle and if necessary move quickly to another topic if things don't go well.

Cross-examinations of opposing witnesses must be organized so that the jury sees exactly what you are doing. They begin by getting any favorable material that the witness has for you in a friendly spirit. This works for witnesses who are ostensibly or truly neutral. It is usually a waste of time with partisan witnesses such as the party on the other side.

Then you must make sure that you have in hand all the prior statements of the witness. In civil litigation this is done through discovery. But if you have any doubts, clear them up. "You were interviewed by Arnold Witkin, the insurance investigator. Is that right? How many times?"

Having got those preliminaries out of the way, announce what you are going to do. "I want to ask you about the telephone calls you made on the evening of April 15, 1995, and then about some of the working conditions there at XYZ Corporation." This is for the jurors' benefit.

Remember, you promised in opening that you would make your case in part by cross-examination. You have just done that by getting the favorable things from the witness. Now you turn to the attack.

When you cross-examine, show the witness documents and objects that bolster your case and make the witness look at them. If these are in evidence, they do not need to be the witness's documents.

- "I am showing you what has been admitted under the pretrial order as Defendant's RR [a telephone company record]. Here is page 15. Will you look at that and just read to the jury the third telephone call on that page. You made that call, right?"

You now have the telephone call linked to a record.

- "You called Ms. Smith?"
- "You called her at 6:15 P.M. and you talked for 37 minutes?"
- "And you talked about what she was going to say about Mr. Jones?"

- "That was on April 15?"
- "On September 19, 1995, you were interviewed by an investigator named Neil Bellows? You told him that you did not talk to Ms. Smith that evening?"

Get out the investigator report. Have it in front of you. Using FED. R. EVID. 612, take the witness over the inconsistencies, refreshing recollection as you go. If this is not collateral, and the witness will not give you the needed answer, make sure you have the inconsistency clearly in mind and ask:

- "Do you deny that you said that?"
- "On your oath?"
- "But you don't deny that it happened?"

As a plaintiff, you should be well ahead of the game when you rest—I don't mean just enough to get by a motion for directed verdict or judgment as a matter of law. I mean that there is enough there that the jury will feel comfortable returning a verdict for you. By contrast, I believe that the defendant who expects to win must have done enough work during the plaintiff's case to be ahead in the jury's mind going into the defense presentation.

Regardless of where the plaintiff stands, the defense case is a chance to make some points by using the "keeping promises" ideas presented earlier. It is also important to use cross-examination to deflect, to repel attack. You cannot, with lay witnesses, "compare testimony." You cannot ask witness X, "Well, if witness A saw it this way, would she be lying?" You can use the device of publishing materials from other witnesses while a given witness is testifying.

You can compare expert testimony. That is, your expert will already have been heard, and it is permissible to ask if the defense expert has considered the work of your expert. Of course, you won't do it in such an open-ended way, but you can broach the subject.

You can also repel attack and do almost the same thing as comparing witnesses, by putting the witness in a location or situation about which others have testified in your case.

- "You know Phil Wilson?"
- "He sits at the desk right next to Ms. Smith?"
- "Your desk is not even in the same office, is it?"

Or in another setting:

- "You were standing on this corner right here?" [Using perhaps an acetate overlay or a copy of the same diagram on which other witnesses have marked]
- "Would you just mark that spot with your initials?"
- "This was at 5:00 in the evening?"
- "And you were looking in this direction?"
- "That's west, isn't it?"

That is, make sure you put defense witnesses in a context that you have already established. They then seem to have a burden to dispel an impression already created.

EXHIBITS AS SIGNPOSTS

I have written that in trials we always navigate by dead reckoning. On our voyage, we don't know exactly where we are with the jurors. We use exhibits to mark particular trial events so that we can refer to them in argument and so the jurors can, in their deliberations, re-create our story of the case.

Always refer to exhibits by their number. Give key exhibits a name, just as you would give a name to a witness. Thus, Government Exhibit 554 becomes "Government 554, the record of phone calls" every time you refer to it. A contract that is the basis of the action becomes "Plaintiff's Two, the contract." If possible, bind the exhibit in a way that makes it memorable. Exhibits will be in the jury room. If you have used them in memorable ways with witnesses, they have their own power and also serve to help the jurors remember what that witness said.

REVIEW OF DEMONSTRATIVE EVIDENCE

The "courtroom of the future" concept has caught on. Mostly it is nonsense. The investment of time and money involved in such electronic wizardry is usually wasted. I tried a case against lawyers whose every exhibit was stored in a database. Counsel went to the podium to examine each witness with a little black box, connected by a wire to a terminal on their side of the courtroom. Computer-illiterate members of their team had a paralegal at their table using the box. When you pushed the soft-touch keys on the box, or used a bar code scanner hooked up to it, the exhibit appeared on the TV screens placed so that jurors, counsel, the judge, and the audience could see them. The effect was to distance the lawyers, the witnesses, and the jurors from the items being shown.

Granted, one had to use the TV screens. That is, unless the exhibit was too bulky to be shown on the screen, counsel could not simply show it to the jury or pass it to the jurors. There was an ELMO next to the podium. Thus, an object or document could be put on the ELMO and displayed on the screen. So one did not have to use the little black box.

The same lawyers filled the courtroom with giant copies of key photos and demonstrative exhibits. It was all slick as can be. I think they wasted their client's money. I have learned this lesson painfully. I once made an opening statement complete with lovely pictures. The judge's law clerk sought me out at the next recess and said, "Judge says to tell you that opening was slick as boiled okra." This was not a compliment.

We would all prefer to remember than to think. That is why grudges—personal, religious, national—have such an enduring quality. At trial's end, you should be able to place all the evidence into a recognizable form—your story. Demonstrative evidence is supposed to be memorable and to help jurors remember.

Some evidence is admissible only "for demonstrative purposes." That is, it does not go to the jury room. Some things called demonstrative evidence are merely exhibits—charts, posters, diagrams—that you will use in opening statement or closing argument. I am cautious about using demonstrative evidence. I would rather use FED. R. EVID. 1006—the summary rule—to make charts that are admissible. I would rather use a memorandum, map, chart, diagram, photograph, or other tangible item that will go the jury room. Then the challenge is to figure out how to present it dramatically—demonstratively, if you will. You can use an overhead projector, an ELMO device for courtrooms equipped with video monitors, or an enlargement of the actual exhibit.

In this way, all exhibits become "demonstrative." Your job is to learn the courtroom technology so that you can present the exhibits smoothly and in a persuasive way. Of course, you must know exactly which exhibit you will use at a given time and have a method for finding them quickly when you need them.

In short, in every trial there are a few exhibits—perhaps only one—that are central to the case. Examples can include a model, a diagram, a chart, a contract, a set of telephone records, a map. These objects are markers on the path; they become reminders of the journey. At trial's end they go to the jury room. There is no reason to dilute their power by having another set of materials that are slicker and bigger. Rather, your job is to make these key exhibits part of the story you are telling.

MEDIA AND TRIALS

In any case that has been publicized, some jurors come to court with attitudes shaped by the media coverage. In a case that has received no publicity, you may wonder how the media can help or hurt your client. Like it or not—and I mostly do not like it at all—knowing the legal and prudential rules about media contact is an essential part of every litigator's life.

You know the law about lawyer contact with the media. Nonlawyers—including, under the better view of the law, parties to litigation—cannot be restrained from public comment on a case unless the comment raises a clear and present danger of harm to the deliberative process. Lawyers, by contrast, may lawfully be prevented from, or punished for, public comment that poses a substantial risk of undue influence on the case.[3] In making and enforcing rules on lawyer speech, bar associations and courts are limited not only by the first amendment but also by the void-for-vagueness doctrine. That is, restraint must not only be tailored narrowly to achieve its lawful objectives, but the rules must be clear enough that lawyers understand what is and is not permitted.

After all, we know that the public's business is done in more than one forum at one time. That is, a trial may well involve social issues on which public debate is essential to public involvement in decision making. Lawyers who are litigating such cases are logical and perhaps necessary participants in the debate. This, at any rate, is the lesson taught by our history.

When James Otis litigated in 1761 about the writs of assistance—the papers authorizing British officers to conduct general searches for goods on which taxes had not been paid—he was not shy about speaking in public of the injustices he saw in those cases.[4] When John Adams was retained to represent John Hancock in a forfeiture proceeding, his contentions and later a text of his undelivered argument were aired thoroughly in the press of the time, along with running commentaries on the legal issues.[5] While the records available do not always identify the authors of contentious comments on pending cases, the concepts and vocabulary point clearly to lawyers, and indeed to Adams himself, as the source.

There is much more of this history. Although Eleazer Oswald was a printer and perennial litigant and not a lawyer, his pointed and even gleeful attacks on the administration of justice in Pennsylvania are well documented.[6] Oswald not only mocked Chief Justice McKean, but published "A Hint to Grand Juries" on the eve of that body's consideration of politically motivated charges against him. Oswald also warned "every lawyer" not to appear in court against a printer, lest:

> His name should, like his carcass, rot
> In sickness spurn'd, in death, forgot.[7]

The criminal process and related types of actions such as forfeitures were essential means of social control by an increasingly unpopular and beleaguered British colonial authority. The press response to these judicial proceedings was a tocsin to the polity. Colonial and post-Revolutionary history establishes the tradition of lawyer comment on pending litigation.

The *Zenger* case of 1735, that most famous colonial seditious libel prosecution, put the wrong man in the dock. Zenger did not write the material for which he was prosecuted. The strident attacks on the administration of New York Governor Cosby, including pointed references to his manipulation of the judicial process, were written by lawyers.[8]

History aside, the Supreme Court has recognized that "[I]n the overwhelming majority of criminal trials, pretrial publicity presents few unmanageable threats to this important right [of fair trial]."[9] Indeed, the Court's cases "demonstrate that pretrial publicity—even pervasive, adverse publicity—does not inevitably lead to an unfair trial."[10]

The speculative character of such a risk was the reason the Supreme Court, in *Nebraska Press Ass'n v. Stuart*,[11] refused to uphold a judicial order barring the pretrial publication of a defendant's confessions. After all, few criminal cases ever get to trial due to the prevalence of plea bargaining.[12] Recent surveys suggest that less than 10 percent of criminal cases go to a jury for resolution.[13] Even fewer cases attract sufficient attention to give rise to a plausible basis for concern about potential juror prejudice from publicity. And in those isolated cases that do, the risk of juror prejudice from all sources is negligible. Indeed, one study conducted by Judge Bauer of the Seventh Circuit revealed that even in highly publicized cases, only half of 1 percent of prospective jurors could recall newspaper accounts they had read.[14]

In addition to the speculative character of potential juror prejudice, the Supreme Court's *Nebraska Press* opinion held that alternate means of securing a fair trial were available, and the First Amendment required that they be exhausted first.[15] Nor can the burden of employing these means be cited as a rationale for limiting speech. As the Supreme Court recognized in *Terminiello v. Chicago*,[16] the threatened danger from speech must be an evil that "rises far above public inconvenience, annoyance or unrest."

Even when it can be demonstrated that prospective jurors have been exposed to press coverage of the case, they will not necessarily be prejudiced as a result.[17] The director of the seminal University of Chicago jury study in the 1950s, Harry Kalven, concluded from his research that "the jury is a pretty stubborn, healthy institution not likely to be overwhelmed either by a remark of counsel or a remark in the press."[18]

To be sure, there are those cases in which publicity is so pervasive and hostile that juror prejudice may, indeed must, be presumed. In such cases, again as the Supreme Court has said, the remedy is a change of venue. Even when the press coverage is more limited, *voir dire* may show that a fair jury cannot be selected and the case must be moved.[19]

As Scott Armstrong has pointed out in a study cited by Judge Richard P. Matsch in moving the Oklahoma City bombing case to Denver, media people treat stories differently depending on the target market. If a disturbing event has happened in a particular community, that locality's media will cover the story to emphasize its local effects and will focus on the search for resolution, for vindication, and even (in a case involving loss, injury, or death) for vengeance. Media elsewhere, including national media, are concerned with the who-what-when-where of classic journalism, but the local folks want the news to point toward a conclusion.

Armstrong's insight has significance beyond its possible use in a change of venue motion. It tells us that when your case has been the subject of intense local publicity, or involves well-known local people and entities, there is a much greater likelihood that your prospective jurors come to court with a potential "story" in mind. Your job is to unearth the stories that are current in the community and in *voir dire* to identify which of them may have captured a particular prospective juror's loyalty.

Another aspect of this problem is that of protective orders, shielding documents from public release and closing pretrial and trial proceedings to the public—including the media. The standards for sealing and closure are fairly clear. The Tenth Circuit reviewed them in the *McVeigh* and *Nichols* cases, based on arguments that we had presented in the briefs and in oral argument:

> In determining whether a particular type of document is included within the First Amendment right of access, courts engage in a twopronged inquiry in which they ask: (1) whether the document is one which has historically been open to inspection by the press and the public; and (2) "whether public access plays a significant positive role in the functioning of the particular process in question."[20]

None of this law seems to restrain the media. If your case is a matter of public concern, off-the-record statements by lawyers, parties, the police, and a variety of other "insiders" will be used in media reports, the accuracy of which may be questionable. In a criminal case, restraining prosecution and police leaks is a daunting—and without judicial intervention, a hopeless—task. It is nearly impossible to find a case of meaningful discipline being imposed on those entities for prejudicial pretrial comment or leaks. The facts of *Gentile v. State Bar of Nevada*[21] attest to this problem. Gentile, a well-respected lawyer, represented a defendant who had been pilloried by the media before indictment. After the defendant was indicted and arraigned, Gentile held one press conference to discuss the charges and evidence. He then knew that the trial was some six months away. At the trial, no jurors remembered Gentile's press conference, although some recalled the police-sponsored publicity. The client was acquitted. One week later, Gentile was charged with an ethical violation for his press conference; the police and prosecutors were never called to account. Gentile's bar reprimand was upheld by the Nevada Supreme Court and reversed by the United States Supreme Court, by a vote of five to four.

The final element of this picture is television and radio coverage of trials. The United States Supreme Court has upheld the constitutionality of televising criminal trials under some circumstances. In some jurisdictions televising is routine. The federal courts are less hospitable to it.[22] My own view is that while televising proceedings is usually neutral as far as its effect on the proceedings goes, there are cases where this is demonstrably not so.

In the O. J. Simpson case, the district attorney announced early that he would not seek a gag order. He wanted to try the case in the media. Defense counsel organized its public efforts as well. The trial judge even consented to an interview. Media representatives swarmed the participants, even offering to pay for stories from potential witnesses.

As the predictable publicity barrage reached its apogee, the purported remedy of jury sequestration was imposed. Every trial lawyer knows that a sequestered jury behaves radically differently from one whose members can go home at night. The jurors react to confinement with resentment. Sometimes they resent their captors. More often they come to identify with the cops who are guarding them. And as the trial wears on, and the defense case threatens to lengthen their confinement, jurors began to look at defense counsel with baleful eyes.

In all of this, the influence of television and the potential for media stardom—for witnesses, jurors, lawyers, and others in the process—have harmed the process by diverting the trial from its function of making a vital determination about human liberty fairly, justly, and decently.

That said, I reject the idea that trials should not be televised because the public might gain an unfavorable impression of the justice system. If I am photographed doing something silly in public, it is not the photographer's fault that my friends make rude jokes. In any case, statements that televising harms the justice system's image seem unsupported.

It is clear, however, that in trials that the media have already sensationalized, the presence of television influences lawyer, judge, and witness behavior in ways that conflict with the decisional process. In such trials the witnesses are busy thinking about their media contracts, and the general awareness of media attention distracts the jurors from consideration of the evidence. It becomes more difficult for the advocates to focus juror attention on the evidence and rules of law that ought to govern their decision. Particularly if I am an advocate for a controversial position in a high-visibility case, this loss of control over the process disturbs me.

I also advise clients to be careful what they say. While clients are entitled to a greater measure of First Amendment protection for out-of-court statements than are lawyers,[23] taking full advantage of that liberty is always perilous. There is no guarantee that a client's remarks will be reported in context or without unsympathetic commentary. The lawyer's job in court is always to establish a bond of trust with the jury and then to extend that trust to the client. Often the lawyer must plead with the jurors to focus on the evidence and not some preconceived view. If the jurors have seen and heard the client before coming to court, they may be so wedded to a particular view of him or her that this admonition is meaningless.

There are exceptions, of course. A client who is a public figure must stay in the public eye. In such a case the client should be making the same kind of statement that the lawyers are: "We will do our talking about the case in court. That's where it belongs."

Even if there are no cameras in the courtroom, media attention affects the process, and its impact must be considered as part of the advocate's job of persuasion. Jurors come to court having read about the case. During the trial, even if they are sequestered, news reports may filter through to them. In the event of posttrial motions or an appeal, there will be deciders who have been exposed to the media. And if Mr. Dooley is not entirely right in saying that "the Supreme Court reads the election returns,"[24] judges are at least sensitive to the attitudes of the community where they sit.

I define the advocate's media job in stages. Before trial, one must be vigilant that the other side is not conducting media warfare by leak. I am content to have a protective order entered defining with precision the scope of permissible lawyer comment on the case. One cannot muzzle the client, of course, but one can enjoin the agents of the lawyers, including investigators, paralegals, and police.

Because discovery materials are not subject to a presumptive common law right of access, it is legitimate for the court to approve confidentiality orders as to them. Closure of hearings is, however, to be used sparingly. Generally, unless items of sensationalistic evidence are to be discussed, I think that judicial proceedings should be in public. Judges behave better under public scrutiny, and both sides get a chance to say their piece. This helps to guarantee that the media coverage is as balanced as possible.

So much for limiting things. I think it is right for a lawyer to make brief informative statements to the media about issues in the case. Remember, however, that media people have an agenda of their own, and you have no control over the editing process. Media people are shameless in their efforts to get a statement from you. They use flattery, cajolery, suggestions that you will be treated unfairly if you don't talk, and all manner of other devices. You need not fall for these blandishments.

Some lawyers try to make sure their remarks get airtime and ink by making inflammatory or extravagant claims. All that behavior does, in my view, is to create juror expectations that cannot be satisfied. On decision day, such tactics turn against their user.

I like to say to the media: "We intend to do our talking in court. We have faith in the jury system. We think that the jurors who will be selected deserve our respect, and we respect them by letting them hear first, in court and from the witness stand, what the evidence will be. We are not going to try our case in the media. Our position, though, is clear— [and then go on to make a brief statement of your story]."

If you are going to make statements, for example, to comment on the day's proceedings, do so briefly. Remember that the average TV news story lasts only a minute or two. Think up a sound bite before you step before the cameras. Decide whether you will answer questions. If you will, figure out what the questions will be and prepare a short answer.

If ambushed on the way to court, even for a motion hearing, remember the key concept: "You know, Judge Wilson is a great judge. And she likes to hear arguments first from the lawyers standing in front of her and not read about them in the paper or hear them on TV. So we will make our argument in court. That's the best way."

NOTES

1. Terry McCarthy, the Federal Defender for the Northern District of Illinois, has written and lectured brilliantly about "looking good" cross-examination.

2. A hearsay declarant's credibility can be attacked just as that of any other witness. *See* FED. R. EVID. 806.

3. *See* Gentile v. State Bar of Nevada, 501 U.S. 1030 (1991).

4. *See* J. Quincy, Report of Cases Argued and Adjudged in the Supreme Courts of Judicature of the Province of Massachusetts Bay 51–57, 469–82 (1865); *see also* 2 Legal Papers of John Adams 106–47 (L. Wroth & H. Zobel eds. 1965).

5. *Id.* at 173–210. These court cases were "the Commencement of the Controversy, between Great Britain and America," according to an Adams letter of July 3, 1776. *Id.* at 107 n.2.

6. *See, e.g.,* Teeter, *The Printer and the Chief Justice: Seditious Libel in 1782–83,* 45 Journalism Q. 232 (1968); Teeter, *Press Freedom and the Public Printing: Pennsylvania, 1775–83,* 45 Journalism Q. 539–44 (1968). *See also* Levy II 370.

7. Teeter, *supra,* p. 17, at 240. Leonard Levy has cited dozens of examples, though mostly more polite, of contentious, robust, and wideopen debate by lawyers about the justice system. *See generally* Leonard Levy, Emergence of a Free Press 173–219 (1985). The colonial and post-Revolutionary history tells us more than that the press clause has independent significance, although it surely tells us that. *See* Anderson, *The Origins of the Press Clause,* 30 U.C.L.A. L. Rev. 455 (1983).

8. One of the authors was a former judge, Lewis Morris. *See* L. Powe, The Fourth Estate and the Constitution: Freedom of the Press in America 8 (1991); Levy II 37–45.

9. Nebraska Press Ass'n v. Stuart, 427 U.S. 539, 551 (1976). The history of press restraints is chronicled in Bridges v. California, 314 U.S. 252, 263–68 (1941).

10. *Id.* at 554. *See* Murphy v. Florida, 421 U.S. 794 (1975); Beck v. Washington, 369 U.S. 541 (1962).

11. 427 U.S. 539 (1976).

12. Nebraska Press, 427 U.S. at 600 (Brennan, J., concurring)

13. *See* Frasca, *Estimating the Occurrence of Trials Prejudiced by Press Coverage,* 72 Judicature 162 (1988).

14. *Id.* at 168.

15. *Id.* at 563–65.

16. 337 U.S. 1, 4 (1949).

17. *See* Murphy, 421 U. S. at 799; Stroble v. California, 343 U.S. 181 (1952).

18. Gillmor, *Free Press v. Fair Trial: A Continuing Dialogue—"Trial by Newspaper" and the Social Sciences,* 41 N.D.L. Rev. 156, 167 (1965) (quoting Kalven). According to another commentator, "Experiments to date indicate for the most part juries are able and willing to put aside extraneous information and base their decisions on the evidence." Simon, *Does the Court's Decision in* Nebraska Press Association *Fit the Research Evidence on the Impact on Jurors of News Coverage?,* 29 Stan. L. Rev. 515, 528 (1977).

19. *See* the careful analysis by Judge Matsch in United States v. McVeigh, 918 F. Supp. 1467 (W.D. Okla. 1996).

20. United States v. McVeigh, 119 F.3d 806 (10th Cir. 1997), *cert. denied,* 118 S.Ct. 1110 (1998), quoting Press-Enterprise Co. v. Superior Court, 478 U.S. 1, 8 (1986).

21. Gentile, *supra* note 3.

22. *See* Fed. R. Crim. P. 53, prohibiting broadcast of federal criminal trials. *See* United States v. Edwards, 785 F.2d 1293 (5th Cir.1986) (upholding constitutionality of Rule 53 and denying journalist's application to broadcast Louisiana governor's racketeering trial); United States v. Hastings, 695 F.2d 1278 (11th Cir. 1983) (affirming denial of request to broadcast trial of former federal judge Alcee Hastings). The rule is important to "the preservation of the courtroom as a place of dignity, where the quest for truth goes on quietly and without fanfare and where utmost precautions are taken to keep all extraneous influences from making themselves felt." Charles Alan Wright, Federal Practice and Procedure: Criminal 2d §861 (1982). In October 1994, the Advisory Committee on the Federal Rules of Criminal Procedure specifically "declined to approve a proposed amendment to Rule 53 which would have authorized" broadcasting of federal criminal trials. Judicial Conference of the United States, Minutes of the Advisory Committee on Federal Rules of Criminal Procedure, Oct. 6–7, 1994.

23. *See, e.g.,* Bridges v. California, 314 U.S. 252, 263–68 (1941); United States v. Ford, 830 F.2d 596, 598–600 (6th Cir. 1987).

24. Peter Finley Dunne, Mr. Dooley's Opinions 26 (1901).

Chapter Five, Part I

Elements of the Closing

I wrote *Jury Argument: You, the Facts and the Law*,[1] and there set out nine principles of closing argument. They are worth reviewing, as an introduction and because we will see them illustrated in Edward Bennett Williams's *Connally* summation.

1. You are always on.
2. You must be you. Drink deep at the well of others' knowledge, but do not ape their ways.
3. Your credibility is a necessary, though not sufficient, condition of victory. You first exercise this principle in opening statement, telling the jurors there are hard choices to make in this case. In opening argument you must preview these choices and suggest a framework for making them. In closing you pick up the theme and deliver on your promises.
4. You must ask for what you want. If there are special issues, you will describe them and talk about how they lead to a logical and complete result. If there are complex legal rules to apply, you will guide the jury through the judge's instructions.
5. The facts do not announce themselves. You must help the jury "find" them by sifting through the evidence in a certain order and according to suggested principles of choice and discernment. The jurors have just experienced testimony, exhibits, instructions, and argument. This is the proximate reality for

them. Now they are going to find an "ultimate"—in the sense of decisive—reality. They know how to evaluate what people say to them and how to interpret experience in their daily lives. The process of deciding in a court case involves a combination of this familiar process with an alien one, to which latter process you are their guide.

6. The facts must acquire a life of their own. Use objects and verbal forms that contribute to making your points memorable.

7. The law is something the jurors care about. You must stress the important principles of law that guide decision and do so without condescension. All people have a socially determined sense of justice; identify that sense and show how the law permits it to be exercised in your case.

8. The law includes the juror's duty to be independent. Each juror is independent of the others. All are independent of the state's power, guided only by the court's instructions on the law. Note in the *Connally* summation how Williams speaks to the jurors' power.

9. The law includes the obligation of the juror's oath. Each juror takes an oath for *voir dire* and another to try the case "well and truly and a true verdict render." We need to remind the jurors of that oath at key stages of trial—at a minimum in *voir dire,* in opening statement, and in closing argument.

WHEN TO PLAN THE CLOSING

Closing argument is the sketch of that structure of fact and law constructed before the jurors' eyes during the trial. It tells them what you have built and helps them to see its essential features. Thus you begin work on the closing argument the day you take the case.

To say this is to repeat the theme of Chapter One. But what does it mean in practical terms? When I start work on a case, I use the potential closing argument to find holes in the evidence and gaps in legal theory. We work on these, and of course the potential closing changes with each passing day as we learn more.

As work on the case continues, I find myself taking parts of the case and working them over in my mind, perhaps making a note or two along the way and putting it in a file. I have the chronology and witness list always close at hand, to refer to a doubtful point. For example, suppose there is a factual issue about how a contract was negotiated and signed. I go over the details, trying out different ways of describing the evidence. Yes, I talk to myself—in the car, in the shower, while in my office. I pace and plan.

You cannot do too much of this. It is a part of "saying your case." If your docket is like that of most litigators—with several or even many cases, you need to have a routine to look at each one of them on a regular basis and perform this exercise. You cannot meaningfully direct your own work, nor that of the lawyers, paralegals, clerks, and investigators working with you, unless you have this type of command of the case.

Some lawyers think they can leave all this to others, then pick up the file and go to trial. That is the way that some busy law offices do things. For example, it is the way that many district attorney offices must arrange their work due to the caseload. In my first criminal trial, the Assistant United States Attorney had clearly learned the basic facts from the police report and from a hasty interview with the arresting officer who witnessed the alleged offense. We won a not guilty verdict, my client and I, because we had worked at the facts from all directions.

If you are directing the work of others, you cannot abandon the guiding role of shaping the case, and that means doing and redoing your closing argument.

OPENING AND CLOSING—
WHAT IS THE DIFFERENCE?

Opening statement is not argument; closing argument is. Closing argument happens after everyone has seen whether your opening promises could be and were kept. Closing also differs from opening in how the nine principles of argument apply.

The opening statement, as we have seen, contains as its third element a description of what you want the jurors to do. In *voir dire* you will have explored their willingness and ability to follow the law and decide the facts without prejudice. In closing, however, you go into some detail about what you want them to do.

In a criminal case there is no finer example than in the *Connally* summation. Williams makes clear what principles a not-guilty verdict will vindicate and what positive good will come from it. This is vital. For the prosecutor a guilty verdict gets a criminal off the streets, makes us feel safe, makes jurors feel they have done a public service.

A not-guilty verdict is more problematic in this respect. It could be seen as a refusal to do something, an act of nonfeasance. It is hard to dignify such a "nonaction" with the same qualities as a positive step for good. So one must seek out examples of nonactions that were in fact laudable. Refusal to cooperate with unfair and unjust government exactions fills that bill. But one should go beyond that—the jurors are deciding to lift unjust suspicion; they are declaring something about the quality of government proof or the character of police behavior or the tactics that brought a discredited witness before them. Williams sounds nearly all of these themes.

In a civil case a general verdict presents the same dichotomy. The plaintiff is asking for "something," and the defendant is asking the jury to say no. When there are special issues or interrogatories, defense counsel should use these during summation, to show how the answers fit together and how the evidence supports them.

Whichever side you are on, you are asking the jurors to perform a public function on behalf of your client. They are for today the wielders of state power, which gives them great responsibility. Tomorrow you, the other advocates, and the judge will go on to another case, and they and the client will return to their lives. But the decision made will stand. It will mean something. The opening statement describes the evidence that it is to be. The closing must include a fervent reminder of the jurors' power.

JUROR INVOLVEMENT

The jurors will not give you a verdict unless their sense of justice impels them to do so. Your entire effort must be to involve them in the process of decision. Daniel O'Connell, the Irish liberator, told us that "we can't drag the jurors along with us." O'Connell went on to remind us eloquently that sometimes, in some cases, we know that juror feelings run high against our client, our legal position, or both. So when you are, as O'Connell says, "throw[ing] off mere fragments, or seeds of thought" remember also that there are different ways to do this:

> Sometimes you will do this soft and soothing. But there will be times, when you suspect the jury's purity, to remind them of their juror's oath. Then approach and defy them to balance for an instant between their malignant prejudices and the clear and resistless justice of the case.[2]

In every phase of trial you empower the jurors. In closing argument you do this by stating your appreciation for their service and then by making clear what they are to decide. As Williams puts it in the *Connally* summation, you will superimpose the legal instructions given or to be given by the judge over the facts as shown by the evidence.

You involve the jury by letting the evidence speak for itself. The quiet force of fact is your greatest ally. In closing argument, there is room for rhetoric, but the rhetoric must flow from the case itself and not be tacked on like an ornament. The jury must move from its appreciation of the facts, through a sense of its duty, to a conclusion that meets justice.

I like to say that it takes about three trial days to have a chance at victory in a case involving "hot button" issues. It takes time for the jurors to appreciate your credibility as an advocate, to absorb the atmosphere of the courtroom as a place where reasoned decisions based on evidence are made, to internalize the idea that prejudices must be set aside. Of course, you will be using every moment of those three days in the ways described in Chapter Four.

In the case of Terry Nichols, I concluded the closing argument in the liability phase by standing behind Mr. Nichols with my hands on his shoulders and saying, "This is my brother. He is in your hands." Prosecutors criticized this gesture, and I was concerned that some jurors might have reacted negatively to it—although by their verdict one could not say that the majority did. In a penalty phase, as in a damages phases or a punitive damages phase, the facts have spoken and the jurors have spoken about the facts. Therefore, the watchword is deference to what has gone before, with suggestions that the choices are still open to give a result favorable to your client. In *Nichols,* the jurors had acquitted of arson and use of a bomb, acquitted of first and second degree murder, and convicted only of involuntary manslaughter and conspiracy.

I returned to the "brother" theme in closing argument at the penalty phase. Let me share some of the penalty phase closing with you. First the beginning, to set the stage for juror involvement, then the end, where I tried to talk about the jurors' duty to rise above vengeance:

Counsel, Mr. Nichols, members of the jury, just shy of two weeks ago—it was in the afternoon—you came in and you rendered a verdict in this case. And since that time, it would come as no surprise to you to know that pundits and hired lawyers and TV-talk-show hosts and lawyers and everybody has tried to figure it out. But the judge is going to tell you in a few minutes when we're all done that all of that figuring and all of that posturing and all of that parading can't change a fact and it can't change the law.

The verdict that you rendered is your verdict. It is final. It is binding on everybody in this courtroom, including the jurors who reached it. And I am not going to spend any time at all trying to tell you what you decided. I think that would be arrogance for me to tell you what you decided. Rather, I'm going to talk about the things that the judge will, when we're all done here, tell you that are yet to be decided, keeping in mind that there is no going back on what's been done. I won't take long.

When we're done here, this time that we've spent together, which has represented an enormous sacrifice, I know, for all of you, will be done and you'll go back to your jobs and back to the community. We'll all go back to our jobs, the prosecutors to other cases, me back to teaching school, Mr. Nichols to a prison, which is the result of the verdict that you already reached, not a pretrial detention facility but a prison. And one of the things we're here to decide today is whether or not in addition to that, beyond that, over and above that, 12 of you should sign a piece of paper that authorizes a sentence of death to be carried out with respect to Mr. Nichols; that authorizes somebody to come get him one day and carry out a sentence that he be put to death.

What you won't see when you go back, by the way, is any of us on this side joining the parade of talk-show hosts and as-told-to books. I think those things are a reproach to a profession that tolerates them, and I think they are a disgrace to lawyers who do that.

And now the final part:

But, of course, even then, an eye for an eye, conscience of the community? Well, the words do appear, I know, in the Old Testament. They appear at a time when God is instructing the people of Israel about a system of blood feud and vengeance. But later on even at that time when a court was convened to decide who should live and who should die, called the Sanhedrin, it was decided that a judgment of death could only be pronounced in the Temple. And so the Sanhedrin stopped meeting in the Temple. And why? Because in the earliest stages of the development of our cultural tradition, it was recognized that when the law in its solemn majesty directs that life be taken, that can be crueler than deliberate vengeance because it teaches, because it is a voice that comes from a place that is at war with a reasoned and compassionate system of social organization.

I suggest to you that the government wants to drag you back to a time of vengeance. I suggest to you that the FBI agent who said to Lana Padilla on the 21st of April, 1995, before a jot of evidence was in his hand, "Those two guys are going to fry," symbolized a rush to judgment that is at war with what the conscience of the community ought to do and ought to think about.

I submit to you that to surrender your deliberations to vengeance is to turn your back on lessons that we have all learned with great difficulty and a great deal of pain. Nobody knows the depths of human suffering more than those who have been the systematic victims of terror; and yet in country after country, judicial systems are saying that in each case, the individual decision must triumph over our sense of anger. Even the Supreme Court of Israel freed from a death sentence a man found to have no direct participation in the deaths of people that he had been accused of killing. In South

Africa, when Mandela was released from prison, it was decided that it would be very, very difficult despite the record of violence against the black majority to obtain a death sentence and that a system would be put in place to make sure that acts of vengeance and anger were not carried out in the name of the law.

Well, I've gone through the [verdict] form and I've gone through the instructions. And if I've said anything that makes you think that I'm trying to tell you what you already decided or what you ought to think in terms of your deepest convictions, please disregard it. . . .

When I concluded my earlier summation, I walked over to Terry Nichols and said, "This is my brother." And the prosecutor got up and reminded all of us, thinking that he would remind me, that there were brothers and sisters and mothers and fathers all killed in Oklahoma City. Of course, when I said, "This is my brother," I wasn't denying the reality of that. I hope I was saying something else. I was talking about a tradition that goes back thousands of years, talking about a particular incident, as a matter of fact. You may remember—most of us learned it I think when we were young—the story of Joseph's older brothers, Joseph of the many-colored coat,[3] now the "Technicolor Dream Coat" in the MTV version. And they were jealous of him, cast him into a pit thinking he would die, and then sold him into slavery. And years later, Joseph turns out to become a judicial officer of the pharaoh, and it happens that he is in a position to judge his brothers. And his brother Judah is pleading for the life or for the liberty of the younger brother, Benjamin; and Joseph sends all the other people out of the room and announces, "I am Joseph, your brother." That was the story, that was the idea that I was trying to get across; that in that moment, in that moment of judgment, addressing the very human being, his older brother Judah, who had put his life at risk and then sold him into slavery, he reached out, because even in that moment of judgment he could understand that this is a human process and that what we all share looks to the future and not to the past.

Members of the jury, we ask you, we suggest to you, that under the law, your judgment should be that this case go back to Judge Matsch and that he reach the just and appropriate sentence under the law and under the verdict that you've already reached. I won't have a chance to respond to what the prosecutor says, but I know that after your 41 hours of deliberations on the earlier phase, you're all very, very accustomed to thinking of everything that could be thought.

My brother is in your hands.

In this entire summation, I did not raise my voice. At this stage, with this issue, deference and empowerment meant keeping matters at the level of rational discourse.

I am not saying that there was no emotion in this summation, but rather that the emotion was in the force of facts. There was plenty of emotional power in recalling what the witnesses had said and how they had said it. An advocate's becoming emotional is not the same thing as conveying or evoking emotion.

Then, too, when the stakes are high, emotion can be particularly dangerous. If we are to do something really terrible, such as vote a death sentence, it helps to be really angry. Anger—which often in life springs from fear—propels itself into self-righteousness and from there into actions that one would not ordinarily take.

In Terry Nichols's case we had the jurors' verdict, which did not find intent to kill. Had we been faced with a verdict that found such an intent, then the message about life versus death would have to be clearer. In such a case one might remind the jurors that in all the faiths likely to be professed by members of the jury redemption plays a major role. We are all better than the worst thing we have ever done.

In a mock summation, given years ago at the Smithsonian Folklife Festival, I can remember invoking with passion the brutalized childhood of a young man on trial for his life. I was trying to put the undeniable reality of his terrible crime into some kind of context. And I concluded by saying:

> I am done now, members of the jury. When I go home tonight, my little girl will ask me, "What did you do today, daddy?" I will tell her that I tried to save the life of one of God's creatures. And, members of the jury, what will you say when you go home?

You must also involve the jurors in the judge's instructions, even the ones that they may find difficult to follow. You might say: "You all know that Mr. Martinez did not take the witness stand. The judge will tell you that this must not play any part in your deliberations. But suppose you get back there to the jury room and somebody says, 'Well, he didn't testify, so he must be guilty.' You can turn to that person and say, 'We took an oath, all of us, to follow the law as the judge lays it down. And we promised that we would make the government prove their case beyond a reasonable doubt and not put the burden on the defense to prove anything.'" This form of argument reinforces the rule of law without lecturing the jurors on it.

You can in closing argument remind the jurors of *voir dire*: "We all take an oath to do what we do here. I took one to be a lawyer, Her Honor took one to be a judge, and you took your oath to answer the *voir dire* questions and then to try this case. In *voir dire* you told me [or us] that [and here repeat whatever promise it was, for example to return adequate money damages if liability were proven or to acquit if a reasonable doubt remains, or whatever]. And I believed you then."

You can repeat this strophe in different forms if there was more than one promise.

SETTING THE SCENE

When you read the annotated Williams closing, you will see how he sets the scene. He describes what he will do with the facts and law, then talks about Jake Jacobsen, the principal witness, the evidence as a whole, and John Connally, the defendant. Each part is further broken down into its elements, with introductory and transition sentences to move from part to part.

The "scene" is not simply a synopsis of facts. In closing argument it is an entire story, told from a distinct point of view and containing its own dynamic of resolution. The point of view tells us how the view of facts and jurors' duty leads to justice. The judge's instructions on specific and general principles of law provide the dynamic of resolution.

When the lawyers for Queen Caroline of England summed up in the House of Lords, in her trial for adultery, their objective was not simply to show that she was accused falsely. Rather, they suggested that the entire case was brought from unworthy motives, that the prosecutors had connived with the Crown, and that the very stability of the country was at stake. Their discussion of the facts was straightforward—the witnesses for the prosecution contradicted themselves and were in turn contradicted. The major witness suffered a lack of memory as to crucial times and events. But the mainstay of their argument was its attack on the very idea of the case being brought, as some excerpts from counsel's arguments will make clear:

> I begin by assuring your lordships that the cause of the Queen as it appears in evidence does not require recrimination *at present* against the heir apparent to the crown. The evidence against her majesty does not, I feel, *now* call upon me to utter one whisper against the conduct of her illustrious consort. And I solemnly assure your lordships that but for that conviction, my lips would not at this time be closed. In this discretionary exercise of my duty, I postpone the case which

I possess. Your lordships must know that I am waiving a right which belongs to me and abstaining from the use of materials that are unquestionably my own.

If however I should hereafter think it advisable to exercise this right, let it not be vainly supposed that I or even the youngest member in the profession would hesitate to resort to such a course and fearlessly perform his duty.

I once again remind your lordships, though there are some who do not need reminding, that an advocate in the discharge of his duty knows but one person in all the world, and that person is his client. To save that client by all means, and at all hazards and costs to all others, and among all others to himself, is his first and only duty. And in performing this duty he must not regard the alarm, the torments, the destruction which he may bring upon others. Nay, separating the duty of patriot from that of an advocate, he must go on, reckless of consequences, though it should be his unhappy fate to involve his country in confusion.

To begin, I call your lordships' attention to what the evidence in this case does not do. I mean to point out the parts of my learned friend the Attorney General's opening statement which instead of receiving support from the evidence, are rather not touched by it at all or actually negated out of the mouths of his own witnesses. My learned friend should rather have made his *own* statement of the plan and construction of his own case. Rather, my learned friend was, in his statement, directed by the instructions which were put into his hands. His speech must be considered as the mere transcript of his instructions, the mere outline of the documents submitted to him, documents prepared in a way which nobody should be at any loss to guess.

My learned friend almost at the commencement used these words, "I will most conscientiously take care to state nothing which in my conscience I do not think, I

do not believe I shall be able to substantiate by proof."
He need not have so strongly appealed to his conscience, for I fully believed him when he said he spoke
from his instructions. . . .

Now, there was no way for that statement to have got
into my learned friend's brief out of the mouths of the
witnesses, who at first did not hesitate to garnish their
stories, though they were not afterwards found hearty
enough to adhere to their falsehoods when brought to
your lordships' bar. . . .

Having said that I proceed without further apology to
the case itself. But, while I disclaim all personal imputation on my learned friend, I claim the right of advert-
ing with the utmost freedom on his conduct as an
advocate. From the conduct of an advocate not only
may the impressions of his mind be collected, but also
much of the nature of the instructions under which he
acted and of the spirit of which the prosecution has
been conducted.

To have to conduct a case in such a spirit, I conceive
to be a misfortune for which no rewards, no honor
could afford an equivalent. A misfortune which has
weighed down my learned friend, a misfortune to
which I declare before God that nothing within the
scope of human ambition could tempt me to have submitted for a single moment. And I mean the office of
prosecuting this bill of pains and penalties to divorce
and degrade the wife of the King of England.

I turn to the case itself. I will read a few samples of
the difference of the Attorney General's statement and
his subsequent evidence to show the value at which
your lordships ought to estimate that evidence. . . .

And then at the end of the argument:

My lords, I call upon you to pause. You stand on the
brink of a precipice. If your judgment shall go out

against your Queen, it will be the only act that ever went out without effecting its purpose. It will return to you upon your own heads. Save the country. Save yourselves. Rescue the country. Save the people of whom you are the ornaments, but severed from whom you can no more live than the blossom that is severed from the root and tree on which it grows. Save the country, therefore, that you may continue to adorn it. Save the Crown which is threatened with irreparable injury. Save the aristocracy which is surrounded with danger. Save the altar which is no longer safe when its kindred throne is shaken. See that when the church and the throne would allow of no church solemnity in behalf of the Queen, the heartfelt prayers of the people rose to Heaven for her protection. I pray Heaven for her. And I here pour forth my fervent supplications at the throne of mercy, that mercies may descend upon the people of this country richer, I dare say, than their rulers have deserved, and that your hearts be turned to justice.

KEEPING THE STORY AT THE CENTER

For Queen Caroline, the central element of story was "the very idea of accusing the Queen." Few would doubt that her sojourns in Italy were at the least suspicious. But the idea of accusing the queen of adultery was fraught with peril for the nation. In addition, there was a popular sentiment building that the accusations were unfair. Most of the accusing witnesses were foreigners. One of them, Majochi, had said *"non mi ricordo"*—I don't remember—dozens of times under cross-examination. The phrase became an object of derision in the streets. So the queen's lawyers unabashedly deployed xenophobia as a rhetorical device.

Rarely will the rest of us have a case in which community sentiment is so clearly dominating the argument. When we think such a case may be in our hands, we will be careful, for such sentiment when unleashed is like rushing water—hard to keep in its appointed channel. Yet in every case, some ideal of justice will be central to our argument. Perhaps we will be discussing that powerful line between not guilty and guilty, policed by the concept of reasonable doubt. Perhaps we will be saying that the defendant's conduct needs to be stopped, for the benefit of others as well as this plaintiff.

Perhaps we will find that the conduct of our adversary has strayed so far from what is right that we can legitimately ask the jurors to examine it. Such a tactic verges on personal attack, which may call out a reply, or a judicial admonition, or—worse yet—jury resentment. Yet there are times when it must be done. Williams's approach to this issue in the *Connally* summation is masterful.

One should also read every word of Atticus Finch's summation for Tom Robinson, as reported in Chapter 20 of *To Kill a Mockingbird*. In coming to terms with the complaining witness's perjury, he blends the facts the jury saw with a chilling reminder of the reasons that she had to lie.

But all references to justice are the story's penumbra. Or, if you want another metaphor, they illuminate by reflected light like the moon. At the center, running through all the great closings, will be a tale of events told by witnesses and supported by exhibits. This is the star, the sun, of your case. The jurors can internalize an idea of justice—of why your client must prevail. But they cannot argue that idea to a particular result without the evidence. The evidence takes them through deliberations as they argue with other jurors. Indeed, one test of your closing should be whether it provides a juror leaning your way with the material necessary to make detailed and precise arguments against someone who sees it differently.

Notice as you read the *Connally* closing how Williams shifts focus yet keeps the story central. The prosecutor's story is that Connally took money from Jacobsen. There is no question that Jacobsen had money from the milk interests and that he told those people he would give it—and later that he had given it—to Connally. There is no question that milk price supports went up or that Treasury Secretary Connally supported that action by the Secretary of Agriculture. Williams's story is not simply that Jacobsen did not give the money. It is that Jacobsen was snarled in his own difficulties and that he took the money for himself and then began to lie about it. A subtle perceptual shift brings the whole matter into different perspective. The main images on the landscape remain the same—price supports, political turmoil, influence seekers, the main characters. But the shadows cast by lighting the tableau differently, and making a slight rearrangement, give one a different impression entirely.

So your argument must deploy the legal principles about credibility and burden of proof but use those to show how the jurors might view particular witnesses and exhibits. For example, in the *Nichols* case we wanted the jury to think about the testimony of plea bargaining Michael Fortier in light of the judge's instructions on reasonable doubt, which included the standard caution that such a doubt would be one that would cause you to hesitate in the more important affairs of everyday life. Fortier reported that he had never seen Terry Nichols utter a violent word or do a violent act, yet that Timothy McVeigh had often said that Nichols was in on the plan to blow up the federal building in Oklahoma City. Fortier's path to becoming a government witness was neither short nor straight. He had been tape-recorded saying that he really knew nothing about McVeigh's plans but that he would not talk in any event until somebody offered him a lot of money.

Michael Fortier? I asked him: Michael—or Mr. Fortier, you went to the FBI, you stood on the balcony of the motel in Oklahoma City. You had an epiphany, sir—I don't know that he knows what an epiphany is, so I didn't ask him if it was a epiphany; but he had some kind of a conversion—and you told the FBI that you wanted to tell your story. And then you went back in the room and you talked about it some more, and the FBI agents left afterward. Then they came back, and then you turned to your wife and you said, "You tell yours first." So she did, and then he told his. And when he told his, he admitted he didn't put Terry Nichols in it.

Here's a guy who claims to have had a conversion. Conversions should be made of sterner stuff. And when asked, he said: Well, I decided I'd keep on lying about that. Michael Fortier. The Judge is going to tell you that a reasonable doubt is a doubt that would cause you to hesitate in the more important affairs of your everyday life. Words like that. Let's think about it. You open your door. There's Michael Fortier. "Good morning," you say.

"Good morning," he says. "I'm Michael Fortier. There's been a car accident down at the end of the street. You really ought to go look."

"Well, I'm sorry, sir, but I've never met you before. And besides that, I've got my kids here."

"Well, that's all right. I'll take care of your kids."

Well, that's an important decision. "Tell me a little bit about yourself."

"Well, I certainly won't fall asleep while I'm taking care of your kids, because I've been up for three days under the influence of methamphetamine, and I have actually learned about a plot to blow up the Murrah Building. But I haven't really sold my story on that yet. I'm waiting for my million, which means I'm a solid citizen, because when I get my million, I'll be a qualified person. I know I'm talking a little fast, but it is the influence of the drug that I am taking."

And I don't have to go through the rest of the conversation. Would you do it? In that important decision as to whether to leave your house for 20 minutes with that guy in charge of your kids, I submit, members of the jury, that no sensible person would do it. Hesitate in the more important affairs of one's everyday life indeed.

In this example, as in the Connally summation, the legal principles are not abstract—they are integrated into the narrative. The same must be true of the substantive legal rules at issue—the elements of a claim or defense. When there are special issues, in a criminal or civil case, you will have the verdict form in hand. You may use a copy of it—enlarged and on an easel, or on the overhead projector, or on the ELMO for video projection—to let the jurors know how you think their decisions should be reflected in answers to the questions. You may choose to talk the jurors through the form without displaying a copy of it, but the effect is the same. You are using the substantive rules of law as a skeleton for the story. You are reminding the jurors all over again, as you did in opening, of what is and is not in dispute.

That is, a part of your closing argument must consist of taking each element of the claim or defense you are supporting and talking about how the evidence supports the answer you want from the jurors. In this way you empower them to translate the evidence into a result.

You may also keep the story at the center with imagery, analogy and figures of speech that represent the story or aspects of it. In the Air Force major's case discussed in Chapter One, our focus was to be the civilian accusing the distinguished military officer. Our theme focused on the shared values of the military community. The reason for our approach consisted of the seven colonels and lieutenant colonels who formed the military's equivalent of a jury, for when an officer is on trial all the court members must outrank the defendant. We wanted these officers to remember, as they judged our client, that she was one of "their own" and not "the other" or the demonized embodiment of illicit lust that the prosecutors painted.

So in summation, I returned to the words and thoughts of Cicero in his celebrated defense of General Murena:

I know that many of you have studied military history, and therefore you probably know about the case in ancient Rome of General Murena. General Murena was accused of corruption by a bunch of civilian witnesses. For his lawyer, he chose Cicero, the most brilliant advocate and orator of his time. In speaking to the tribunal, Cicero contrasted the profession of lawyer with that of general. General Murena had brought riches to Rome, and helped to guarantee the liberty of its free citizens. By contrast, and in his address Cicero was quite mocking in word and gesture, lawyers are all tied up with their technicalities, their pettifogging. And by this means, Cicero pointed out the importance of honoring those who serve in uniform and make their career doing so, and protecting them against the baseless charges that ill-motivated civilians might bring.

Members of the court, I became a lawyer because I believe in human rights. But I'll tell you something. These days, there are a lot of times when we lawyers run out of words. And that's when we call you. The finest hours of your service today, when you best fulfill the oath you took, are in defense of human rights where they are endangered in so many places in the world.

You know, in *voir dire* we talked about religious beliefs and upbringing. I was raised a Baptist, and was therefore taught that the story of the loaves and the fishes is quite literally, historically true. But whether or not you believe that, there is a powerful image there, a powerful message. And that is that there are two things that do not diminish, but grow greater as they are given away, and those are God's love and human justice.

In every case, we ask jurors to transcend. For twelve of them (or seven to nine members of a court martial, or six in some civil cases) to agree on a verdict, they must find common ground at some level of generalization. They must identify with your client, or with that client's claim for justice. The members of this court martial would not take a public stance identifying with freedom of sexual preference. For some, strong religious conviction would preclude that. For most of them, the command of the Uniform Code of Military Justice had to be upheld even if it seemed harsh in application. In courts-martial, the court that is like a jury sets punishment as well as deciding guilt and often indulges its doubts about the severity of the code in that context.

So we chose three generalizations, each of which is an invitation to transcend the particular issues and make a statement about justice. The first was at the level of proof—a sloppy investigation and less-than-credible witnesses. The second was to reaffirm, in the military context, the rights of service members to be judged fairly when accusations are leveled by civilians; not gay service members, but all service members, becomes the relevant group. Third, I talked about religious values. This was for a double purpose—one was that perhaps some members of the court would be persuaded that these sorts of cases deserve compassionate handling. The other purpose was preemptive: in case religious zealotry found its way into deliberations as an argument for conviction, a countervailing thought would be in the air.

RESPONDING, ANTICIPATING, REBUTTING

If your opponent opens and closes the argument, you must watch out for the rebuttal. If in your jurisdiction the court will insist that the opening be full and the rebuttal be just that and no more, enforce that rule by setting time limits that help to ensure it is respected. If, as in a few places, there is no limit on the rebuttal, you know there will be things said that would not be, if the speaker knew that her opponent had the right of reply.

Under either scenario, you can make discreet objection to matters not in evidence or to other improper tactics. Objections during argument must be softly spoken, accompanied by a brief statement of reasons. Do not object unless you know that in this judge's court there is a reasonable chance to have the objection sustained. Unfounded interruptions during argument look bad.

In the penalty phase summation in the *Nichols* trial, quoted above, I finished with a discussion of the Joseph story and then referred back to the jurors' consideration of the liability phase evidence. In every case, you must tell the jurors in more or less detail that you count on them to make sure that rebuttal does not overwhelm. Of course, there is less chance of this if the jurors have hold of the evidence in context. You might say: "I am almost done here. This is my only chance to talk to you. When I am done, Ms. Winston has another chance. I guess that's fair, since they have the burden of proof here and their failure to carry that burden weighs on their case. But she might say something that causes you to wonder—now what would Mr. Tigar say about that if he had another chance? I won't be able to stand up and satisfy your curiosity about that. I am confident that you, having heard all the evidence, and being the ones with the duty to decide, will be able to figure out the answer to anything any of these lawyers throw at you—and that includes me."

In your middle-of-the-sandwich argument, how much anticipating should you do of what the rebuttal will be? If you have not heard a major theme sounded in the opponent's opening argument, you can be pretty sure it will be there in rebuttal. If the gap is obvious, say so: "Now we did not hear about the doctor's report from Ms. Winston in her argument just now. Maybe we will hear about it in rebuttal. But let me talk about it right now."

The general rule, however, is: Make your argument, set out your theory, answer strong points that might be raised on the other side, all as though there were to be no rebuttal. Do not seem to be answering your opponent directly nor to be warding off blows not yet struck. Your case, in closing as in opening, stands by itself.

If the rebuttal argument is yours, the canons of fairness dictate that you shall use it properly. Attempts to smuggle in prejudicial material free from any response by the opponent are unethical. And if your opponent objects, the judge may sustain the objection in terms that cast your credibility and therefore your whole case into doubt. She might even let your opponent make a brief surrebuttal.

Jurors do not like lawyer tactics that look like attempts to overwhelm their judgment. They don't like lawyers who don't play fair. Time and again, when my opponent has used rebuttal to rile up the jurors or to introduce some issue or line of argument that is over the line, I have heard jurors express resentment toward such behavior afterward.

In rebuttal, tell the jurors why you have that right: "We are allowed to make this rebuttal argument because we have the burden of proof. As I said in opening statement, we accept that burden. And we have presented evidence throughout this whole trial to meet it—to satisfy you by a fair preponderance of the credible evidence that Ms. Smith was targeted for sexual harassment by Mr. Jones and the XYZ Corporation. I want to spend my last few minutes with you talking about some of the issues that have just been raised— questions for which the evidence you have heard and the law the judge will give you readily provide the answer."

You will notice in the *Connally* case that the prosecutors had said in their closing that they would not set out their theory of a particular event but would wait to see what the defense had to say about it. As my notes to the summation point out, this is a bad tactic. Williams could not have known exactly what the prosecutors would say on this subject but was certainly prepared to address it.

The lesson is that there will always be issues that are "optional" in the sense that one would not raise them unless the opponent did or are in the "must include" category but will be handled differently based on the opponent's approach. For those issues the argument notes must have some reminders of the issues and then alternative formulations. A closing argument should be prepared so that all the foreseeable contingencies are addressed. It is dangerous to depart from one's plan based on an idea of the moment. The risks are too great that one will fail to see the context in which things are happening.

A final caution: in responding or rebutting, rhetorical questions are a bad idea. They invite bubble-bursting responses. In a jury trial involving alleged terrorists falsifying firearms purchase reports, defense counsel strode to the prosecutor's table in closing argument and picked up a handful of government exhibits that he was claiming were of doubtful relevance.

"And what does all this prove?" he declaimed.

"Illegal dealing in guns," said a juror in the front row.

One trouble with advocates is that we are so convinced that our cause is just that we forget that this is not obvious to the onlooker. So don't ask such questions.

NOTES

1. 14 LITIGATION 19 (Summer 1988).

2. KEVIN MCCARTHY & MICHAEL E. TIGAR, WARRIOR BARDS, scene 1 (1989). This one-act play in six scenes depicts Irish and Irish-American advocates.

3. *Genesis* 44–45.

Chapter Five, Part II

Closing Argument—An Example

This is Williams's summation in the *Connally* trial. In the trial, the AMPI representatives had testified that they gave Jacobsen money to give to Connally. Jacobsen had said he gave $10,000 of the money to Connally. He had described a day in Houston when Connally, in a meeting at Connally's Houston office, gave him back $10,000 to put in his safe-deposit box so that he could claim that he had never given the money to Connally.

Nineteen witnesses from the Federal Reserve and related entities had said that the money in Jacobsen's box *could* have been in circulation on the date Jacobsen said he got the money from Connally. It was clear, though, that much of the money could not have been in circulation at the time Jacobsen got funds from AMPI and that Connally of all people would have known that. Forty-nine of the bills Jacobsen said he got from Connally bore the signature of George P. Schultz, who succeeded Connally as Secretary of the Treasury.

Jacobsen also claimed that Connally, having given him the $10,000, became worried that the bills were not old enough to make the story plausible and so gave him another $10,000 more than a month later at the home of George Christian, a Connally friend and former press secretary to President Johnson.

In the defense case, Connally testified, and a parade of character witnesses appeared.

* * * * * * *

May it please the court and ladies and gentlemen of the jury.

You have been sitting here for almost three weeks in what has been up to now a silent role as the triers of the facts in this somewhat unique criminal trial.

Following the argument of counsel and the instructions which His Honor will give to you, you will take this case to your jury room to begin your deliberations, all to the end of arriving at a verdict that is fair and right and just.

It is my purpose in the time that is allotted to me to review with you the significant parts of the evidence, and to superimpose, as it were, over that evidence the instructions on the law which His Honor will give to you, so that together we may see the points of coincidence, because I believe in that way I can be of maximum help to you in your deliberations.

COMMENTARY

In every summation, as Williams notes, you must put together the law and the facts. Note where Williams begins. He is going to be "of maximum help." He is going to "superimpose"—using a gesture of one hand over the other—the instructions over the evidence.

First of all, I want to thank you. I want to thank you for the attention that you have given to this case for the past three weeks. At times the evidence was tedious and at times it was complex and almost incomprehensible.

COMMENTARY

He is referring to the Federal Reserve evidence on money in circulation. It was at times mind numbing. I had done the research on this issue and prepared cross-examination outlines and exhibits for the banking witnesses. At one point even Williams became frustrated with how long it was taking. He came over to counsel table and whispered, "I'm dying out there. Is this going anywhere?" I said things looked fine, and he continued. Many times, in complex cross-examinations, we all get that feeling that we will never get through it to the point we are trying to make.

> Most of the time you will get through it, because your plan of attack gives you several places to fall back and gives you a good ending no matter what happens.

And I know I speak for all the parties when I say to you we are deeply grateful to you for your service.

I have never served as a juror and I suppose I never shall, because I am a trial lawyer, but I have always deeply believed that it is the highest form of public service, that it is the highest function a citizen can perform. It is the most God-like function that you will ever be asked to perform in your lives, because you are being asked to make judgments on a fellow human being.

COMMENTARY

Note the progression here. He thanks the jurors, without sycophancy. Jurors do believe their job is important. Even those reluctant to serve come away with a sense of pride and a new attitude toward service. In a celebrated case, jurors feel this sense of pride more easily. Indeed, during *voir dire* you may want to weed out those who are too eager to serve. You will seldom want a juror who comes to the case with an agenda already fixed.

In a case that has not attracted media attention, one purpose of *voir dire* is to tell jurors just how important the case is—to your client and to the justice system. You pick up this theme in argument.

The final step in this progression is to speak of the "God-like function," which one would do often in criminal cases but less often in civil ones. This jury included deeply religious people. Their faith may cause them to hesitate to "judge" another human being. If you were not going to use this image, you could use a softer one to the same effect: "The importance of this case is shown by the very fact you are here. For all the most important decisions in our society, in all disputes between individuals, or between individuals and corporations, or individuals and the government, we don't trust the lawyers, the judges, and the bureaucrats. We trust you. We ask for people from the community to come and give up their time and render judgment."

G. K. Chesterton apotheosized the jury by saying that all important matters are resolved by calling twelve ordinary citizens from different walks of life. As he recalled, the "father of Christianity" had done the same thing. I have never used this image, because I think it might be offensive to some jurors. The image of Jesus calling on the apostles may strike some as more talk about male-dominated institutions. Some devout Christians may think that equating juries with the apostles borders on sacrilege. Non-Christians will think the image inapt for other reasons.

On the day when we first met I said to you when I made the opening statement on behalf of the defense, that an opening statement by a trial lawyer is not like a politician's speech, because a politician seeking high office could stand before you and promise the moon, knowing that he didn't have to deliver on his promises or his commitments until after the votes were cast.

I said to you that day a trial lawyer has to deliver on his commitments, that he has to prove to the jury before they begin their deliberations, before they begin their consideration of the case and before they ballot.

I say to you, I hope with humility, and I know with sincerity that I think we have met that responsibility.

─── COMMENTARY ───

Here Williams is reminding the jurors of the promise.

I want now to canvass the evidence with you, so that you can make your own determination.

─── COMMENTARY ───

This is empowering—you make up your mind whether we have met our obligation.

Let's look in the first instance at the charges that have been filed here. There are two charges against John Connally which you will consider in your jury room. The first is that on May 14th, 1971, while he was Secretary of the Treasury of the United States, he took $5,000 from Jake Jacobsen.

And the second, members of the jury, is the identical charge, except only the date is different.

He is charged with having taken another $5,000 on May 24th—on September 24th, I misspoke myself—on September 24th.

Now, His Honor is going to tell you as a matter of law when he gives you your instructions on the law, that the burden rests squarely upon the prosecutors to prove to you, members of the jury, beyond any reasonable doubt that John Connally is guilty of those charges.

He will tell you also that under your sacred oaths as jurors taken on the very first day when you were selected by all counsel from all the prospective jurors who sat in that room, that under your oaths as jurors, unless the prosecution has carried the burden of proving to you beyond a reasonable doubt that John Connally betrayed his trust and took $5,000 on May 14, 1971, that under your oath you must return a verdict of not guilty; and that the very same thing is true with respect to the second charge.

COMMENTARY

How many times does he say "oath", and "law"—two evocative words? And he couples that with a reminder that all the lawyers chose these jurors from among all those assembled for jury selection.

Unless they have proven in this court of law that John Connally betrayed his trust on September 24, 1971, and bargained away his honor to Jacobsen, it is your duty, under the oaths that you took on the first day, to return a verdict in this case of not guilty.

COMMENTARY

The charge is accepting a gratuity "for or because of" an official act performed. There is no allegation of bribery, which would involve "corrupt" intent and a *quid pro quo*. But Williams is upping the ante—making this a question of "honor" and "bargain." He is doing so because the defense rests critically on the difference between Connally as person (and public servant) of honor and Jacobsen as liar and thief. To make the distinction work, Williams intensifies the rhetoric of the charge. In the next two paragraphs, Williams contrasts the image of Connally with that of Jacobsen.

Now, I ask you members of the jury at the very outset before we go any farther, can you say in your minds and in your hearts that the quality of the evidence offered in this courtroom by the prosecution has met that burden, that the quality of the evidence offered by the government through the lips of a man whom they have characterized in an indictment as a fraud and a swindler, whom they have characterized on two occasions, once in the United States District Court for the Western District of Texas, and once in this very courthouse here as a perjurer?

Can you say that a witness, branded by the government in those terms, who proclaims himself to be a liar under oath, can you say that that evidence meets the burden of satisfying you beyond a reasonable doubt of the guilt of a man who came into this courtroom with an impeccable reputation for honor and integrity after almost three scores of his life? I don't think you can say that.

I don't think you can say that. I don't think right at the threshold, you say that—

THE COURT: Mr. Williams.

MR. WILLIAMS: —the government has sustained that burden.

THE COURT: You may suggest, you may not think.

COMMENTARY

Williams continues unfazed by this. He adjusts his language. Did he step over the line by saying "I don't think"? An advocate cannot express a personal belief in the client's cause. He or she may, however, say what the evidence shows. What Williams said does not, in my view, cross that line. He is admonishing the jurors, pointing them to a result based on evidence—or the lack of it. This is not expression of personal belief.

As a matter of tactics, however, one should be careful to inject a personal view. You want the jurors to see their way to a conclusion, the better to hold on to it.

The most common form of the error, to which objection must usually be made, is "vouching" for a witness's credibility by saying in effect that you would not have put the witness on if you did not think her credible.

MR. WILLIAMS: I say, members of the jury, that they offered a witness here who cut a cynical deal for himself to avoid his misdeeds, to avoid the punishment for those misdeeds, a punishment that in the aggregate might have been 40 years in the penitentiary, and came in here and bore witness against this defendant.

I say that if that kind of evidence can support the burden that the prosecution must meet in a court of criminal justice, God rest the American Bill of Rights, because it can happen to you and me.

Supposing one of our co-workers was caught in criminal conduct and, faced with the penitentiary, could be told, oh, you can mitigate this, you can eliminate the consequences of your misdeed if only you give evidence and lay culpability on another.

Have we reached that point in our society where scoundrels can escape their punishment if only they inculpate others? If so, we should mark it well, that although today it is John Connally, tomorrow it may be you or me.

COMMENTARY

This is a necessary attack on the turncoat witness. Remember, though, the usual reply by the adversary: We did not select Mr. X; the defendant did.

Now, I want to talk to you about Mr. Jacobsen. I want to talk to you about Mr. Jacobsen the man, and about Mr. Jacobsen the witness. I want to talk to you about Mr. Jacobsen the witness before he had an interest to falsify, and about Mr. Jacobsen the witness after he had a motive to falsify.

COMMENTARY

For Jacobsen, it is "before and after." That is the key duality whenever a key witness has changed his story. In this paragraph, Williams characterizes the prosecution's case. You will do the same in every summation, civil and criminal: You will in a deft paragraph state a key to understanding the opponent's case— and its flaws. Here the government's case rests on Jacobsen. The prosecutors would deny this, pointing to what they claim to be corroboration. The defense says none of that corroboration rises higher than Jacobsen's credibility. For example, if it be proved that AMPI gave Jacobsen money, we have only the latter's word that he gave it to Connally.

Standard jury instructions include a charge that the testimony of an admitted perjurer be received with caution and weighed with care. They include a similar instruction for an alleged accomplice and for a plea bargainer or immunized witness. We asked for, and got, all three instructions in this case, so the jury was told in three different ways to be careful of Jacobsen's testimony.

Then I want to talk to you about John Connally the man, and then John Connally the accused, and the nature of the case against him.

COMMENTARY

This, too, is classic. Your case is in triplets—the person, what happened to that person, and what are we going to do.

First of all, let's look at Mr. Jacobsen, the man. The evidence has shown, members of the jury, that on February 6th, 1974, he was indicted. Normally it wouldn't have significance in a case that a witness had been indicted, but it

COMMENTARY

Williams is careful here. An indictment is not proof. Jacobsen is still presumed innocent of these charges. One cannot undercut that presumption, for it is important to Connally as well.

has significance here, members of the jury, because he was excused from this indictment when he agreed to give evidence.

What does the government which offers him as a witness before you say about him in this indictment? Covering a time, precisely the time frame with which we are concerned and interested here.

It said in that indictment, members of the jury, that Mr. Jacobsen and his associate, Mr. Cowan, and a man named Herring, conspired to misapply for their own personal gain the monies of the First San Angelo Savings and Loan Association, of which Jacobsen was a controlling shareholder, board member, chairman of the board, with the intent to injure and defraud that association; that they did it by false documentation; that they fraudulently took funds from the depositors and shareholders of that bank over a period of time, precisely coincident with the time with which we are dealing here.

COMMENTARY

The government did indeed dismiss these cases against Jacobsen as a part of its bargain. The district judge in Texas was offended by this, and tried to keep the cases alive. He appointed special prosecutors to continue the case because the Justice Department would not. The Fifth Circuit held that the court did not have the power under these circumstances to deny the government's motion to dismiss. The court likened the dismissal power to the common law nolle prosequi, and said that judicial supervision of such action is quite limited. *See* United States v. Cowan & Jacobsen, 524 F.2d 504 (5th Cir. 1975).

And it becomes highly relevant, members of the jury, because at the very time, as I will show you as we move along when he was embezzling his client, stealing his client's money in 1971, he was misapplying the funds of this bank in 1971.

In Count Two he is charged with misapplying $825,000 of their funds.

In Count Three it is recited that he and his partner, Mr. Cowan, diverted $115,600 to Mr. Cowan.

Count Four, $93,677 to Mr. Jacobsen.

Count Six, $10,000 to Mr. Jacobsen.

And it is a litany of fraudulent conversion by Mr. Jacobsen during 1971. That's what the government said about him in this indictment,

---

COMMENTARY

Is an indictment an admission by the government that certain conduct happened? If so, this is evidence under FED. R. EVID. 801(d)(2)(D). The cases say that the indictment is usually not evidence in that sense, but that many other statements by government counsel, such as those in jury argument, would be. *See* United States v. GAF Corp., 928 F.2d 1253 (2d Cir. 1991); United States v. Salerno, 937 F.2d 797 (2d Cir. 1991), *rev'd on other grounds,* 505 U.S. 317 (1992). When the government—or any adversary—takes an inconsistent position, even through counsel, this is a powerful subject of comment. We are not contradicting the presumption of innocence here, only raking the adversary for its own inconsistency.

---

that he was betraying his trust to his shareholders and to his depositors, and pilfering their funds.

Now, two weeks later they brought another indictment against him. They brought that indictment right here in the District of Columbia, and what did they say about him then?

They said that he had committed perjury before the grand jury here because he had testified that the money which he received from Mr. Lilly was still in his safe-deposit box in the Citizens National Bank in Austin, Texas, at the time he testified before the grand jury, when in fact it was not.

This was the second time the United States government had indicted Mr. Jacobsen for perjury in two weeks; and that only a year ago.

Now, what is perjury? Perjury is lying under oath.

The words "lie" and "liar" do not flow easily from my lips, and I think they flow very uneasily from the lips of most people. They are words at which most of us recoil. We don't like those ugly words, and, so, we use softer words all the time when we can.

We say falsehood, and untruth and prevaricator, we say perjury, when we mean liar under oath.

I think perjury may be one of the most heinous forms

COMMENTARY

In a re-creation of the Jacobsen cross-examination in 1992, I began with "You are a liar, are you not, Mr. Jacobsen?" It was an approach that seemed to work, given the amount of follow-up material there was. *See generally* James McElhaney, LITIGATION 175 (1995). Williams is right, however. You need to be careful when calling somebody a liar. Maybe the jurors will think the person is merely mistaken, and if you can win on that theory so much the better for your case. Here, however, Jacobsen's falsehood is a centerpiece of the defense. Why, then, is Williams being careful? He is letting the jurors see the evidence and make their own judgment. He is trying not to appear to be dictating what they should think about the evidence. My mock cross was designed to get to the same place by letting the jurors see Jacobsen admit many lies and then wiggle around about the characterization.

---

of crime in the whole United States Criminal Code. We all can understand when someone in a moment of weakness or a transport of anger or passion may break the rules of conduct that are proscribed in our federal criminal code, but for a man to walk up there, put his hand on the Bible, raise his hand, swear to God that he is going to tell the truth and then to spew forth a litany of lies, is conduct so despicable to be beyond description.

COMMENTARY

The characterization of perjury is a rich vein in the history of trial law. The perjurer is, in one view, worse than the assassin, for he commits his crime by sullying his oath to God. Williams evokes the biblical tradition in the next paragraph with "false witness."

Of course, the "informer" in Irish literature is the most despised of creatures. And Irish advocates have given us the richest rhetoric on the subject. In our play, WARRIOR BARDS (1989), Kevin McCarthy and I put these words in the mouth of Daniel O'Connell, the great Irish advocate, though in truth we took them from the actual arguments of both O'Connell and his colleague John Philpott Curran. They are typical of Irish lawyers' attacks on informers:

> If it was not known by unfortunate experience, and particularly in many recent instances, it could scarcely be conceived that such abominable turpitude could find place in any human being. It could scarcely be conceived, that any being, imbued with a rational and immortal soul, would deliberately come forward to forswear himself in the a court of justice when if he is believed the life or liberty of the accused will be forfeited.

> Look at him. He admits to treason and proudly carries the pardon in his pocket. Yes, his pardon in his pocket, so that he will not be executed as a traitor. And more, his bribe—not yet in his pocket. Yes, yielding up the tie of friendship, to watch the steps of his friends for the bribe of government.

> I have heard of assassination by sword, by pistol, and by dagger; but here is a wretch who would dip the Evangelists in blood; if he thinks he has not sworn his victim to death, he is ready to swear, without mercy and without end: but oh! do not, I conjure you, suffer him to take an oath; the hand of the murderer should not pollute the purity of the gospel: if he will swear, let it be on the knife, the proper symbol of his profession!

And another example:

> I speak not now of the public proclamation for informers, with a promise of secrecy, and of extravagant reward.

> I speak of what your own eyes have seen, from the box where you are now sitting; the number of horrid miscreants, who acknowledged, upon their oaths, that they had come from the seat of government—from the very Chambers of Dublin Castle [headquarters of British rule in Ireland]—where they had been worked upon, by the fear of death and the hope of compensation, to give evidence against their fellows. Oh, yes, the mild, the wholesome, the merciful councils of this government are perched over catacombs of living death, where the wretch that is buried a man, entombed till his heart has had time to fester and dissolve, is then dug up a witness!

Especially so when those lies are false witness against another.

Now, the government said he was a liar. What does he say about himself? What does this man say in this very case? Not under hostile cross-examination by me, not under the fire of rapid questioning, but under the friendly interrogation of the prosecution.

COMMENTARY

The power of the symbol. Williams insisted that the transcript as delivered by the court reporter, with a blue ribbon and cover sheets, be left in its pristine condition. You could make a copy, but you had to put it back just the way it was. No pencil marks on it, no highlighting. Thus, when he picked up the transcript, he was handling the official record, imbued by its appearance with authority. The same idea is often used with deposition transcripts or key exhibits.

At page 264 of the record:
"QUESTION: Did you appear before the grand jury that week?
"ANSWER: On November 2nd.
" QUESTION: Did you testify falsely on that occasion?
"ANSWER: Yes, I did."
Page 265:

"QUESTION: The day after your grand jury appearance did you talk to Mr. Weitz?"

That's the lawyer for the Ervin Committee.

"ANSWER: Yes, I did.

"QUESTION: Did Mr. Weitz talk to you about the money?

"ANSWER: Yes.

"QUESTION: Did you lie to him?

"ANSWER: Yes.

"QUESTION: Later on in the next week, I think November 2nd, which was a Friday, the following week, did you testify in depositions in Texas in a lawsuit, *Nader v. Butz?*

"ANSWER: Yes.

"QUESTION: Were you asked about money on that occasion?

"ANSWER: Yes.

"QUESTION: Did you tell the truth about it?

"ANSWER: No, I did not."

At page 280:

"QUESTION: Did there come a time subsequently when you testified before the Senate committee under oath?

"ANSWER: Yes, sir.

"QUESTION: Once again, did you lie?

"ANSWER: Yes.

"QUESTION: Did there come a time when you appeared before the grand jury here in Washington for a second time?

"ANSWER: Yes.

"QUESTION: Do you remember when that was?

"ANSWER: No, sir.

"QUESTION: Was it in January '74?

"ANSWER: I believe so.

"QUESTION: Did you testify falsely on that occasion?

"ANSWER: Yes.

"QUESTION: Were you questioned about the $10,000 which was in your safe-deposit box?

"ANSWER: Yes.

"QUESTION: Did you say that the $10,000 which was in your safe-deposit box was the same $10,000 that you received from Mr. Lilly in May, 1971, and you left it there untouched?

"ANSWER: Yes, sir.

"QUESTION: Was that truthful?

"ANSWER: No, sir."

Now, you will all remember that Jacobsen went into bankruptcy in June of 1972.

COMMENTARY

Williams is turning the corner here. First, we have the government and Jacobsen admitting he is a liar. The specific lie Williams chooses is about whether or not Jacobsen left the AMPI money "untouched." Of course Jacobsen went on to say that in fact he took the money and gave it to Connally. That is the problem with many examples of turncoat testimony—the proponent can claim that there is a simple change of story occasioned by nothing more than a desire to "come clean." Williams is going to argue that Jacobsen lied about touching the money to protect himself from charges of embezzlement, not to protect Connally. Hence, the transition from lying to bankruptcy. He will now show just how desperate were Jacobsen's financial straits.

Now, he had been asked before the grand jury at a time when he now says he was telling the truth about his assets, and of course the purpose of it was to show that Jacobsen was a very wealthy man, and he had no need for funds, and wouldn't have considered embezzling his client's funds.

He was asked what his net worth was, what his assets over his debts were, in January of '71 and he said $3 million.

Then they asked him if it was about the same in January '72 and he said, "Maybe less than $3 million, but around there."

Now, members of the jury, just six months later he filed a petition in bankruptcy in the Western District of Texas, and he said that his debts exceeded his assets by $8 million, and I asked him about that, and he said, oh, well all this had taken place in six months.

He had gone from plus $3 million to minus $8 million.

And then I showed him a letter and I asked him if in fact he hadn't begun his bankruptcy in March, and at page 309, he said: "Yes, that refreshes my recollection."

Now, I'm not surprised that counsel for the government spoke for almost two hours this morning to you reviewing the facts of this case without ever referring to this document which is in evidence for reasons that you will see.

COMMENTARY

These bankruptcy exhibits are "markers." Williams wants the jury to remember them. He is handling, among other exhibits, Jacobsen's bankruptcy petition and its attachments. These show a detailed history of Jacobsen's finances during the months just before his 1972 filing. The jury will remember these papers, and ask to have them identified for them during their deliberations. We were heartened when the jurors focused in a note on the very payments that Williams is now discussing. Note that he repeats the identification of the crucial section. As it happened, the exhibit went to the jury room with the paper clip still attached to the important page.

First of all, in this document he was asked, members of the jury, about his various safe-deposit boxes. What did he say?

"Safe-deposit box Number 865 has been empty for the last two years."

This is the box referred to in Government's 7-B which he went into on October 16, 1970, April '71, May 4, '71, May 13, '71, October 5, 1971, June 12, '72. Empty said he. And you will see, members of the jury, that he had a reason for using those boxes.

Empty all the time he was going in and out, said he, under oath, in his petition for bankruptcy in the Western District of Texas.

Significant. Significant, that on October 5, 1971, right after he came back from Washington, after he says that he gave money to Mr. Connally, he went into that box. And even more significant: four days before he filed the petition for bankruptcy in which he said that box had been empty for two years, he went back in. Why do you think he went in? To clean it out before the trustee in bankruptcy saw what was there.

That's not all in this document which tells a whole tale.

We find, members of the jury, that during 1971 Attachment Ten shows you that almost every week he had a note coming due. It shows, members of the jury, by a wild coincidence, on the very day that he took $10,000 from Mr. Lilly, allegedly for John Connally, he borrowed $100,000. He borrowed $100,000 from the National Bank of Commerce in Dallas, Texas.

It shows, members of the jury, that on the very day that he took the last $5,000 from Mr. Lilly, which he lied about in front of the grand jury and the Ervin Committee, and now says he remembers about which I shall have much to say, on the very day he took that $5,000 from Lilly, what did he do?

He paid $5,000 on an indebtedness to the Security State Bank, 201 West Main Street, Fredericksburg, Texas.

At the very time that he says he was giving John Connally $10,000 in the summer of 1971, he paid off $10,000 on another indebtedness at the Capital National Bank in Austin, Texas.

Members of the jury, Schedule 10 of this petition is ten pages long of notes that were in default, on which he was being forced to pay during all of 1971 to a roster of banks in Texas. There was no chance that this man took $10,000 and didn't apply it to this cascade of debts that he had.

Schedule 11. Schedule 11 is even more interesting, because Schedule 11 shows in this petition in bankruptcy, four pages of forced sales that he was making of stocks in order to meet note payments that were in default.

The house was crumbling. His financial empire was gone. The sheriff was practically at the door during 1971. And he was in constant default on his indebtednesses, all during those very months when he says he was taking money from Mr. Lilly for Mr. Connally.

Small wonder that this document played no part in the government's case, Defendant's Exhibit Number 2, because it tells the story of financial disaster. Because it shows that the man told a falsehood on May 25, 1974, in this courthouse, at a time when he swore in this case he was telling the truth, because he said, during that '71 period he had a net worth of $3 millions of dollars.

Jacobsen was a desperate man. He was embattled and beleaguered.

If you will recall at the very end of my cross-examination of him, I asked him at page 513:

"QUESTION: Now, I asked you yesterday whether or not you were indicted on February 6th in San Angelo. I now want to ask you, Mr. Jacobsen, when you were negotiating with the prosecutor with respect to your testimony and the disposition of the pending criminal cases against you, you asked the prosecutor, did you not, whether they would dispose of the other cases in which you were being investigated in Texas, did you not?

"ANSWER: Yes, sir. I did.

"QUESTION: And you asked them that right at the end, did you not?

"ANSWER: Yes, sir.

"QUESTION: You were talking, were you not, about the Los Lomas case, were you not?

"ANSWER: I don't remember what cases I was talking about. My lawyer in Austin asked me to ask him that.

"QUESTION: Well, did you mean the Robert Taft case, the Harold Hill case, the Patchett Bus and Transportation Company case, the Los Lomas case, and the Sharpstown Loan case?

"ANSWER: I don't remember what I was referring to.

"QUESTION: Is it your testimony, Mr. Jacobsen, that when you asked Mr. Tuerkheimer

---
COMMENTARY

Frank Tuerkheimer was the lead prosecutor on this case and a member of the Watergate Special Prosecutor's office.

---

whether your plea bargain ended the Texas cases on which you were being investigated, you don't know what cases you were talking about?

"ANSWER: No, Mr. Williams. I knew that I was talking about a number of cases, because they had investigated a number of cases. And I knew they had investigated cases other than the ones you mentioned. But I just wanted to know if the plea bargain took care of all the cases they were investigating in Texas.

COMMENTARY

This had been a calculated risk on Williams's part during cross-examination. Jacobsen had been indicted in the case Williams first mentioned, involving Cowan and Herring. He had not been charged in the other cases, but at least his lawyer felt there was some risk there. We did not have really solid information about these other cases, but enough to open the subject on cross and see what Jacobsen would do. The risk was that Jacobsen would deny everything about any investigations except those in which an indictment had been returned. The principal witnesses who could contradict him were part of a discredited Justice Department that had been tainted by the Watergate scandals.

Williams is not deterred by Jacobsen's repeated efforts to end the inquiry by pleading that he doesn't remember. So Williams is willing to accept the risk that Jacobsen will continue in this vein. He decides to list every case that was the subject of investigation, making it less and less credible that Jacobsen would not remember some of them. Finally, Jacobsen sees that he has lost the battle and he caves in. Had Jacobsen persisted, the "is it your testimony" answer could have been used as an example of an incredible answer.

In short, members of the jury, the man who was brought here upon whom the prosecution asks you to predicate a verdict of guilty in this case, beyond all reasonable doubt, it is a man whom they have charged with swindling and fraud, a man whom they have charged with perjury, a self confessed habitual liar and I suggest to you a proven embezzler.

But I will go into that in more detail in a moment.

What does the prosecution do about this man? Well, first they agree to drop all the felony charges pending against him down in Texas. Then they agree to drop the charges here in District of Columbia. And they agree not to prosecute him for that $5,000, about which we will speak in just a moment.

And then what do they do? They put him on the stand. He takes the same oath that he says he has defiled a hundred times.

And they asked of you, the jury, to bring in a verdict of guilty beyond a reasonable doubt on the testimony of Jacobsen.

Inscribed across the portico of the Supreme Court of the United States are the magnificent words, the bedrock of our system of government, "Equal Justice Under Law." Rich or poor, old or young, friend or foe, neighbor or stranger, man or woman, red or yellow, brown or white, black, whatever. "Equal justice under law."

Before the law, we all stand equal in justice. I see no equal justice under law when the government asks the return of a verdict of guilty beyond a reasonable doubt on the testimony of an alleged swindler, an alleged and avowed perjurer, a man who has bargained his way out of the consequences of his misdeeds, and about whom the prosecutors are concerned with respect to his law license.

— COMMENTARY —

Another transition. Williams is moving on to capitalize on the startling—to us, at any rate—revelation that the prosecutors did research to establish that the federal felony to which Jacobsen pleaded guilty deals with conduct that is a misdemeanor in the Texas Penal Code. Thus, Jacobsen had some assurance that he would not be disbarred, and this assurance came in large measure from the prosecutors.

Defendant's 5. Jacobsen wasn't satisfied getting the felony charges dropped, he wanted a disposition of his case that would help him save his license to practice law. And Defendant's 5 shows that the prosecutors said the following to him:

We told Jacobsen we could understand he was concerned about disbarment proceedings in Texas. We told him we were not his attorneys, that he would have to conduct his own research on the consequences of a 201(f) plea, but that our preliminary and scanty research shows that the conduct he was pleading guilty to was not a crime in Texas at the time he committed it and was made a class A misdemeanor by the new Texas Penal Code, which went into effect on January 1, 1974.

COMMENTARY

This letter was producible in discovery because it discussed the terms on which Jacobsen would plead. In it, prosecutors are saying that giving an unlawful gratuity, which was a two-year federal felony under 18 U.S.C. §201(f) as it then stood, was not a crime in Texas. Under the Texas Penal Code, a payment was unlawful only if corruptly made with a quid pro quo. Later, as the letter reflects, gift or receipt of such a gratuity was made a misdemeanor. There probably were election law violations to which Jacobsen would be liable as well. The important thing is that the prosecutors are coming as close as can be to giving Jacobsen an assurance that he can continue to practice law.

I say for shame. I blush in embarrassment at that man practicing law, and I blush in embarrassment that the prosecution would be concerned that a man who was an avowed perjurer, a man who was an alleged defrauder and a swindler, I blush in embarrassment that they would be concerned that he stay in the practice of law.

That's the kind of deal that Mr. Jacobsen made for himself—tried to make for himself—and that's the kind of concern that the prosecution showed for this man. They agreed to drop that piranha back in the tank.

COMMENTARY

At this point, Williams was on the move. He approached the prosecutor's table and brandished the letter. Of necessity, he was standing behind the prosecutors. They could either continue to look straight ahead at the jurors, or they could turn and look at Williams. They chose the former alternative. In either instance, he was in their territory as he leveled the accusation. As he held the letter in his left hand, with his right hand he enacted picking up a fish and dropping it into a tank.

I say, members of the jury, that if that is equal justice under the law, we should strike from the portico of that grand building, that magnificent expression embedded in those words.

I want to talk to you about Mr. Jacobsen, the witness.

COMMENTARY

A transition—the before and after of Jacobsen is a basic contradiction, but the treatment of Jacobsen is a triplet—the man, the witness before, the witness after. Williams has finished one topic and uses a transition to introduce the next one. This is essential to the flow of the argument. Sometimes you will add to the verbal transition by turning a page of notes and sometimes by some other gesture.

You have seen the evidence on Mr. Jacobsen, the man. Let's look quickly at his testimony before he had an interest to falsify, before he was cutting that cynical, sordid deal that he finally made on May 23 of 1974, which is spelled out in Government's Exhibit 12.

COMMENTARY

Now Williams will read from a series of prior statements. He asked Jacobsen about each of them. He did not simply single out a sentence or paragraph of each Jacobsen appearance or interview. He read from them at length and simply asked Jacobsen if had said these things. This was the part of the cross-examination that some found dull. Now, in closing argument, is the time to use them and make the point.

He went before the grand jury. He went there on November 2nd of 1973. What did he say?

"I talked to Secretary Connally about whether or not he wanted to give money to somebody, or what he wanted to do with it, and he said he didn't have anybody he wanted to give any money to, so he didn't use it.

"What did you do with it?

"Well, I kept it."

On that same day:

"Are you saying on the second occasion you asked Secretary Connally if he wanted the money?

"Yes.

"And again he said no?

"That is right.

"QUESTION: Then what did you do?

"ANSWER: I just left it in my safe-deposit box and forgot about it. Frankly, for a little while."

One of the grand jurors suggested a question.

"Without any formal meaning to this word, isn't that a form of stealing Mr. Lilly's money or deceiving him?

"No, I am going to return it to Mr. Lilly."

The very next day, on November 3rd, he went to the Select Committee for an informal interview. He was interviewed by Mr. Weitz, and he was interviewed by Mr. Chinny of the Ervin Committee.

What did he say to them?

"In mid-1971 Jacobsen asked Lilly if he could provide $10,000 in cash which Jacobsen was going to make available for Connally's disposal.

"Shortly thereafter Lilly gave $10,000 in cash to Jacobsen, who put it in one of his two safe-deposit boxes in the Citizens National Bank. Jacobsen told Connally that he had $10,000 in cash from AMPI for his use. He says that Connally told him he didn't want to give any money either to Democrats or to Republicans. As a result Jacobsen said he just kept it in his box. A year later, after Connally left office and headed Democrats for Nixon, Jacobsen says he asked Connally again about the money, and Connally did not use it. Jacobsen said he broke the bills into smaller denominations, and that the money is still in his box."

What did he tell the Ervin Committee under oath? First he went into a deposition, in *Nader v. Butz.* Under oath:

"Do you know of any money being transmitted by Bob Lilly to John Connally?

"ANSWER: No.

"QUESTION: Have you ever heard of any such transaction?

"ANSWER: No.

"QUESTION: Do you know of any AMPI or TAPE money ever being delivered to Connally?

"ANSWER: No.

"QUESTION: In any way?

"ANSWER: No."

Under oath.

Under oath again before the Select Committee on Capitol Hill, December 14, 1973:

"When did you talk to Mr. Connally about this?

"ANSWER: I think it was in June or July.

"QUESTION: What did you tell him?

"ANSWER: I told him I had $10,000 that was available for him to give to any politician he wanted to give it to."

"What was his response?

"His response was that he did not want to make any contributions.

"Was anything said about the transaction or the availability of the money?

"ANSWER: No. Except that he did not want it.

"QUESTION: But he didn't tell you to return it?

"ANSWER: No, he did not tell me to return it.

"QUESTION: Did he give any reasons to explain why he didn't want it?

"ANSWER: He did explain why. Briefly he said, 'I'm a Democrat and in a Republican administration, and I do not want to be giving money to Democrats since I'm in a Republican administration, and I do not want to be giving money to Republicans since I'm a Democrat, so I would just not rather give anything.'

"QUESTION: Did you ever deliver any money to Mr. Connally?

"ANSWER: No, sir. I did not.

"QUESTION: The matter of $10,000, was that ever discussed again by you and Mr. Connally?

"ANSWER: Only during the Democrats for Nixon campaign.

"MR. WEITZ: When was that? Not the campaign, the conversation?

"MR. JACOBSEN: I do not remember.

"QUESTION: Was it in '72?

"ANSWER: Yes, in '72.

"In the second half of '72?

"Yes, sir.

"Sometime between August, for example, and the election?

"Yes.

"What was Mr. Connally's position at that time? Was he still in government?

"No, he was head of Democrats for Nixon.

"And you brought up the subject spontaneously?

"I told him I still had that $10,000 and I would be glad to put it in the Democrats for Nixon campaign.

"Did he ask you about what $10,000 you were talking about?

"I do not remember if he did.

"What was his response?

"He didn't want it.

"Did he say why?

"He didn't want any money from AMPI because I suppose, the publicity they had received as a result of a series of small donations."

Then he came before the grand jury here.

"What do you remember about what you said to Secretary Connally about the money, and what he said to you?

"Well, I remember I said that I had $10,000 available from AMPI, and that he could do with it what he wanted, thinking he might want to make political contributions with it. And he said he did not want to make political contributions, he was a Democrat in a Republican administration, and that as a Democrat he didn't want to make contributions to Republicans, and his being in the Republican administration he didn't want to contribute to Democrats.

"QUESTION: And what did Secretary Connally say and what did you say, on the second occasion?

"ANSWER: Well, I said, after he formed Democrats for Nixon, I asked him if he wanted the $10,000 in that capacity in the Democrats for Nixon, and he said he didn't want it."

That's his testimony before he had any motive to falsify.

One more time he gave evidence, the day after he was indicted in West Texas for conspiracy and fraud. He was interviewed by a lawyer of AMPI, Mr. Edward Wright,

---

COMMENTARY

Note that Williams is not being so fulsome in his description of Mr. Wright as he was in opening, when Chief Judge Hart stopped him.

---

and he was asked about the money that had been given to him by Lilly in 1971, and this is what he said:

"In May or June of 1971 I received $10,000 in cash from Bob Lilly. This was delivered to me personally. I still have this money in my safe-deposit box. I will return the money to AMPI when I get clearance from my attorney, Arthur Mitchell of Austin. The safe-deposit box is in the Citizens National Bank of Austin. This money was made available to John Connally for political purposes. Connally never wanted the money. I set it up with Connally. I got the money on the theory that Connally could use it for political purposes. When I told Connally I had it, he said he didn't want to make any political contributions.

"Later I offered the money to Connally again. This was for a contribution to the Democrats for Nixon campaign. Connally again refused.

"I was never a party to giving any money whatever to John Connally, and I have no knowledge of milk money going to him."

That's what he said before he had a motive to falsify. Now, members of the jury, let's look at his switch.

Let's look at this case and see how it came into existence, its origin, its beginning and its development.

COMMENTARY

Another transition, coupled with an invitation to the jury: "let's look."

I think it was the beginning of the last century when the poet, Sir Walter Scott, wrote the often-quoted lines, "Oh, what a tangled web we weave, when first we practice to deceive!" Oh, how many problems we build for ourselves when we tell the first significant lie.

COMMENTARY

Not every juror knows of Sir Walter Scott, but on average a few will. Williams's theory is that Jacobsen got himself so ensnared in his own lies that he had to keep inventing. He wants to use the complexity and detail of Jacobsen's story against him. For these purposes, the imagery is perfect.

That's how this case came into being, members of the jury.

Jacobsen told two lies in November of 1973, and they have spawned thousands more, and he can't extricate himself.

I want to show you how it came about, and how he now finds himself in the horrible, horrible, despicable state of bearing false witness against another man under oath in a court of justice.

On November 2nd he was called to the grand jury, and he told his first lie. They asked him about the $10,000 that he got from Lilly.

"And then what did you do with it, after Secretary Connally turned it down?

"Well, I kept it.

"Where is it now?

"It's in my safe-deposit box.

"Still in the same bank?

"Yes, sir."

Then, members of the jury he told the second lie. The second lie was this:

"Is that the only payment made by Mr. Lilly to you which was ostensibly for Mr. Connally?

"Yes, that's the only one.

"Was there not a later $5,000 payment also made for the same purpose?

"Not that I recall, sir. All I got was $10,000."

In that same appearance before the grand jury they asked him again:

"What did you do with the money?

"ANSWER: I just left it"—meaning the $10,000—"in my safe-deposit box and forgot about it.

"Did it ever occur to you that Mr. Lilly's intention was that the money got to Secretary Connally, not to your safe-deposit box?

"Certainly, that was Mr. Lilly's intention.

"Without any formal meaning to this word, isn't that a form of stealing Mr. Lilly's money?

"Oh, no, I'm going to return it to Mr. Lilly.

"Before we excuse you"—they asked him—"before we excuse you, does anything refresh your recollection as to whether or not the following October or November of 1971, Mr. Lilly gave you another $5,000?

"No, sir, he didn't give me $5,000."

He told two lies. He said he still had the $10,000, when indeed he didn't because he used it, and he said he never got what has now been called the third $5,000.

He feared, members of the jury, the charge of embezzling his client's funds. He feared that with a passion. And, so, a case that was conceived in greed, was born in lies.

COMMENTARY

This is a truly masterful gloss on those grand jury appearances. To be sure, Jacobsen's denial about the $5,000, which he never claimed he gave to Connally, is significant. But look how Williams has reinterpreted the matter. The government admits that Jacobsen lied, but its version is that he lied about giving money to Connally and that his difficulties began with that falsehood. Williams must convince the jury that Jacobsen's lies had a different purpose—to shield him from prosecution for embezzling AMPI funds. He is thus able to concede that the money Jacobsen had in his safe-deposit box at the time of his grand jury appearance was not the original AMPI money received from Mr. Lilly. This, too, meshes with the government's theory. But Williams suggests that the money came into the box not because Connally gave it to Jacobsen to put there as a cover-up of the illegal gratuity, but rather that Jacobsen put it there to cover his misappropriation. This is the theory of minimal contradiction at work: Williams has accounted for all the conceded facts and needs only a relatively slight perceptual shift to put the entire matter in a different light.

Now, he was trapped, trapped by his own mendacity before the grand jury on November 2nd. Two lies, his troubles began to pyramid. Soon he was indicted. He was indicted for his swindle down in West Texas.

MR. TUERKHEIMER: Objection, Your Honor. That assumes facts, and that's an allegation, only.

MR. WILLIAMS: He was indicted for swindling.

THE COURT: Wait a minute. I expected you to bring this up some time ago, but you didn't. As I told you, ladies and gentlemen of the jury, Mr. Jacobsen was indicted in Texas. The matter is still pending. He is still presumed to be innocent until proved guilty beyond a reasonable doubt, as any defendant in any case.

However, with regard to his credibility you can consider the facts that he did have an agreement that that case would be dropped if he pled to the charges here.

Now, go ahead, Mr. Williams.

COMMENTARY

The net effect of this judicial interjection is not hurtful to the defense. One can avoid the entire issue by telling the jury just what the judge tells them here. Of course, the indictment is just a charge, but it is a charge brought by the same government that is charging Mr. Connally, and it was worrisome enough to Mr. Jacobsen that he wanted it settled. And therefore, as the judge will instruct the jury, it gives him a motive to lie and may, nay must, be considered for that purpose.

MR. WILLIAMS: Your Honor, I said he was indicted for fraud. He was indicted in West Texas on February 6, 1974, and he was indicted here in the District of Columbia on February 21, 1974.

He was indicted for the falsehood of saying that the money that he got from Lilly was still in his box. And he saw the walls coming in on him. And one week from that day, one week from that day, he was in the prosecutor's office negotiating a deal.

What was the deal? Get the Texas case dropped. Get the District of Columbia case terminated. Get the $5,000 transaction eliminated. Try to save his license. And lo and behold what else? He came in and he told the story about John Connally, but he told the story with these conditions.

Defendant's Exhibit Number 34, a memorandum from Mr. Tuerkheimer, to the files.

"Initially I told Morgan and McNellis, Mr. Jacobsen's lawyers, that the only restrictions, as a result of this meeting, would be that none of us would testify in any proceeding against Jacobsen about what was said during the meeting, and that we would not subpoena Morgan and McNellis to testify either."

COMMENTARY

I still wonder at times how we ever got this document. A prosecutor's notes about a tentative proffer like the one Jacobsen and his lawyers, Morgan and McNellis, were making may be off limits as attorney work product. The Supreme Court's decision in *Goldberg v. United States,* 425 U.S. 94 (1976), holds that work product claims do not shield material from production under the Jencks Act, 18 U.S.C. §3500, but Jencks material includes only "statements" of the witness. 18 U.S.C. §3500(e). We argued that the entire record of the plea bargain, including the sessions where potential testimony was proffered, were producible as potentially exculpatory. When such material is produced, it can be very helpful, because most plea bargains for testimony in complex cases take place in stages as the prosecutors and the turncoat's lawyer explore what each side will gain from the bargain.

In the *Nichols* case, we did not have the prosecutors' notes of the bargaining sessions, but we did have a number of FBI reports of interviews that tracked the changes in Michael Fortier's story. Fortier was the witness who said that Timothy McVeigh had told him that our client Terry Nichols was in on the bombing plot. However, Fortier brought Nichols into his rendition only belatedly. In summation, I summarized this progression: "The Marine Corps builds men. The FBI builds witnesses."

What does that tell you? He was tentative, he was trying it out. But if it didn't work, he didn't ever want to hear about it again. He didn't ever want anyone coming forth and saying he told this story about John Connally if he didn't wash himself out of all his troubles.

Here was an embattled, beleaguered man, bankrupt and indicted, driven by his initial lies, even bearing false witness against his friend, but only if it worked.

Nobody must say a word unless the deal is cut. And how did it go thereafter?

Well, the evidence shows that they had him there day after day for hours. This is long prior to preparing him for this trial. Government's Exhibit 13 shows all his visits over there. He was there for ten solid days before they put him in front of the grand jury.

COMMENTARY

Williams is handling an exhibit as he says this—the record of Jacobsen's visits with the prosecutors. These days all sorts of records are kept of comings and goings, especially in public offices. This sort of material can be very important in recounting the construction of the witness's tale.

Finally, on the 21st of March the deal was made.

Government's Exhibit 12. They dropped the Texas case. They dropped the District of Columbia matter. The $5,000 will not be a subject of any indictment. And Jacobsen now has gotten himself freed from the prospect of an aggregate possible 40 years in the penitentiary, on a plea to an offense, the maximum punishment for which is two years, and which gives him encouragement that he may hopefully keep his law license.

He came to the stand, he testified. He testified, I say, like a programmed robot. It took him one hour and 20 minutes on that clock to tell you in staccato fashion, things that happened over a three-year period.

COMMENTARY

This is accurate. It is important not to overtry one's case, and the prosecutors were trying to make Jacobsen a small target. But he made a terrible appearance on the stand—reluctant, withdrawn, quiet. The prosecutors had clearly failed to work with him to make his demeanor confident, his expression clear, his voice natural. Jacobsen was, after all, an experienced lawyer and lobbyist. He knew how to persuade. The cross-examination took five times as long as the direct.

Thank goodness there is the instrument of cross examination, the oldest instrument in the world for getting at the truth.

The first cross-examination in the history of the world is recorded in that book on which you took your oaths in the Old Testament, the book of Daniel, when he cross examined the accuser of Susannah, the famous episode of Susannah and the Elders. He showed by the fact that her accusers couldn't tell a straight story when pressed for details, that they were bearing false witness against a beautiful and virtuous women who was about to be condemned under the law of Moses. The first recorded cross-examination in the history of the world.

COMMENTARY

The story of Susannah and the Elders, not a part of King James but in other editions of the Bible, was Williams's favorite story about cross-examination. *See* Daniel 13:51–62 (Oxford Annotated Bible, 1962). This is an abbreviated version. Daniel separates the two witnesses and asks one where the act took place. He says under one tree, while the other says under a different tree. The contradiction dooms the accusation. The story is not in the King James version.

I say to you, members of the jury, in every single detail of Jake Jacobsen's story, he collapsed under cross-examination. And I want to show it to you because it may have been so subtle as not to be apparent immediately as it was happening.

COMMENTARY

I have stressed that cross-examination cannot do the work of closing argument. Now we are learning the same lesson from a different perspective. Do not assume that the jurors got every point you were making in cross-examination. Use final argument to put it together.

Let's look at every significant date in this case. He said, members of the jury to you that on April 28th of 1971,

John Connally asked for money, sitting in the Treasury office of the Secretary of the Treasury.

```
——————————— COMMENTARY ———————————

We are well into this summation, and this is the first nod given
to the details of these accusations. All that precedes has been to
prepare you to disbelieve the government's version, which
Williams is now beginning to recount.
```

And he said:

"I fixed the amount in my mind of $10,000."

It doesn't say that John Connally said any amount. He says:

"He asked me for some money for the help he gave on the price support question."

He doesn't explain to you why this conversation was put on April 28th, a month and three days after price supports were raised, when he had seen John Connally on March 30th for an hour, on April 16th and talked to him on April 19th.

Now, explain that. He has to put it on April 28th because he has to tailor his story to fit as closely as possible to the time he took the $10,000 from Lilly which was May 4th. The same day he made a $100,000 loan from the bank in Dallas about which the bankruptcy shows you.

He says he fixed $10,000. Then why in the name of reason did he take $15,000 from Lilly if he fixed $10,000? And if he fixed $10,000, why in the name of reason did he carry $5,000 to Connally? Oh, well, he came up with two envelopes and one was empty and one was full, and we heard the greatest mumbo-jumbo on that to which you were exposed during the trial.

And what does he say $10,000 for? Because at that time when he first told the story, he didn't know that they knew that Lilly was talking about the third five. That's why he said ten. He was trying to explain that ten that he got, and that he said he kept.

Now, the other five popped out, and he explodes his whole story of April 28th, 1971. He tailored his story to fit the records. And you will see as we go through this date by date, that he architected a story every foot of the way to dovetail as closely as possible to records that would corroborate some facet of the falsehood.

Let's look at the next one. He says he went on May 14, 1971, to the Secretary's office, he took $5,000 out and handed it to him. Mr. Connally went into the lavatory and came out with no money. That's the story that he told.

COMMENTARY

This is, of course, a dramatic story. The media had been full of Jacobsen's version, including money changing hands in the secretary's office, and Connally going into his private bathroom, presumably to flush the wrappers down the toilet. In preparing for the case, Williams and I went to the Treasury Department (when the incumbent was absent), and reenacted Jacobsen's alleged version, even to finding out whether one could hear the toilet flush while sitting in the guest chair at the secretary's desk. This is one instance of Williams's devotion to detail. You read later that Jacobsen disavowed the toilet flush on cross-examination.

He didn't quite explain satisfactorily, I should think, why he held back the other five.

He said after he gave him five, he went to the American Security and Trust Company and opened a safe-deposit box and put the other five in.

What did he say when he was telling his story to Mr. Sale? He told Mr. Sale because he couldn't keep the facts straight, "I purchased a box, put five in, took five with me."

Now, he found out that the box entry didn't quite jibe with that so his story was changed, and he tailored it.

COMMENTARY

The government claimed that Jacobsen's story was corroborated by such things as his safe-deposit records and his opening a safe-deposit box the same day as the first alleged turnover to

---

Connally. This evidence was difficult, for Jacobsen had no
apparent need for a safe-deposit box in Washington except as a
home for the Connally money. Yet even this piece of favorable
news for the prosecution is blighted by Jacobsen's unaccount-
able statement that he decided for an unexpressed reason to give
the money in two payments and by his having changed his story
as to the order of things when it turned out that the bank's
record of his gaining access to the box was at a later time of day
than the Treasury log of his visit to Connally.

Now, what about the rest of that? At page 434 of the
record

COMMENTARY

Whenever speaking of the record, Williams is handling the actual transcript.

I asked him the following:

"QUESTION: When Mr. McNellis submitted a proffer of
what you would say on March 4, 1974, you said you
would say that when you gave Secretary Connally the
$5,000 it was in wrappers, and that he went into the lava-
tory in his office and he flushed the wrappers down the
toilet bowl. Isn't that what Mr. McNellis said?

"ANSWER: Yes, sir.

"QUESTION: But your testimony here in Court is that
you never told Mr. McNellis, your lawyer, that.

"ANSWER: No, sir.

"QUESTION: You never mentioned that to him?

"ANSWER: No, sir."

And then I said, and His Honor rebuked me for saying
it to him in cross-examination, but I may say it to you in
argument, I said that had to be a figment of his imagination. He disclaimed his lawyer.

Now, why the [safe-deposit] box? Why the box? We
have heard so much about the box. Because the box is the
thing upon which the prosecutors lean so heavily as such

vital corroborative evidence. They say, well, he wouldn't be going in and out of that box. That's what they said this morning, if it were empty.

Well, I say he would. I say he would have had a very, very good reason. I say he kept this box after he said it was empty and that's proven from government's Exhibit 6-A.

If it be true, that he went in there in May and put $5,000 in after seeing John Connally, and that he went back there in September and took $5,000 out before seeing John Connally, and if it was empty why in the name of reason did he pay rent on it for the following year in May of 1972?

Why? Because he was worried then.

He wasn't plotting against John Connally in 1971. He was worried about explaining to Mr. Lilly what he had done with the money that he kept, and he was building a trail. He was building and architecting a defense.

I say to you members of the jury, as I said to you on the opening day, he knew perfectly well John Connally wouldn't take $10,000 or $10, from him. And, so, when he got $10,000 from Mr. Lilly it was a bonanza at a time when he desperately needed it, as you will see from the Defendant's Exhibit the petition in bankruptcy.

He was still worried about it. So, just in case, down range he always wanted to have some record tying it in as proof that he hadn't taken it. And if you will look with me at September 24th, you will see that his whole story of September 24 is tailored around an entry into this box.

If it was empty after September 24, 1971, why did he keep paying rent on it until it was blown open two years later?

And look, members of the jury, at the other box, 865, which he says in his petition for bankruptcy had been empty for two years. Six entries into that box during the two-year period.

The most significant one, however, being after he comes back from Washington to Austin, when he enters in October '71, at a time when he swore it was empty, and back he goes in there four days before he files his petition for bankruptcy in the Texas Court.

What does he say about September 24, 1971? He told Mr. Sale, "I called him." Meaning John Connally.

"I asked him, are you ready for the rest of what I had for you?"

Members of the jury, you know that's false. All you have to do is look at John Connally's logs for September 24, 1971. He was at a cabinet meeting at 9:00 o'clock to 9:30, from 9:30 to 10:30 with the President and Dr. Burns in the White House, and at 11:00 o'clock he was on Capitol Hill in the Senate Foreign Relations Committee.

When in the name of reason could Jake Jacobsen have called him? But he didn't hesitate to spill that out until the records exploded that story, as he architected his tale.

Now, let's talk about the third $5,000. Counsel said he wasn't going to say much about that until he heard what I had to say about it.

COMMENTARY

The prosecutor declined to give a version of the third $5,000 in his closing, preferring to save it for rebuttal. If you have the right to open and close the argument, rebuttal is a useful place for some arguments. It is never a place to introduce difficult subjects that the other side is sure to bring up. This third $5,000 was an issue in the case, and the prosecutor knew it. It was a problem for their side. The jury expects the lawyers to tell them problems with their case and then to talk about why those problems do not prevent the verdict the lawyers want. It is almost never a good idea to hide from one's difficulties, and never wise to tell the jury you intend to wait and see what the other side says before committing to a theory of the facts. If you are not going to argue the point, don't. Then you can use rebuttal to speak of it as a red herring, a desperate argument by the opponent to avoid the main issue.

So I'll say what I have to say about it right now.

On November 2nd he went before the grand jury, and he said to the grand jury three times that he never got a third $5,000 from Mr. Lilly, and at the very end, as a last question, he's asked by Mr. McBride:

"Does anything refresh your recollection? Does anything refresh your recollection that you asked and got $5,000 from Mr. Lilly in 1971, in November?

"ANSWER: No, sir. Absolutely not."

Then he goes up to the Ervin Committee and they ask him two times:

"Did you get another $5,000 from Mr. Lilly?"

He denied it. He denied it. Then he went before the grand jury on May 23rd of 1974, and after a process which I am going to show you, that is what he said:

"The records reflect I did get $5,000."

Now, he has been confronted with the records.

"I don't remember giving it to Secretary Connally, but I must have given it to him, because I brought it to Washington for that purpose."

Now, let's look at this memorandum, members of the jury, because here is proof positive of the way this man architected his story over a period of months in meetings with the prosecutors.

This is Defendant's Exhibit 15.

"John

COMMENTARY

Speaking of John Sale, a prosecutor. Note again that these notes are an invaluable guide. If one cannot have them produced initially, one might take the witness through the developing version of the story as reflected in the material at hand and then call repeatedly on the other side to produce any evidence that the witness's version of his changing story differs from what was told the proponent's lawyers. They have an ethical obligation to acknowledge such contradictions. The passages on which Williams is now relying identify what is said as coming from Jacobsen, so there is a strong Jencks Act argument for their production.

---

asked Jacobsen if Lilly's version of the facts refreshed his recollection of the receipt of the money. Jacobsen said he still had no recollection of getting the $5,000.

"Jacobsen stated at this time, however, he had an inkling regarding the third payment. He had a gnawing inkling concerning the third $5,000. He had a feeling that on an occasion other than May of '71 he brought cash to Washington and kept it in the briefcase overnight at the Madison Hotel.

"From this inkling Jacobsen felt he could now state that a third $5,000 payment must have been made to John Connally. When pressed by John to account for his seemingly newfound recollection, Jacobsen stated that his mental processes had operated in the following manner.

"First, Jacobsen started with the premise that if he asked for and received money on the premise that it would be paid to somebody, that somebody received it.

"Second, although he had no recollection whatsoever of receiving the money from Lilly, he accepted the fact that he must have received the money from Lilly in the manner in which Lilly stated.

"He concluded that his recollection of coming to Washington with cash in his briefcase and keeping the cash in the briefcase overnight must have related to a third $5,000 payment to John Connally.

"However, Jacobsen stated he was unable to reconstruct any of the events surrounding the actual transfer of the $5,000 in his office.

And Mr. Quarles,

COMMENTARY

James Quarles, the junior prosecutor and scrivener for these meetings.

who wrote that memorandum, said:

"I understood Jacobsen to be saying that the only aspect of the transaction which he had any recollection of, and spoke not of a recollection but of an inkling, was the fact of having cash in his briefcase on a trip to Washington. From that inkling Jacobsen was able to infer he made the third $5,000 payment to John Connally."

We saw this afternoon in his petition for bankruptcy, that on the day he got that $5,000 he paid off a $5,000 note to one of the many banks to whom he owed money in Austin, Texas.

What I have to say about that third $5,000, members of the jury, in response to what the prosecution asked, that third $5,000 is like the 13th stroke of a grandfather's clock in the night. It casts doubt on everything that went before it.

―――――――――― COMMENTARY ――――――――――

This is from A. P. HERBERT, UNCOMMON LAW 28 (3d ed. 1937). One might also say that the third $5,000 casts doubt not only on itself but also on everything that has gone before.

Would Your Honor take a short recess?

―――――――――― COMMENTARY ――――――――――

A good place to take a break. The argument has begun softly and treaded through some emotional territory and now into and out of perceived difficulties in the defense case. The jurors need some time to stretch, to absorb the complex series of facts, if the rest of the argument is to have maximum impact.

THE COURT: All right.

We will take a ten-minute recess at this time.

MR. WILLIAMS: May I proceed, if the Court please?

THE COURT: Yes.

MR. WILLIAMS: Now, we come to the next episode in Jacobsen's story.

He told you about a phone call that he had on September 24 of 1973 with Mr. Connally.

―――――――――― COMMENTARY ――――――――――

Williams is starting a new theme. Jacobsen says that when the investigation began, he called Connally and the latter agreed to give him $10,000 to put in Jacobsen's safe-deposit box so he could say he never gave the money.

They put in a telephone bill that showed a call to 713-236-2222, and from that telephone bill he spun out a conversation, he spun out a long conversation with John Connally, just the way he spun his story from everything to which he could find a point of departure.

What do the facts show? When finally Jacobsen comes up with the only record that he has been able to produce of his activities for the relevant years, a scratch sheet of phone calls for October 1973, it shows that on that day he talked to Beverie Ware, Beverie Ware, but maybe that's not persuasive enough.

Maybe he writes down names of the secretaries of the persons he calls, maybe that's the way he keeps his records.

COMMENTARY

This may be difficult to follow. The phone company records show a call from Jacobsen's number in Austin to this Houston number. Jacobsen says it is a call to Connally. But his own notes reflect that he spoke with Beverie Ware, Connally's secretary, and the phone itself would have rung at her desk or that of the other secretary Cynthia McMahon. And the records show that Connally was not in Houston at that time but in his hometown of Floresville, Texas, south of San Antonio, attending a bank board meeting.

But then we get to the bill which we offered yesterday from Southwestern Bell Telephone Company.

Who is the call to? Beverie Ware or Cynthia McMahon? And what are the facts? The facts are as they have developed here, that Mr. Connally had left Houston to go to Floresville, and he was at a board meeting in Floresville that afternoon and had lunch in Floresville.

He spun a story out of the telephone bill that is belied by his own records, belied by the only record that he has produced throughout this whole period of investigation.

Now, I ask you, members of the jury, you have heard about what has been produced by John Connally, logs, appointment books, telephone records, itineraries of his every movement during the relevant period, and what do we get from this man? We get one scrap of paper that he found in January of 1975, he says, and flew up in an air express to the prosecutors.

The only piece of paper, the only piece of paper that we got from him.

No wonder that he has produced no records after the experience that he had with this one, when this one came forth and gave the lie to his whole story about his telephone conversation on the 24th of September 1973.

COMMENTARY

Williams is on the move again. There is a stack of exhibits on the counsel table, which he has placed so that he must stand behind the prosecutors when he goes to get them. The stack includes every daily log kept by Connally's office for the relevant period, every telephone record, every diary calendar. Williams hefts this pile of documents and lets it back down on the table. Then he takes the single piece of Jacobsen's records, which has Beverie Ware's name on it, and holds it between his thumb and first finger and waves it.

Now we come to the meeting on the 29th, October 29th, 1973. He met with John Connally at John Connally's office in Houston, and that is the meeting at which he says Mr. Connally left and he came back with this money in a cigar box, piled up on top of each other, and with rubber gloves on top of the money, and he handed him the cigar box, and threw away the rubber gloves, he, Jacobsen, says, and Jacobsen took the money in the cigar box back to Austin.

On the witness stand in this trial he told the story for the first time that there were gloves, rubber gloves.

Always before it had been a glove. He began to think about it, and he realized how absurd it was to suggest that someone had counted money with a rubber glove on one hand up to $10,000.

When he thought about that one he changed it. He colored his story, he architectured a new story so by the time he came to trial it was two gloves.

───────── COMMENTARY ─────────

See the Preface for a discussion of this episode.

Now, what did he say to Mr. Tuerkheimer when he was first telling the story?

Defendant's Exhibit 13-B, talking about this very meeting in Houston:

"Cigar box and glove in it, left it in JC office."

Now, I suggest to you that that means he left the cigar box in JC's office, although he testified on the stand he took the cigar box with him in the airplane in his briefcase, and I ask you reasonably could any man forget if that story were true whether he carried $10,000 to Austin, Texas, in a cigar box or left the cigar box in John Connally's office?

He doesn't say anything about the rubber gloves.

Now, what else does he say?

Two times he said in this courtroom that when John Connally gave him this money he said it's all old enough.

And I asked him on cross-examination what did he say to you when he gave you the money? He said, it's old, older money.

That's what he said on cross.

This morning Mr. Tuerkheimer called John Connally a very smart man. They have said a lot of things about him in the pleadings that have been filed here.

They have charged him with felonious conduct and a breach of trust. They have charged him with some pretty heinous conduct, but no one has suggested that he is stupid.

I ask you if John Connally would hand $10,000 to Jacobsen in Houston and tell him it's old enough to be money that was passed from Lilly in 1971, and have in that pile of money 49 bills signed by his successor in office, George Schultz, who didn't take office until June 12, 1972?

I ask you.

Now, it might be that if he were of such a mind to do that that he wouldn't have thought about whether the money was old enough. That might have gone by his mind.

But to say it's all old enough, and Mr. Tuerkheimer stood here this morning and he caressed these bills and kept telling you how crisp they were, how new they were, they are all new and crisp.

And he tells you, Mr. Jacobsen tells you, that John Connally gave him $10,000 with all new, crisp bills saying they are all old enough and 49 of them are signed by a man who didn't take office until Connally was back in Houston practicing law.

I say that beggars intelligence, but that is the story he told on the witness stand.

It's all old enough. And then he says something else.

He tells you that while he had that money in his [safe-deposit] box in Austin, Texas, that John Connally says, Oh, oh, there are some Schultz bills in there.

COMMENTARY

In an effort to explain the presence of bills too new to have been in circulation when Jacobsen said he gave Connally the money, Jacobsen said Connally had called him to tell him that there were Schultz bills in the box.

How in the name of reason would John Connally know if they were in his box in Austin, Texas, that there were some Schultz bills in there? Who had access to that box?

I will tell you who had access to that box: Mr. Jake Jacobsen, and Mr. Jake Jacobsen told you and he told the grand jury that he went into that box frequently, frequently without ever putting his name on the card.

He didn't have to put his name down to go in there.

That is the kind of story that Jacobsen architectured, it's all old enough.

And he says that John Connally went out of his office and he came back with a cigar box, came back into his office after being gone ten minutes, and gave it to him.

Beverie Ware took the stand and Cynthia McMahon took the stand and they both testified that he never left his office.

Are they going to ask you to take the word of a self-styled perjurer, of an alleged swindler, of a man who has testified perjuriously by his own affirmation, scores of times over two secretaries who came in here and testified under an oath which they respect?

Every time that there was an opportunity for someone to see Mr. Jacobsen do what he said he did, it was false.

Corroboration? There is no corroboration for Jake Jacobsen except what he architectured to cover up his embezzlements.

That is what they ask you to do, make no doubt about it.

They say to you, ladies and gentlemen of the jury, reject those girls taries on the other must mean that the secretaries are lying. Juries understand that employees may lie for their employers and that secretaries may routinely do so when the employer wants to duck a telephone call or an appointment. But in this case the two secretaries made an excellent appearance, and pinning the liar label on them is more than the prosecutor needed to do. They might have stepped out for a bit. They might have had an errand to run. It was a long time ago. They had no reason to remember at the time.

as giving false evidence and take this alleged self-styled perjurer, take this alleged swindler at his word, and our burden is to prove beyond a reasonable doubt the essential elements of this offense, that is what they say.

Now, you heard the first day that the money will leave a trail. In the opening statement by the prosecution they said the money will leave a trail.

The money left a trail all right, but let us see the trail that it left.

For one and a half days, members of the jury, they put on, I think, 19 witnesses. I thought they were trying to bore us to death for a while, but they put 19 witnesses on to prove what?

They now tell us they put those witnesses on to show that it was possible for this money to have been in circulation at the time that Jacobsen says that John Connally gave it to him.

COMMENTARY

This was the evidence discussed earlier. Williams is now going to make good on the cross-examination of the 19 banking witnesses, with their charts and summaries. Basically, these witnesses described the road that money travels from being printed to its distribution to commercial banks. For $100 bills, the track is easy because at that time every such bill was traceable. For smaller denominations, one had to trace the money by batches and based on sampling techniques. But six weeks of work—trying to track every bill—paid off, as this part of the summation shows. Jacobsen cannot have got that money from Connally on the day he said he did.

They are so unconfident about this man's word and his oath that they brought 19 witnesses to say, well, it was possible, and he said if there is one bill—this morning— one bill that wasn't in circulation in October 29, 1973, then Jacobsen is a liar. That is what he said. That is what he said this morning to you.

Well, look at Government's Exhibit 43. There are two of these bills, two of these bills, $20 bills, where are they? They hadn't even been put into circulation for the public on October 9 of 1973, 20 days before they weren't even in circulation for the public.

Where were they? They were in the case vault of the Oklahoma City Federal Reserve Bank.

Oh, says the prosecutor, be of good cheer, the money runs through that Oklahoma City cash vault very fast, and he stands up and he says most bills come in one day and out the other.

Well, let us look at the record.

Here is the record of how long those bills stayed in the Oklahoma cash vault before they go out into circulation to a bank, a commercial bank. You will see this exhibit. I am going to pick them off here.

The second bill 30 days. The fourth bill 22 days. The fifth bill 22 days, 24 days, 28 days, 30 days and 25 days.

There are some on here that go in and out on one day, but I say to you if you strike an average, and these bills went out on the average, they would only be hitting an Oklahoma City commercial bank on the day that Jake Jacobsen has them being handed to him in a cigar box in Houston, Texas, in John Connally's office.

Now, he set that test. I didn't set it. Is there a reasonable doubt in your minds that the bills that went out on

October 9 to the vault in Oklahoma City could have been in circulation in a commercial bank in Houston, Texas [on October 29]?

COMMENTARY

"Is there a reasonable doubt?" We are getting to the end now, and Williams is emphasizing the burden of proof. Reports show that the foreman of the jury began the deliberations by stressing "beyond a reasonable doubt."

They want it both ways.

For one purpose they are hot off the press. They are crisp and brand new.

But for another purpose, they are all older bills.

I say that that story was exploded, the story of November 25, 1973, when [Jacobsen] said he went to George Christian's home, and he says he walked out with John Connally and he got into John Connally's car and John Connally took $10,000 more out and he wrapped it in newspapers, and Jake Jacobsen carried that newspaper-wrapped $10,000 in his short-sleeved sport shirt and slacks so that nobody could see it.

Now, are they going to ask you ladies and gentlemen of this jury to believe a self-styled perjurer and an alleged swindler, a man twice indicted by the government for perjury, over George Christian?

COMMENTARY

George Christian testified that no money changed hands and that Jacobsen was dressed so that if he had been carrying money it would have been visible.

Is that the kind of evidence that they have brought into this courtroom and on which they ask you to convict a man who has been impeccable for three-score years of his life?

His Honor will tell you when he instructs you all the cautions about taking the testimony of a perjurer, all the cautions of taking the testimony about a man who says he was an accomplice, all the cautions about taking the testimony of a man who has made a deal.

COMMENTARY

When an admitted or convicted perjurer testifies against your client, you are usually entitled to a cautionary jury instruction that such testimony must be received with caution and weighed with care. When a plea-bargainer testifies, the standard instruction speaks of such a witness having a motive to falsify. A similar instruction is given when an alleged accomplice testifies. In this case, we tendered and were granted all three instructions. Under FED. R. CRIM. P. 30, the trial judge had made those rulings before final argument. Now Williams is weaving them into the fabric of his presentation.

And I say when those cautions are considered their case is in shambles on the courthouse floor.

I want to speak to you about the defendant. This is the kind of case that they have brought against him.

Is he some captain of crime so that they had to make a deal with a scoundrel because it was so important to get him?

COMMENTARY

Some jurors may and probably do think that using turncoats is a good idea in at least some kinds of cases. The prosecutor would argue that their use is vital in this very kind of case, for there is no victim to complain. From there, we get the argument that "sting" operations are also appropriate in political corruption cases.

Is he some captain of crime that would induce them to apply the philosophy of the end justifies the means?

Is it? No, it isn't.

I want you ladies and gentlemen of the jury to give John Connally only one thing. I want you to give him equal justice under the law. I want you to give him the same treatment that any man in America would get.

He isn't entitled to any consideration whatever, none at all, because of his public service or his service as Secretary of the Navy or Secretary of the Treasury or Governor of Texas or his military service, it doesn't mean a hoot, and I don't want anything in the way of consideration for that.

COMMENTARY

This is hyperbole. It works here, but must be used sparingly and with caution.

I say to you he is entitled to special consideration for only one thing which every other man and woman who came into this courthouse would be entitled to, and that is this:

I suppose that some of you wondered when I called a number of witnesses to the stand the other day to attest to his honor and his integrity it may have gone through your minds, oh, well, anybody can get five or six people to come in and say that he is an honorable man.

Six people came in here, Congresswoman Jordan; Mrs. Lyndon Johnson; Secretary Rusk; Secretary McNamara; Dr. Graham; Mr. Rose, chairman of the opposite political party from him.

COMMENTARY

The character witnesses were a tour de force. One may, of course, in any case, put on character witnesses to testify to veracity—from opinion or reputation. FED. R. EVID. 404(a), 608. In a criminal case, character evidence is risky, for it opens the door to a "have you heard" cross-examination that can reveal uncharged and even lawful misconduct. Justice Jackson's *Michelson v. United States,* 335 U.S. 469 (1948), remains the leading case. But as Williams points out, most judges will give you the instruction that character evidence alone raises a reasonable doubt. Prosecutors will argue in rebuttal that we all know people of the most sterling character who turn out to have done terrible things, against all expectation.

In the *Connally* case, the selection of character witnesses was difficult, but our search focused on those who had known

Connally in different capacities and who disagreed with him in important ways. Barbara Jordan, an African-American member of Congress, had been a state senator when Connally was governor of Texas. They had political disagreements, but Connally seemed to her a person of honor in all their dealings. Her appearance in the courtroom was a dramatic moment, and a District of Columbia jury knew her from her bravura performance on the House Judiciary Committee during the Nixon impeachment inquiry.

Lady Bird Johnson was another star witness. She enjoyed great popularity in Washington, D.C., independent of her husband. On the stand, she answered the questions about Connally's character, giving her opinion and speaking of his reputation for honesty and integrity. She then turned to the jury, without a question pending, and said, "There are a lot of people who don't like John, but nobody ever said he isn't honest." In that sentence, she captured a major aspect of the case. Connally was in many ways more articulate—some said smarter—than Lyndon Johnson, but some thought of him as somewhat cold, arrogant, and distant. Mrs. Johnson captured a point we were trying to make.

Reverend Billy Graham was also an impressive witness, although one took a risk putting him on. He had been identified closely with the Nixon administration and if pressed in a certain way would defend Richard Nixon in ways that would harm his credibility with this jury. No such questions were asked, however. Graham is most memorable for his answer to the question "And what is your business or occupation?" He replied, "I preach the gospel of Jesus Christ all over the world." One juror said loudly, "Amen!"

Many of them had differences with him, they had logical political differences, but every last one of them said his reputation for integrity and honor is unquestioned when I put them on the stand under the rules of this Court.

If there had been one mark on his life, if there had been one ugly rumor, if there had been one accusation, if there had been one scandal, if there had been anything that stained or sullied or tarnished his name in the slightest, they could have brought it forth before you, and with the vast resources at their command, the FBI, their own staff, you can be sure that if there had been such they would have brought it out here in this courtroom.

From the fact that they did not, you can infer that the man on trial who has been made the object of obloquy, the target of slander by this self-styled perjurer, is a man who has had no stain in 58 years of his life on his record.

And His Honor will tell you as a matter of law that the facts alone, apart from other considerations or in the light of all the evidence, may be sufficient to raise in this case a reasonable doubt.

Now, let us talk about John Connally, the accused.

Yesterday they brought out, oh, well, you know, he gave all those records, but they were subpoenaed. They were subpoenaed.

Members of the jury, under our system of justice, no one is forced to give evidence. It's an elementary principle of our criminal justice system that no one has to give evidence in an investigation of himself.

COMMENTARY

Anyone who read Williams's book *One Man's Freedom* would know of Williams's eloquence about the adversary system. This argument is a spirited defense of a prospective defendant's right not to testify or produce personal records. Let us examine its parts.

Williams first takes the position that Connally had a right not to produce his diaries, telephone call records, and similar documents. There was in 1975 more to that position than perhaps there is today, for there are sharp limits on Fifth Amendment protection of papers. *See generally* WAYNE R. LaFAVE & JEROLD H. ISRAEL, CRIMINAL PROCEDURE §§8.12–8.13 (2d ed. 1991) [LaFave & Israel]. But one can still make something of not resisting a subpoena, of voluntary acts of cooperation.

This leads to the second point: What do jurors think about a suspect's obligation to come forward and help the authorities, and how do they judge him if he slips up on some detail? Testifying or being interviewed raises the stakes considerably, for one may be charged not only with the substantive offense but with lying about it as well—as though one's defense is already certified unbelievable by the grand jury or prosecutor.

I think many jurors will find Williams's analysis persuasive. In the trial of Terry Nichols, jurors understood how Nichols might have been mistaken about details, and they appreciated that he had taken the initiative in contacting law enforcement. They were critical of the FBI's practice of not tape-recording the interview and of keeping Nichols for nine and a half hours of interrogation in a basement room. Jurors are less likely to be sympathetic to a well-heeled defendant, with lawyer in tow, who makes an appearance in a formal setting—such as the grand jury, a deposition, or a prosecutor's office—and tells untruths about important matters.

As Williams has already proved he knows, jurors do not easily forgive liars.

They have a right not to. It is founded on a simple philosophical principle that there is something unfair to confront a man with confessing his guilt, committing perjury or facing contempt if he refuses to answer.

In our system of justice we regard it basically as dealing with a small boy and saying to him, if you suspect that he took the loose change out of your pocket, I am going to punish you for stealing if you say you took it, for lying if you deny you took it, and for disobedience if you don't answer.

So we have an accusatorial system. No man has to come forward with evidence.

John Connally, from November the 14th, began cooperating with the prosecutor's office, he was in their office all morning for interrogation, voluntarily.

He went in the afternoon to the grand jury beginning at one o'clock.

The next day he was in front of the Ervin Committee for four hours interrogated by six lawyers as he told you.

Then after they had begun their deal with Mr. Jacobsen, after Mr. Jacobsen had been in their office negotiating himself out of eight felonies, negotiating himself out of the $5,000 prospect of embezzlement, negotiating to try to preserve his license, they called John Connally back for three hours and they had him in front of the grand jury, and they took his whole defense and then they charged him.

COMMENTARY

> That is, the prosecutors already knew what they were going to do, and they simply wanted to get some discovery to which they were not entitled. There are some older cases on the "perjury trap" grand jury subpoena, but most courts think that the Fifth Amendment privilege is protection enough. A perjury trap refers to the subpoena of a witness solely for the purpose of eliciting testimony that is intended to be used in a later perjury prosecution of the witness. *See In re* Poutre, 602 F.2d 1004, 1005 (1st Cir.1979); Bursey v. United States, 466 F.2d 1059, 1079 n. 10 (9th Cir.1972); Brown v. United States, 245 F.2d 549, 55455 (8th Cir.1957).

They charged him with two felonies.

He gave them all his phone records, he gave them all of his calls, his itineraries, his logs, his appointment books, both while he was in government and while he was in private practice in Houston.

He gave them 400 pages of testimony to 3,000 questions, he gave them all of his phone records for his home and his ranch and his office, all of his bank records.

You didn't hear anything about safe-deposit boxes of John Connally or cash of John Connally.

They tried to suggest to you this morning, in what was a foul blow, I say, that somebody else gave him the money in that office.

COMMENTARY

> This argument is in response to the prosecutor's suggestion in summation that a friend of Connally's came to Houston and gave him the money that he in turn gave to Jacobsen. The prosecutors were tantalized by this prospect and spent a great deal of time investigating Rex Cauble, a Connally friend from Denton, Texas, who was principal stockholder of a bank. While there was plenty of evidence that Cauble had access to cash, there never was proof that he gave it to Connally. The only evidence consisted of records of toll calls between Connally and Cauble.

Where is the evidence of that? Where is there one line of proof?

And they have been at this case for 18 months.

But that was the innuendo that was dropped here this morning. They were helping to charge him.

There was no effort to block. There was no stonewalling here. There was no effort to keep any taped conversations from you. Everything went in.

Now, contrast that with Mr. Jake Jacobsen's offering, that is what they got from Mr. Jake Jacobsen, for three years, and I ask you who had something to hide here.

COMMENTARY

Again, Williams rifles through Connally's records in evidence and holds up the single Jacobsen exhibit.

At the end, at the very end, what were they reduced to? When John Connally sat on the witness stand yesterday, in one of the greatest demonstrations of nitpicking that I have seen in my 30 years in courtrooms, they picked at little answers here and there that he had given in hundreds of pages to try to suggest that there were inconsistencies.

And they brought out that he neglected to tell them about the October 26th meeting in Austin, Texas, with Jacobsen.

And he said, I understood the question, sir, to mean what was my last meeting.

There was no reason for him to conceal it.

Now, what do we have? We have the summary that John Connally dictated when he came out of the grand jury room on November 2nd of all the questions and answers that were put to him which he sent off to Temple,

---
COMMENTARY

Larry Temple, a prominent Austin lawyer and friend of Connally, to whom Connally sent the summary.

---

which Jacobsen turned over to them, and they have been sitting here with that for a year and it is right there for you to see what John Connally understood the question to be.

"When did you last talk to Mr. Jacobsen?

"ANSWER: Approximately two and a half weeks ago," and so forth.

It was perfectly clear to them. He understood the question, and yet we went through 30 minutes of nitpicking here yesterday.

And then the question was whether or not he falsified when he said that he saw Jacobsen in the hotel in the late afternoon on the 26th, instead of for breakfast.

Here was his itinerary, this is the record he had. The record showed that he didn't get back into Austin, the itinerary says, until 9:00 A.M. Friday.

This caused him to believe that his meeting with Jacobsen was in the late afternoon.

When Mr. Barnett came to the stand and said he remembered serving breakfast, there was no further question on it, because this itinerary had been departed from, and the aid to memory on which he had relied had been invalid because it had been discarded.

--- COMMENTARY ---

Williams is here answering the two points on which the government claimed that Connally had lied to the grand jury—as to when he had met with Jacobsen and as to the time of day of another meeting that Connally admitted having. The first matter is disposed of by noting that Connally had dictated notes after the grand jury appearance that supported his statement that he understood the question in a certain way and answered it on that understanding. The moral here is that if your client is going to talk to somebody, have that talk recorded verbatim. And debrief the client afterward.

The "time of day" problem was a puzzler for the defense for the longest time. Connally clearly remembered meeting Jacobsen on a certain day at the Crest Hotel in Austin. He refreshed his memory with the typed itinerary that his office always kept for him and concluded that the meeting took place while the

Connallys were getting ready for a formal dinner. In his mind, Connally associated the meeting with getting dressed. As it turned out, Connally was mistaken. He had departed from his typed itinerary and actually met Jacobsen in the morning, while he was putting on his tie and preparing for morning activities. The light went on for Connally, and for all of us, when the room service waiter, Mr. Barnett, walked in to take the oath. Barnett had served coffee to Connally and Jacobsen. On direct examination, Connally readily admitted this error, which did not seem to make much difference anyway. The moral here is that calendars and similar documents can be misleading and can actually help to create false memories. Admitting such an error at the earliest possible moment is obviously important to the advocate's—and the client's—credibility.

That is the kind of thing that they were reduced to at the end of this case, nitpicking the witness who had given them all of his records over a period of months in an effort to discredit him and divert you from the main issue in this case about which they never asked him a question, John Connally, did you take any money from Jake Jacobsen.

If they can divert you on this nitpicking you maybe won't notice that their case is on the courthouse floor in shambles, a wreck.

My time is almost up. I hope that I haven't taxed your patience by my persistence or by my zeal. I have never learned to talk about human liberty or human reputation concisely or complacently.

--- COMMENTARY ---

The rhythm of this summation varies. Sometimes it is soft, sometimes coldly logical, sometimes emotional. Some jurors may resent lawyer emotion, because they think it interferes with their rational processes. Not every summation will carry you to emotional heights. But when you go there, you must reassure the jurors that you don't require them to pick up your feelings. It respects and empowers jurors to make the statement that Williams is making here. Another form might be: "I have gone on for some time. I have talked about the law and evidence as we see it from over here. If in my zeal I have seemed to go too far, please don't hold that against my client."

Denigrating the lawyer's role is a stylistic embellishment as old as Cicero's defense of General Murena, as noted in Chapter One. For hints from the air force court martial summation on dealing with this theme, see Chapter One.

We have been together now for three weeks, and for you the case is just three weeks old. But for this defendant it is over a year old. It has been a year of accusation, of humiliation, of anguish, as the result of this assault that was made on his integrity.

Three weeks from now the case will have perhaps faded into the recesses of your recollections, the far recesses of your recollection. You will have gone back to your other concerns, the prosecutors will be on to new matters, and the court will be handling new cases.

But what you do in this case in your jury room will place an indelible mark for the balance of life.

Nothing in a life that has been filled with glory and tragedy can so mark as what you do in your jury room on this evidence and on this record.

COMMENTARY

This theme is available to you in almost any setting. Consider "Tomorrow, or next week, when you have given your verdict, this case will be over for you. You will, with the deep thanks of all of us, have returned to your homes, your jobs, your families. The lawyers and His Honor will go on to other cases. But for Mary Smith, this will be her one and only one chance for justice. This will be for her a defining moment in her struggle for recognition of her dignity and honor." Empowering the jury requires some reminder of their obligation and of how important this all is to your client.

It is an awesome responsibility. But His Honor will help you discharge that responsibility when he tells you that the burden in this case, as in every case of this kind, rests squarely on the prosecution to prove to each and every one of you beyond all reasonable doubt the defendant's guilt.

And if they have failed to sustain that burden, there is only one verdict under your oath as jurors, and that is a verdict of not guilty.

I want to say to you just two last things.

You know, I think in life you can bargain for and buy almost everything. You can bargain for and buy mansions and villas and priceless works of art. You can bargain for and buy fine jewelry and all the creature comforts that you can conjure up in you mind.

But thank God there are some things you can't buy and you can't bargain for. You can't buy or bargain for wisdom. You can't buy or bargain for justice, because if you do, it's injustice. You can't buy or bargain for love, because if you do, it isn't love that you get. And you can't buy or bargain for truth, because it isn't the truth that you get, it's the truth with a cloud of suspicion over it.

COMMENTARY

This is an almost perfect triplet. Beginning with "wisdom" means there are four elements in the sequence, but there is no counterpoint to "wisdom" as there is to justice, love, and truth. In the closing strophe of a summation, one tries to summon images of fairness and of the jurors being fair.

You can buy and you can bargain for testimony,

COMMENTARY

The contrast between "truth" and "testimony" was sharp and dramatic.

---

and that is what the prosecution did in this case, and that is why their case is in the state it is in at the present time.

This case is styled United States, United States against John Connally, but I want to tell you something. The United States will win this case. The United States will win this case.

I saw one day on the wall of a courthouse, the oldest courthouse in England, the words, "In this hallowed place of justice the Crown never loses because when the liberty of an Englishman is preserved against false witness, the Crown wins."

After tramping for 30 years across this country in federal courthouses all over the land, I tell you the United States never loses because when the liberty and reputation of one of its citizens are preserved against false witness, the United States wins, the United States wins the day.

COMMENTARY

This is a magnificent way to put the government's position in a criminal case. The quoted language may or may not be on a courthouse in England. I remember that it is on the wall of the Justice Department inner courtyard.

I think, members of the jury, the greatest experience, the greatest exhilaration, the greatest fulfillment that a human being in this life can have is to lift the pain and anguish off another if it can be done in justice.

I ask you at long last to lift the pain and anguish, the humiliation, the ostracism and the suffering from false accusation and innuendo, vilification and slander from John Connally and his family, and if you do, the United States will win the day.

I ask you tomorrow to return a verdict in this case of acquittal for John Connally on both counts of which he is charged.

COMMENTARY

The jury did so, in about four hours.

Chapter Six, Part I

Elements of Argument to Judges[1]

WHAT IS THE SAME

Many lawyers think that arguing to a judge or judges requires a completely different set of skills from arguing to jurors. There are differences, as the next section of this chapter discusses. But the similarities must first be understood. Invention, arrangement, style, memory, delivery—one must think of each of these in preparing for any argument to any tribunal.

The judge or judges must have a context for decision, just as jurors must. They are influenced by arguments that are arranged in a sensible way and delivered within the canons of style that govern their tribunal and the particular issues being argued. Some of judges' context comes, as does that of jurors, from their background and social position.

One understands this kind of context by the equivalent of *voir dire*. That is, since judging is a public function, your judge or judges will have issued rulings, and run their courtrooms in particular ways. One can therefore know what they bring to the process of deciding. One can know, that is, the prejudices that a given judge may bring to the bench.

Judges are also influenced by context in the sense of story—the story of a particular case or issue. Judicial opinions in the Anglo-American tradition begin with a recitation of facts, then an analysis of the legal principles at stake, then a conclusion. Even the midtrial rulings of a judge are contextual, for they provide more or less amplitude to the advocates' actions in telling the story.

In crafting a brief or an oral argument, therefore, the factual context of decision—the impact of decision on ordinary lives—must be the first consideration. You learn to "say your case" for an appeal as for a trial. You should say it in the introduction to your brief. And you should say it in oral argument. In *Alderman*,[2] the story is not what the petitioners allegedly did—that has become irrelevant as the issues on appeal and *certiorari* have been framed. But there is a story nonetheless. It is the value of adversary inquiry in detecting and deterring illegal government conduct, particularly in the realm of electronic surveillance.

In *Ivanov,* the companion case, the story is somewhat about the espionage done by the petitioners—this is inescapable because by the time the Supreme Court gets the case the defense is not challenging the sufficiency of the evidence. The story is why the claim of national security should not defeat an effort to uncover and redress government illegality in the criminal process. It is related to the *Alderman* story, but overlain with the national security implications necessarily supplied by the espionage charge.

In another case, the story might be that the cumulative effect of errors robbed the defendant of the right to a fair trial in certain defined ways.[3] Indeed, an appellant is always saying in one form or another that there were errors. But this is never enough of an assertion. One must go on to say why these errors make this appellant entitled to certain relief. This is not simply a question of harmless error or standard of review, both of which concepts may operate to restrict the relief available even when an appeals court is convinced the trial judge was wrong.[4] One must go beyond these rules of decision to say that the client is "entitled" to this relief, that it is just that he or she receive it.

By similar token, the appellee who defends the judgment may take solace from rules that insulate the trial judge's rulings from scrutiny or reversal but must also assert that the result obtained in the lower court is just.

Some appellate arguments are cast largely in terms of impact on particular individuals who are worthy of being helped. Other times, the party will not evoke our sympathy. He or she (or the entity-client) may have done terrible things. For such a client (like Alderman and Ivanov), the argument is rule-oriented. Upholding the rule contended for is seen as conferring so great a good as to make trivial the harm that might be done from applying it. Williams expressly makes this argument in *Alderman* and especially *Ivanov*.

The reader may remind me that dozens of judicial opinions contain statements that the judges wish they could rule another way but are confined by precedent or standard of review from doing so. Most of these observations are in my opinion makeweight. They are slogans behind which to sound a judicial retreat. The harmless error invocation is even more clearly thus: Something wrong was done, but the appellate judges don't disagree enough with how things turned out to be moved to help.

Some advocates and many judges downplay the role of advocacy, and particularly of oral advocacy, in decision making. Some judges claim that they are moved to change their minds in only 5 percent of cases. I say not so. Appellate judging is a collective deliberative process. Oral argument forces the judges to go through that process face to face. In a jurisdiction where you don't get oral argument in every case, the nonargued cases are often decided by a phone conference or even by an initiating judge who drafts an opinion and sends it on to the other panel members. When judges meet in person, there is a chance for all the influences on decision—briefs, law clerk memos, and oral argument—to work together at once. Experience has made me skeptical of the 5 percent figure.

The influence of argument is one of the ways in which judging and jury decision are similar and therefore in which the same advocacy principles will hold sway. There is one way—grim though it be—to gauge the effect of good advo-

cacy on decisions. That is the proliferation of waiver doc-
trines in appellate decisions. If the advocate did not make the
argument cogently at the right moment in trial, the point is
lost on appeal. If the argument is not made in the opening
brief, but saved for the reply, it is lost. If it is in a footnote
and not made prominent enough, it may also be forfeited.[5] It
seems inconsistent at best for judges to say that advocacy
makes little difference in a positive way when they clearly
think it makes a big difference in these negative ways.

WHAT IS DIFFERENT

The similarities noted, there are some differences between
appellate and trial advocacy. These differences are made
clearer when we read the same advocate, Edward Bennett
Williams, in both trial and appellate mode. Some of the difference is about the judges themselves. As Judge Patrick
Higginbotham likes to say, judges are—or regard themselves
as—professional deciders. They take pride in quickly grasping
the essence of an issue and then resolving it. This self-pro-
claimed expertise may sometimes make judges seem impatient. It certainly means that the lawyer must get to the point.

This professional mien is the key to another context of
judicial decision, and that is the judge's image of a set of
legal rules within which a particular decision must fit. This
set of rules is only imperfectly captured by the word *precedent*. Judges are certainly governed by *stare decisis*. Yet the
rules they administer are open textured enough that they
have a great deal of discretion, and within that discretionary
zone their own sense of where the law ought to be holds
sway. The open-textured quality of legal rules gives room
not only for the judge's views but also for your argument
about the justice of ruling for your client.

Judges are not chosen as are jurors. *Batson v. Kentucky*[6]
and its progeny have helped guarantee that jury panels are
a cross section of the community. Judges, by contrast, are
almost all lawyers and are not as a group anywhere near rep-

resentative of all the tendencies and groups in the community.

Argument to judges is interactive. Unlike jurors, judges can ask questions, and they expect responses. This is not as big a difference as you might think, because in jury argument we try to see things through jurors' eyes. We do as Williams did in the *Connally* summation and try to empower them by acting as their surrogate in uniting fact and law. It is well, however, to remember this idea, for sometimes the judges do not ask questions, and you must then try to focus the argument on areas that you believe reflect their concerns, just as in a jury case.

THEMES OF ARGUMENT

Legal argument arises in several settings, yet the principles of it are fairly constant. Some arguments are made on the spur of the moment in trial; for example, in rulings on objections. While you may not have the chance to make a detailed argument on admissibility, being prepared to do so ensures that your objection is well grounded and well expressed.

A second type of argument is on case management issues to a trial judge, where the scope of judicial discretion is widest. Examples include discovery, scheduling, severance and joinder, and some routine aspects of pleading. Your argument on these issues must be grounded in your own good faith, in the way that efficient and just administration of the case will be affected by the court's ruling and by a firm foundation in the lore of procedure. For example, you might seek a pretrial conference to set a discovery schedule. You will have filed a memorandum of law; the judge may or may not have read it before the argument. You will have found out the judge's habits in this respect. In any argument to a judge or judges who have not read your brief, your discussion of the facts and your analysis of the issues must be more extended.

And so in our case, we might argue: "If the Court please, we are here today on our motion to conduct discovery in phases, as a means of saving the parties time and money and sharpening the issues in dispute. There are two issues that, if resolved in favor of the defense, will terminate or sharply limit this lawsuit. These are exposure and statute of limitations. If we prevail on either issue, the case is effectively over, and yet the discovery necessary to present dispositive motions on these issues can be done quickly and efficiently. Then we know if we have a lawsuit. The alternative is that the parties must spend a lot of money and time on all the issues framed by the complaint and on such things as expert witnesses who may never be needed. We estimate that all discovery on these issues could be completed within ninety days. We are prepared to tender our relevant documents within thirty days."

This form of argument is not an abstract plea to limit discovery—it is a discussion of how best to find out the story. It is underpinned by the defendants' story, which is that its product did not cause the harm, and if it did, it was too long ago. The plaintiff's story is about harm, the defendant's story about the irrelevancy of that harm to liability. This is familiar terrain, as the prior chapters attest.

But when we think of "argument to the court," we usually think of the more formal setting of a court of appeals or of a dispositive motion argument in trial court or argument in a judge-tried case. The last-named kind of argument partakes most clearly of the techniques and principles of a closing argument to the jury. But it has its own peculiar emphasis on legal rules, to an extent not seen in jury argument.

As you build your argument, remember that judges need memory prompts too. If you are in district court, you will often use charts and diagrams. In some appellate settings, such things are used, particularly in complex cases. Certainly in your brief you may use such devices to summarize difficult material.

In most instances your argument will be limited in time. You must therefore choose the issues that you intend to present orally. In preparing, have enough material to fill the allotted time, but be able to present all the key issues in one-third of that. In choosing issues, heed Judge Alvin Rubin's advice, which he attributed to legendary quarterback Joe Montana: "Throw deep."

In most appellate courts these days, the judges have read the briefs. They don't need you to restate the facts and in fact will resent your taking the time to do so. If one or more of your arguments is fact based, limit your analysis to the key points. Even if you are arguing sufficiency of the evidence, you need to compress your factual analysis to avoid using up your time to no effect. If the court is interested in the point, the judges will have questions about particular factual matters. You will also get clues on focus from your opponent's presentation.

Let us see how this works in a real case. Assume you have twenty minutes to argue for the appellant; this is about average in federal courts of appeals. Even in the United States Supreme Court, you have only thirty minutes on a side. Multiple appellants and multiple petitioners usually split the time. If there are multiple appellants in your case, try to get an agreement that one lawyer will argue for all. If you wind up with two lawyers doing it, try to get the time extended to thirty minutes a side. You probably won't get more than that, and if there is one advocate on the other side, you will already have done him or her enough of a favor by getting thirty minutes.

If you have twenty minutes, you need to save some for rebuttal. I would save four minutes. If you run over a little on the top side, you will still have three minutes, and that is usually plenty.

How should you plan to use the sixteen minutes? The "first cut" of issues should be those that will result in reversal of the whole case. From those issues, which ones benefit from oral argument? Here are some questions to ask:

- Is there a factual dispute that illuminates an issue, on which you are sure the judges will have questions?

- Is there a doubtful issue of circuit law, where judges may be wondering which direction to go in—in this case to be sure, but for the future?
- Is there an issue that highlights or exemplifies what is wrong with the case? In one oral argument, literally dozens of issues were presented by a six-month multidefendant criminal trial, but two of them seemed to illustrate the government overreaching that we said was at the center of things: the prosecutor's ignoring circuit law about the contents of a conspiracy indictment and the prosecutor's leak of inflammatory and false information about the defendants on the eve of jury selection.[7] These issues, we said, were suggestive of an entire course of conduct and provided an introduction to more complex and difficult matters touching on alleged bank fraud. They were the themes of oral argument and became main themes of the court's opinion.
- Is there an issue on which your opponent has made a misstatement of the record or the governing law? This may be a good candidate for oral argument, but of course you will not engage in personal attack when you argue it.
- You will probably know who is on your panel a week before argument. Is there an issue with which one or more of the judges has become identified? Of course you will Shepardize all the cases, and you will use Westlaw or LEXIS to find relevant opinions by panel members. This will help you approach an issue you have chosen. But the composition of the panel may help you choose the issues to begin with.

In choosing issues, allow about one-third to 40 percent of your allotted argument time. That is, figure that questions from the court will take up the rest of the time. That way your "must argue" points are almost sure to be covered.

When you have chosen the issues, you need to make a notebook with (1) an introduction tab with your "say the case" story line, (2) a tab for each issue you plan definitely to argue, (3) a tab for each optional point—the ones you will argue if your time is not consumed by questions, (4) a tab for each additional issue in the brief so that you will have notes to respond to questions by the judges even if you did not plan to argue that point, (5) a conclusion line to end the argument.

In addition, you will want a folder with copies or summaries of the leading cases and a copy of your index to the record. Don't make a full copy of every case—use summaries except for the ones that are truly important.

With these materials, the briefs, and the joint appendix or record excerpts, start by learning to navigate through the paper. That is, practice with colleagues being asked a question or hearing an opponent's argument, then quickly finding what you need to make your response.

If you are the appellee, your notebook looks the same, although your optional issues become more important to you. You have the advantage of hearing your opponent argue and hearing the court's questions. In that process, some of your "must" issues may become compressed, and some optional ones elevated.

RESPONDING AND REBUTTING

Argument styles have changed. Times are limited. In other countries, such as Canada, there is much more emphasis on oral advocacy than on written briefs. With these limits, we have seen rhetorical styles change as well. Lawyers do not have the time for so many rhetorical devices as once they did, and this has marked another change between arguments to juries and those to judges.

Of course, one way judges try to control advocates is by trivializing the value of advocacy and seeming to react unfavorably to arguments delivered with passion and conviction. Sometimes, when one probes these judicial harrumphings, one finds a distaste for the content of the advocate's argument. Judges criticized William Kunstler for rhetorical excess, though Bill was a superb oral advocate. Most of the time, this was displaced criticism of Bill's politics or his choice of clients.

More legitimately, judges criticize lawyers who substitute bombast for substance. I have heard a lawyer emote for twenty minutes on a point of procedure, spouting exquisite generalities about unfairness. The issue was whether a particular statute and rule of federal civil procedure applied and if so what they meant. The lawyer's job was to make a plausible argument that he had read those things and that they permitted the result he sought. Only in that context does his claim for justice—his story—acquire meaning.

And here is the key: don't be afraid to invest your story with conviction, but make sure that there is substance at the center of it. This is a general observation on advocacy to judges, but it fits here because we are talking about responding and rebutting, two places where it is easiest to use the wrong tone.

When your opponent says something with which you disagree, and perhaps utters it disagreeably, your response must be based firmly on the factual record and the legal rules. Just as in jury argument, the judges may not know enough about the case—or may not care enough about the issue to share your sense of outrage. You have to bring them to a point where they can share it.

Example: Your opponent says, "These appellants never so much as visited the property before they did their land swap, and the appraisals they got were clearly phony." Your turn comes. You say, "At transcript page 742, Mr. Wilson says all these defendants visited that property, and at page 1015, we find that the appraisers they used were approved by the Bank Board. This misstatement of the record is unfortunately typical of what happened at trial, and as we have pointed out in our brief, in this court as well."

The hardest time to use in argument is rebuttal. The judges probably think they have heard it all. They say they like it when lawyers stand up and say they have nothing to say in rebuttal. Again, this is an advocate control device as much as anything.

If you are appellant or petitioner, you should have two perorations prepared, one for the end of the main argument and one for the end of rebuttal. These should be one-sentence statements that sum up your case. One could call them ornamental, in the sense that one cannot put a lot of substance into a sentence. But they mark out your claim for justice. "In sum, if the court please, due process may cost something—it always costs more than no process. But it is the hallmark of procedures worthy of respect." Do not declaim the summation; say it simply, with conviction.

For rebuttal, however, your main purpose is not to deliver your one-sentence statement. You yield to the judges' expressed preference by saving only 15 percent or 20 percent of your time for rebuttal. What do you do with that time? First, use pinpoint citations to the record, the briefs, or cases cited in the briefs, to skewer points made by your opponent. The judges' law clerks are taking notes. The court clerk is probably recording the argument for the judges and clerks. The judges may be taking notes: Remember, as my South African friends say, to watch his lordship's pencil. So your citations are shorthand ways to make significant points. If very brief quotation from a case or the record will make the point, you can use it.

If your opponent has raised, and the judges seemed to be interested in, an issue that was an "optional" and that you did not argue on the top side, rebuttal is your chance to do it. Your preferred form of response is "the issue of reliance has come up. We dealt with that at pages 21 through 24 of our brief. I add only this in reply. . . ."

THE VALUE OF QUESTIONS

I was once at an oral argument where an assistant attorney general told a questioning judge to be patient; he would "get to that later." He was rebuked. He lost. Questions are usually windows to the judges' thought process. They are therefore valuable. I say "usually" because some judges ask their law clerks to provide a few good questions for argument as part of a bench memorandum. These questions are not valuable guides to anything, but you cannot know whether the odd question you are hearing is one of them. So you have to take all the questions seriously. It may be that the odd question you hear means that you have truly miscalculated the strength of your position.

Some questions are asked by judges who may be thinking of ruling a particular way but who want some ammunition against their colleagues. So they ask things that seem to reflect a view other than their own. Whatever the basis for the question, it must be taken seriously and answered directly. Questions define a major and important difference between jury argument and appellate argument. Some judges have been known to write to the advocates before oral argument, noting questions that will be asked during oral argument. Some trial judges post tentative or proposed decisions. Welcome all such help. Try to get the judge to tell you what is on his or her mind.

Sometimes the judge asks a question in a hostile way, either because the judge wants to challenge you or because the judge does not in fact think much of your position. If it were an adversary speaking to you in such a tone, you would be tempted to respond in kind. Don't. Some judges deliberately bait advocates. I have heard "questions" like "Oh, that rule is the bastard child of misplaced dicta from another circuit, don't you think?"

A judge who asks such a question is not interested in your abstract views about justice, nor ready to receive your anger or sarcasm in reply. Your answer must be given as though the question had been asked politely. In the example given, the advocate replied, "Whatever the provenance of the rule, it has become circuit law, and it is not open to this panel to undo it. Only the en banc court could do that."

In your argument notebook, there should be a note about everything that might come up in oral argument. Under the appropriate subject tab, find that note. Use it to craft your answer to the question. As the examples from Edward Bennett Williams show, sometimes answering the question saves time because it deals with an issue you were going to treat anyway.

Whether or not you have a note, the question needs a short and direct answer, preferably "yes, Judge X," or "no, Judge Y." There is usually more to say, by way of explanation, but give the inquiring judge a clear signal as to where you are headed. Too often I have heard answers to oral argument questions that begin somewhere in the middle and leave one puzzled as to just what the advocate contends.

If you don't know the answer to the question, say so. "I don't remember what the record contains about that, but. . . ." The "but" is that your colleague is just now looking it up, that you will have an answer in your rebuttal argument, that you will seek leave to file a supplemental brief, or some combination of these.

The rapid-fire exchange of questions and responses sometimes leaves an advocate at a loss. He is afraid of making a concession fatal to his cause. Sometimes, by not thinking matters out beforehand, an advocate does stumble in that way. It will probably happen at some time in your career, and the only way out is to acknowledge it and go on: "I see now where the court's questions are heading, and I think I made an error back there. If the question is X [restating the first question that got you in trouble], the answer must be Y [putting yourself back on track]. The reason is . . ." If you are out of time or realize the error only after the argument is over, seek leave to file a supplemental brief.

Preparation is better than a cure. In preparing for oral argument, focus on probing questions that point up difficulties with your position. Some lawyers and law firms conduct moot court arguments to prepare. For some lawyers and particularly for those without experience, this is indispensable.

My own preference is to sit around with colleagues and be peppered with questions. I will also try out the main themes of argument in this group. I do not rehearse the precise words I will use or the manner of presentation. I want those aspects of the argument to be fresh. "Don't leave your fight in the gym," the boxing trainers say.

Sometimes in argument you will get a helpful question— perhaps even a restatement of your position. Beware, for the seemingly favorable question could be setting you up for a more probing one. Helpful questions have several purposes. The judge may be trying to get you to restate an argument for the benefit of a doubting colleague. She may be trying to get the argument back on track. Your response should be "We agree with that, Judge X. And the reasons are not hard to find." Then complete the answer briefly. Do not fawn.

NOTES

1. The ABA Section of Litigation has for sale a set of videos and materials called *Effective Argument to the Court*. The materials are based on a very successful one-day program that covered argument in district court, the court of appeals, and the United States Supreme Court. These can be ordered from the ABA toll-free at 1-800-285-2221. In MICHAEL E. TIGAR, FEDERAL APPEALS: JURISDICTION & PRACTICE (2d ed. 1992) (third edition to appear in 1999), I talk about all aspects of appeals, including briefs and oral argument. Much of what we say there about persuasion in a written argument applies also to oral argument.

2. 390 U.S. 165 (1969).

3. *See* United States v. Riddle, 103 F.3d 423 (5th Cir. 1997), in which Samuel J. Buffone of Washington ably wove a series of alleged errors into a tableau of unfairness requiring reversal.

4. The subject of error, harmless error, and plain error is discussed in MICHAEL E. TIGAR & JANE B. TIGAR, FEDERAL APPEALS: JURISDICTION & PRACTICE ch. 5 (3d ed. 1999).

5. Briefing and arguing federal appeals is discussed in detail in FEDERAL APPEALS: JURISDICTION & PRACTICE chs. 9–10. My favorite quote on the "If you bury your argument, you will lose it" theme is from Judge Posner of the Seventh Circuit:

The government contends that Dunkel's conviction is not affected by Cheek. First, the prosecutor contends, Dunkel waived any objection to the district court's ruling by burying it in a single unreasoned paragraph of his brief on appeal. A skeletal "argument," really nothing more than an assertion, does not preserve a claim. . . . Especially not when the brief presents a passel of other arguments, as Dunkel's did. Judges are not like pigs, hunting for truffles buried in briefs.

United States v. Dunkel, 927 F.2d 955, 956 (7th Cir. 1991), *aff'd,* 986 F.2d 1425 (7th Cir. 1993).

6. 476 U.S. 79 (1986).

7. United States v. Adkinson, 135 F.3d 1363 (11th Cir. 1998).

Chapter Six, Part II

Persuading Judges—An Example

The *Alderman* and *Ivanov* cases, in which Edward Bennett Williams argued for the petitioners, came to the Supreme Court in a most unusual way. Early in the Kennedy administration the FBI, without benefit of the authorizing legislation that was eventually passed in 1970,[1] installed bugs and wiretaps[2] in the rooms and on the phones of several Las Vegas figures. Among those overheard was Ruby Kolod, an officer of the Desert Inn, whose office suite the FBI had bugged.[3]

Kolod invested money with a Denver promoter named Robert Sunshine. Sunshine did not handle the investment properly, or so Kolod believed. So Kolod, in an effort to collect what he thought was due him, sent Willie "Icepick Willie" Alderman and Felix Antonio "Milwaukee Phil" Alderisio from Nevada to Colorado to explain the situation to Sunshine. Kolod, Alderman, and Alderisio were convicted of conspiring to make murderous threats in interstate commerce. The Tenth Circuit affirmed. Among the issues on appeal was Williams's contention that a thorough review of all logs and tapes of overheard conversations at Kolod's premises would prove that no plan was ever hatched to make threats. That is, the unlawful electronic surveillance should be produced because it was exculpatory.

The Williams firm filed a petition for *certiorari,* which was denied on October 9, 1967. While the petition was pending, a lawyer in the Williams office heard from a Justice Department source that there had been a bug or tap on

Alderisio's business premises in Chicago. I drafted a motion
to stay the mandate pending filing of a petition for rehearing.[4] Petitions for rehearing of *certiorari* denials are seldom
filed and almost never granted. Our argument was that if
there were unlawful electronic surveillance, the government
had a duty to disclose it and to have an adversary hearing as
to whether the unlawfully obtained evidence had tainted the
government's case.[5] When I went to file the motion, the
deputy clerk was most brusque and wanted to know if Mr.
Williams—whose bold signature adorned it—had really
known what he was signing.

The Acting Solicitor General Ralph Spritzer replied to the
motion, saying that the Justice Department had set up a
review committee, which would review all illegal electronic
surveillance. Only if that committee found the unlawfully
obtained material to be "arguably relevant" to a pending case
would disclosure be made.

Our petition for rehearing thus presented the issue squarely: should taint determinations be made by a Department of
Justice committee or by an Article III judge? While the
rehearing petition was pending, an unrelated case came into
the office. We were retained to represent Igor Ivanov, a
chauffeur for the Soviet trading company Amtorg who had
been convicted of espionage. Ivanov was caught at a transfer of information between an American engineer and two
diplomats from the Soviet United Nations mission. The diplomats had immunity and were expelled. Ivanov did not have
immunity.

I drafted a *certiorari* petition for Ivanov, raising the issues
that had arisen at trial and on appeal to the Third Circuit. But
I added a footnote to the questions presented, saying that no
question is presented concerning unlawful electronic surveillance, on the assumption that if there were any, the solicitor general would disclose it, and citing the Kolod rehearing
petition.[6]

The solicitor general, replying to the *Ivanov certiorari*
petition, added a footnote saying that no disclosure would

be made and cited the government's opposition to the Kolod rehearing petition. In reply, we filed a motion to amend the petition for *certiorari* to add the question posed by the exchange of footnotes.

The Supreme Court, *per curiam,* granted rehearing in Kolod and ordered that taint issues be subject to adversary determination.[7] The solicitor general filed a "Motion to Modify the Order of the Court" challenging the *Kolod* opinion. He claimed that forcing the government to disclose illegal wiretapping in all cases would harm the privacy interests of third parties whose conversations were overheard. For example, if a citizen not under suspicion wandered into the ambit of a bug on Alderisio's premises, revealing that citizen's conversation to Alderisio and his lawyers might even be dangerous. In the related *Ivanov* case, the solicitor general seemed to argue that national security was a sufficient basis for warrantless electronic surveillance, although he did not squarely ask the Court to decide this. He did note that revealing the fruits of such surveillance might put intelligence information at risk.

The Court responded by ordering reargument in *Kolod* and by granting *certiorari* in *Ivanov* limited to the wiretap disclosure issue. Thus the stage was set: Williams against the new solicitor general, Erwin Griswold. The *Kolod* case was now called *Alderman* because Kolod had died. It would be argued first, followed by *Ivanov.* The Court, in its order-setting reargument, asked the parties to brief the issue of standing. That is, who would be able to suppress the fruits of electronic surveillance at Alderisio's premises: only Alderisio and any persons overheard, or an expanded group that might include alleged co-conspirators? Or should the Supreme Court take the position that had been adopted by the California Supreme Court[8] and hold that anyone against whom unlawfully obtained evidence was offered had standing to challenge its use?

Because the solicitor general was the movant in *Alderman* and the respondent in *Ivanov,* Williams would have two arguments almost back to back. *Alderman* would be argued first, with the solicitor general going first and Williams second. Then *Ivanov* would be argued with Williams going first and then the solicitor general.

A Supreme Court argument is like, but unlike, any appellate argument one can make or imagine. The Court's argument chamber is on a massive scale, and yet the advocate stands close enough to the justices to engage them in a kind of conversation. The justices vary widely in their style, and some ask many more questions than others. As in all advocacy to judges, the questions are a window to the judges' concerns. They are to be welcomed and answered without evasion. Yet the advocate in most American courts has only a limited time and must use the questions to move the argument along.

Supreme Court arguments differ from others because the Court takes only a relatively few of the several thousand cases brought to it on *certiorari* each term. The justices choose cases to make rules and policy and not particularly to see that justice is being done to individual litigants. They are therefore alert to the broader consequences of proposed rules of law and want the advocate to tell them the effect of particular decisions and not simply to rest on precedent.

Following are the texts of Williams's arguments in *Alderman* and *Ivanov*. You notice that he deploys similar rhetorical devices to those he used in jury argument but that his language and tone are more magisterial. He is speaking in this case against a backdrop of his own Supreme Court cases, several of which were landmarks of Fourth Amendment law.[9] He is putting this case in the context of his own passionate commitment to the values of an adversary system. And he is speaking to a Court whose members had helped to remake constitutional criminal procedure in the terms just past: Chief Justice Warren and Justices Black, Douglas, Brennan, Stewart, Harlan, White, Marshall, and Fortas.

To prepare for these arguments, Williams spent time every day for weeks, poring over the record, the briefs, and the cases. He made notes and outlines on yellow legal pads with a #1 Defender brand pencil in his bold handwriting and then laid them aside and began again. Groups of us would sit with him and listen to proposed themes and to forms of words that he would use to express them. We would pose questions. He would argue with us. We would work on answers. The meetings would often break up while we went to the library for more research. At the next session Williams would have redone his yellow pad notes, and we would begin again.

In every one of the thirteen cases Williams argued before the Supreme Court, he came to a formulation of his position that was filled with passion. Many of the cases involved criminal procedure, and many dealt with church-state issues. In the latter cases, Williams had generally been retained by a religious organization.

Williams had not, in most of these cases, participated heavily in writing the briefs for the Court. He had reviewed the drafts and determined which issues should be presented and how. For him, however, oral argument required taking a new look at the case. After all, what was the use of argument if one was just going to parrot the briefs?

Always, Williams strove to put a position clearly in the first few minutes of argument, the better to invite challenge and question from the Court. In his preparation, there was never a formal "moot court." Rather, he would invite one or two or three people in the office in to argue the issues and pose questions.

The Court's members respected him greatly. This was clear from the arguments themselves and in their private and public comments. I was honored to help Justice William J. Brennan, Jr., write his dedication speech for the Edward Bennett Williams Library. The justice and I sat in his office at the Court with transcripts of Williams's arguments, and he commented how cogently Williams had presented his positions. This was great praise from a justice who, after all, had written several opinions rejecting Williams's position in the church-state cases.

We begin with the argument in *Alderman,* followed immediately by that in *Ivanov.*

* * * * * * *

Mr. Chief Justice,

COMMENTARY

This is the usual way to start. I begin by saying "Mr. Chief Justice of the United States," which is the statutorily proper title. 28 U.S.C. §1, enacted in this century.

---

may it please the Court, from the briefs that have been filed in this case and from the oral argument of last Term, we can begin a consideration of the issues raised by the Court from the premise that the petitioner Alderisio's constitutional rights under the Fourth Amendment have been violated by federal agents when they employed electronic surveillance equipment to overhear his private conversations.

Q: Did he make this argument whether or not the place where they were overheard were his premises?

COMMENTARY

At first the government had conceded that the bugged premises "belonged" to Alderisio, then retreated somewhat from that concession. The retreat raised the issue of standing, although if he were permissibly on the premises, *Katz v. United States* would establish that his rights were invaded if he were overheard without his express or implied consent. Implied consent would arise if, for example, the true owner had given permission for microphones to be installed.

A: Yes, sir.

Q: Do you think that has any bearing on the scope of it?

A: No, sir, I do not, and I propose to develop that fully. I think so long as he has a proprietary interest in the premises that were electronically monitored, he has clear standing to move to suppress—

Q: I am assuming the government was able to establish he has no proprietary interest in the premises?

A: Whether he had a proprietary interest or not. I believe it is immaterial with respect to his own conversations, or those of others when he was not present.

--- COMMENTARY ---

The "others when he was not present" raises the standing issue.

Q: So, the question of standing becomes very important?

A: Yes, sir.

Q: As to the scope of what he is entitled to depending on whether or not he had an interest in the premises. Is that it?

A: Yes, sir; and I must say to footnote Your Honor's observation, I was surprised—and I use the word surprised consciously as an understatement—to hear the Solicitor General say Alderisio had no standing with respect to monitoring premises in which he had a proprietary interest when he himself was not present because in the very brief filed by the government at page 21 of the government's brief, they say, "In our memorandum filed last Term, we assumed that a criminal defendant would have standing to challenge unconstitutional electronic surveillance if (1) he was a participant in conversations overheard in this manner or (2) although not a participant, the overhearing occurred in premises owned by him or in which he had some other interest at the time. We adhere to this position."

If the Court please, what is the government saying here?

--- COMMENTARY ---

Williams almost always said "government," not "the Solicitor General," surely not "the people," and sometimes "the prosecutor" or "the prosecution" to describe the other side. He pronounced all the syllables, giving the word the sense of an entity asserting great power and in need of restraint.

It says we have the logs, memoranda and records resulting from this illicit electronic surveillance, and we are not going to give them back to the victim of this electronic surveillance. Rather, we are proposing a procedure by which we make a confession to the trial judge of the nature, the time, the place and the fruits of our transgression and let the district court evaluate that confession and determine in camera ex-parte what is arguably relevant to the pending prosecution.

COMMENTARY

This is the heart of the case: Will the defense get the transcripts to review them and make claims about taint? Williams was interrupted right at the outset before he could state the issue as he saw it. But he did what one must: He answered the questions. He also took the opportunity in answering to point to a contradiction between the solicitor general's brief and oral argument. He had made this note during the solicitor general's argument and was prepared to use it whenever the occasion arose. But now, having answered the questions, he returns to the argument he came prepared to make.

What is the reason for which they had advanced this procedure?

They say in the case at bar because these logs, memoranda and records may contain arrant gossip without claim to truth and injurious to third persons.

So, we say then to the government as the logical next question, "Well, what about those logs, records and memoranda that are obviously and patently and palpably not injurious to third persons, and what does the government say to that?

What I suggest to the Court is a rather cavalier and bizarre disregard for consistency.

They say, "The practical problem is that neither the government nor the Court can ever know with certainty when disclosure to the defendant of an overheard conversation might be harmful to other participants in the conversation."

I say mutatis mutandis.

―――――――――― COMMENTARY ――――――――――

Latin for "things being changed that must be changed," that is, with the necessary changes. Williams uses this phrase to say that the solicitor general's position logically leads to another question, which in turn exposes the solicitor general's position as flawed. Now watch what he does as he follows the sequence.

How can the judge know whether the failure to disclose the logs, memoranda and records of the conversations might be harmful to the defendant in the vindication of his constitutional rights?

They go on to say at page 15:

―――――――――― COMMENTARY ――――――――――

Why give the page number? Williams had a passion for precision in argument, whether it was the record, a case citation, or something in the brief. Remember that the judges may or may not be taking notes, but the law clerks surely are and the argument is usually tape-recorded.

"There are decisions where even the disclosure of a conversation that is innocuous on its face can prejudice third-party defendants."

I say mutatis mutandis. I say there are conversations which are perfectly innocuous on their face which may be lethal in suggesting leads to evidence gathered by law enforcement evidence for presentation to the Grand Jury and for subsequent presentation to the Trial Court.

They say at page 15, "The experience of the Department of Justice in reviewing cases involving electronic surveillance to determine when disclosure must be made has indicated that because the factual situations are so varied, it is almost impossible to draw a general rule of disclosure that can be applied to a broad class of cases and will avoid the possibility of injury to third persons."

To that we say Amen and it is impossible to draw a rule of demarcation that will avoid through an ex-parte sys-

tem—that will avoid injury to the defendant in the vindication of his constitutional rights under the Fourth
Amendment.

COMMENTARY

This progression is masterful. He has stated the case for disclosure, answered the key points of the government's argument,
and has the balance of his half hour left to develop these points
or to move on to the standing issue as the Court and he may
wish. The rhetorical form is a triplet. Williams could as easily
have used *mutatis mutandis* for the third strophe, for he was
really saying what the Department of Justice finds difficult will
also be difficult for trial judges in an *in camera* inspection. He
chose instead the "Amen" formulation to signal that this was the
third and final element of his argument. In addition, the *amen* is
a prosaic and ordinary conclusion to the elegance of the Latin. It
is not what one expects to hear and therefore punctuates the
argument.

The only safe course, says the government at page 15,
we submit, is to decline to order disclosure whenever it is
clear that nothing in the material is arguably relevant to
the prosecution.

We say, if the Court please, the only safe course, when
we are talking about the vindication of constitutional
rights and when conceivably the trial judge cannot make
this determination in camera ex parte without the aid of
the defendant and his counsel, is to make these conversations, which have been illegally seized, available to the
defendant and his counsel.

COMMENTARY

In any criminal case, *safe* is a powerful word. The prosecution
always means "public safety," which means a curtailment of the
defendant's asserted rights to protect the public or some governmental interest. The defendant must say that this formulation
turns *safe* on its head, for the Constitution exalts individual
rights. The "safety" of all is guaranteed by compelling respect for
the rights of each. Chief Judge Richard S. Arnold of the Eighth

Circuit eulogized Justice Brennan's contributions to criminal justice by saying that Brennan's decisions make us "safer and freer." The cases being argued involve a prominent alleged Mafia hit man ("Icepick Willie"), an alleged major organized crime figure (Alderisio), and a convicted spy (Ivanov).

We say, if the Court please, the Constitution, the law and the basic rules of fair play require the disclosure of these materials to the victim of the search.

If the Court please, as was pointed out earlier this morning, it could not reasonably be argued by the government that if there had been a search of the defendant's premises, a ransacking of his premises and a seizure of his papers and records and letters, it could not reasonably be argued by the government that those materials which were seized from him should not be returned to him, but rather, should be handed up to a District Court Judge to determine whether any of them had arguable relevance to the pending prosecution.

————————— COMMENTARY —————————

The "inventory" requirement in a physical search is discussed in LaFave & Scott §3.5(1).

We say, if the Court please, that the same basic principle applies with respect to conversations which are protected within the Fourth Amendment.

Q: It is not quite that easy because what you are talking about in the case before us, at least one aspect of it, relates to conversations between two strangers, let us say, who happen to be on the premises of the defendant, and those two strangers may have had a reasonable expectation that their conversation would be private, and they have a kind of interest in this. So, it is much more complex and subtle, it would seem to me, in a case where the government would unlawfully seize letters or documents belonging to the defendant. I wonder really if the issue between you and the Solicitor General does not relate to technique—what is the proper technique as to balance between these. It would seem to be obviously competing values or determining whether or not the material is relevant to the prosecution of the defendants.

A: May I address myself to the question I understand Your Honor has raised.

COMMENTARY

The justice has not asked a question; he has made a statement. This often happens in oral argument. One must treat the statement as though a question had been posed, lest the argument take on a too-personal tone. So, one begins the "reply" with words like "the question contained in Your Honor's comment is a difficult one. We would say . . . ." A related observation: In general, it is dangerous to restate the question before answering it. Williams courts that danger and conquers it, for his answer sets up with a hypothetical the government's own "worst case." What if we give over these materials to a crime captain, and they contain conversations of those against whom he or she may take retribution? He knows these questions are coming, and with his hypothetical he is attempting to set the terms of debate.

The answer is masterful, but as we shall see not quite complete. Williams has a series of answers to the government's "no disclosure" position, and before the argument is over you will see them all. His first is to say that the rights of those on the premises, who are not being prosecuted, are derived from the common law and do not have the same dignity as those of a defendant invoking the exclusionary rule and seeking a hearing at which the rights of confrontation and compulsory process will be invoked. This is not a wholly satisfactory answer, for there is an excellent argument under *Katz* that the bystanders' Fourth Amendment rights have also been violated. However, it was not clear in 1969 when this case was argued that there was a federal judicial remedy for that incursion, so it is perhaps accurate enough to speak of their rights as common law. A leading case on such incursion had been litigated by the Williams firm in state court. *See* Elson v. Bowen, 83 Nev. 515, 436 P.2d 12 (1967)(rejecting federal agents' claim of executive privilege in civil suit concerning FBI unlawful wiretapping), and was eventually settled.

Williams quickly moves to a central thesis, which he will maintain and which the Court will expressly adopt in its opinion, Alderman v. United States, 394 U.S. 165, 185 (1969):

> In addition, the trial court can and should, where appropriate, place a defendant and his counsel under enforceable orders against unwarranted disclosure of the materials which they may be entitled to inspect. *See* FED. R. CRIM. P. 16(e). We would not expect the district courts to permit the parties or counsel to take these orders lightly.

To concretize it, in the case where the defendants premises are electronically monitored and the monitor picks up conversations of A and B when the defendant is not present, the question is what is the defendant's standing to get those conversations. I suggest there are competing social interests and there are competing legal interests.

What are they? On the one hand we have a defendant charged with a criminal offense who is seeking to vindicate a constitutional right. We have a situation here where the government has violated his Fourth Amendment right by invading his premises in which he has a proprietary interest.

As a result of that invasion, they have reaped certain benefits, they have gathered certain fruits, they have gathered certain evidence against him, and they say you have no standing because it was not your conversation.

On the other hand, you have the competing social value of the two persons who thought they were talking privately, maybe even against the defendant himself.

Now what is their right? We are weighing a common law right of privacy of these people against the constitutional right of the defendant. What can be involved in that common law right? It may be a pecuniary interest.

I am sure the Court would agree it should be subordinated to the defendant's constitutional right and the right to privacy can be safeguarded effectively, I submit to the

Court, insofar as protective orders can be fashioned and ordered by the trial judge to protect those third persons from unnecessary disclosure.

It has been our experience that, if the Court please, in every one of the hearings which have been conducted as a result of an illicit electronic surveillance, the defendant himself has asked for protective orders because he does not want to proliferate the government's opportunity to invade his privacy. And so, too, can protective orders be fashioned to protect as far as possible the right for protection from further damage as far as third persons are concerned.

Q: In a sense, that is what we are talking about here in one of these protective orders. Is it necessary to give the court the power to examine the logs in camera and to suppress them? For example, A and B, in the situation you are talking about, in the way that you put it, if A and B were talking about bumping off the defendant, I think that is the kind of situation that people will think about in connection with cases of these types. Shouldn't there be some mechanism by which the court can examine the log in camera? To me that is rare. I don't know anything about this.

A: Your Honor, I think you have pinpointed the situation that may constitute one-tenth of one percent of the cases. I think even in those cases the rights of the participants in the conversations can be effectively safeguarded. If in fact, we have a realization of the bizarre hypothesis that two [people are] talking about eliminating the proprietor,

---

COMMENTARY

First he minimizes the possibility as a practical matter. This is what one must do with any *in terrorem* argument, even when suggested by a question. First note the true extent of the risk. Then Williams puts out another key element of his argument: the government can always dismiss rather than disclose. He does this in answer to a question. There is no follow-up question on the subject, so he saves the point and returns to it later with case citations. Certainly this has been a theme in the briefs.

then the government, I suggest to the Court, has the choice of providing those persons with the same sort of protection that it provides to material witnesses in many cases where these interests are at stake, or alternatively, if it does not wish to do that and wants to exalt their rights over and above the interests of sovereignty to go forward with the prosecution they can dismiss the prosecution.

But I suggest to Your Honor that it is not practical, it is not feasible, it is not practical for a trial judge sitting in camera to make a determination as to whether any of the logs, memoranda or materials resulting from the electronic surveillance were used by the government in developing leads.

I want to give the Court just one illustration of that and it is cited in our brief. We have a case where there is a boilerplate indictment for income tax evasion charging the defendant in the typical language with evading taxes for a given year. The only thing they ever change in those indictments are the year and the amounts of money.

COMMENTARY

In an indictment under 26 U.S.C. §7201, it is generally alleged that the defendant attempted to evade and defeat a large portion of the income tax due and payable for a given calendar year, understating his taxable income by X dollars and underpaying tax by Y dollars.

Unlike the Jencks Act materials, if you please, unlike grand jury testimony, if the Court please, when we talk about a trial judge looking at the logs, memoranda and records of an electronics surveillance, we are talking about packing cases filled with materials, not sheaves of paper. We are asking a trial judge to do the superhuman task of juxtapositioning packing cases of electronically monitored conversations against the skeletal averments of a criminal indictment, using the wildest flights of his powers of imagination, as suggested by the Solicitor General, to determine whether the government seized any of those and developed leads.

Here is a case where the trial judge spent four weeks reading the documents. They were voluminous. They were so voluminous that he had to delegate the job to another judge who he had read them, and they came up with the answer that there was nothing relevant.

When the trial came on, one conversation turned out to be the origin of a lethal chain of proof. What is the conversation? "How are you. You are coming on the TWA? I will get ahold of Cliff. I will call him right now. Charlie won't be there. His wife is being operated on. I will have a room there for you and your wife. You are going to stay through Sunday? Okay, buddy."

Now I suggest to the Court that no trial judge sitting before trial or after he had heard all of the proof in a three-week trial could have determined in camera ex parte that the conversation was, as it turned out to be, the origin of a line of proof that was devastating.

COMMENTARY

This was an example of an overheard conversation that the prosecution used in Baker v. United States, 401 F.2d 958 (D.C. Cir. 1968), aff'd after remand for further hearings on unlawful surveillance, 430 F.2d 499 (D.C. Cir.), cert. denied 400 U.S. 965 (1970). Although Baker's conviction was later affirmed, after extensive hearings on electronic surveillance, the example was compelling, because the seemingly innocuous conversation showed that Baker—who was secretary to the senate majority— had stopped in Las Vegas on his way from picking up money in Los Angeles and taking it back to Washington, D.C.

What is more, if this Court please, when this Court and other courts design to deter lawless law enforcement, we find more sophisticated methods are devised to countervail the rules of disclosure. For example, when the Jencks decision came down and when the Jencks statute was subsequently enacted by the Congress, we found well-motivated law enforcement over-zealous in the pursuit of their duties who found ways to put on paper in narrative form statements that were not susceptible to turn over under Jencks.

COMMENTARY

Jencks v. United States, 353 U.S. 657 (1957), is the decision requiring turnover of prior witness statements to the defense. The holding was codified, some would say "limited," by the Jencks Act, 18 U.S.C. §3500. Then there was extensive litigation over whether an investigator's report was a "statement" of the witness. *See, e.g.,* Campbell v. United States, 365 U.S. 85 (1961), 373 U.S. 487 (1963).

When the Dennis case came down

COMMENTARY

Dennis v. United States, 384 U.S. 855, 872–23 n.20 (1966), a decision that also reaffirmed the "disclose or dismiss" teaching of United States v. Coplon, 185 F.2d 629 (2d Cir. 1950), *cert. denied,* 342 U.S. 920 (1951) (L. Hand, J.) (the government must turn over all logs of unlawful wiretaps in a suppression hearing in the espionage case or suffer dismissal of the prosecution), and United States v. Andolschek, 142 F.2d 503 (2d Cir. 1944) (L. Hand, J.).

and grand jury testimony was ordered to be turned over to the defense after the direct testimony, we found and are finding across the country well-meaning, able, zealous and competent prosecutors who seek to avoid this advantage to the defendant having grand jury minutes no longer transcribed.

Now, in this instance, when we have a *Kolod* rule, what has happened and what can happen? It isn't any longer necessary, if the Court please, to make logs, memoranda or records of an electronic monitored conversation. We cite in our brief a situation where the agent in charge of the investigation monitored the premises of the suspect 24 hours a day. He listened to the conversations each day, and if he saw anything in those conversations which he believed to be of interest to him, he would telephone to another field office the information gleaned, and he would ask field operators to run down those leads. The basis of the lead would be ascribed to a confidential informant protected from disclosure by McCray against Illinois

---

COMMENTARY

386 U.S. 300 (1967).

---

and a lead would be developed and a trial would be created and there would be nothing of a written nature to turn over to the trial judge for an in camera ex parte examination to determine whether or not there had been a fruitful violation of defendant's rights.

So, I suggest to the Court that it is not possible for a defendant to vindicate his constitutional rights in the area of electronic surveillance without an adversary hearing, a full open adversary hearing and without a disclosure to him of the nature of the surveillance and the time and place of the surveillance and the fruits of the surveillance.

COMMENTARY

Williams has now laid down his main attacks on secrecy: first, without adversary inquiry, you cannot know the extent of government misconduct; and second, only the defense can tell whether a particular overheard conversation might have led to some item of prosecutor's evidence. The prosecutors have a motive not to find a connection, and district judges don't have the factual basis to make such a determination without a hearing. This echoes a sentiment in the *Dennis* case, 384 U.S. at 874–75:

> In our adversary system, it is enough for judges to judge. The determination of what may be useful to the defense can properly and effectively be made only by an advocate.

Q: I am still puzzled a little bit by what seemed to concern Justice Fortas's question to you, given the case of a conversation between A and B on the premises of C, and C is the defendant in the subsequent criminal prosecution. You suggested in your answer that C's right was a Fourth Amendment right, a constitutional right, whereas the right of A and B was something less. I think you characterized

---
COMMENTARY

The justice sees the weakness in Williams's initial position. Williams must now be wary.

---

it as a common-law right to privacy.

A: I think I can explain that.

Q: Take the *Katz* case, for example. I assume that the telephone booth was the property of the telephone company, so it is Fourth Amendment right, I suppose, that was violated. As to Katz, however, this Court held rightly or wrongly that he had not a common-law right but a Fourth Amendment right on those premises.

A: I would like to answer both questions. I don't think the telephone company had any right because they leased that telephone booth to Katz, and it was his privacy that was invaded. On the other, I said that C's constitutional rights were invaded. A and B's constitutional rights have already been invaded just as C's.

But when we came to the question posed by the government as to whether A and B's conversation should be made available to C, the defendant, then, in that case as between A, B and C, we are not talking about constitutional rights. We are then talking about a right to privacy which they have against him with respect to conversations which have already been seized unconstitutionally.

I say that their right to privacy as against C, must be subordinated to vindicate his Fourth Amendment rights. I am not here to denigrate that A and B's constitutional rights have been invaded. That is an accomplished fact. Fortunately, they are not defendants. The difference is that this is the post-indictment stage.

COMMENTARY

This analysis is complex. Williams now concedes—as he must under *Katz*—that A and B are victims of a Fourth Amendment violation. He then makes explicit what was inherent before. We are talking about remedy, not about rights. C is indicted, and the issue is his right as against those of A and B. If C has a Fourth Amendment–based right to exclude unlawfully obtained evidence, he must have a procedure to vindicate that right. The procedure involves calling witnesses and cross-examining them. Ultimately, the government has the burden of proving that its case is free from taint. So whose rights will win? A basic assumption of the right to compulsory process is that inconvenience to a witness does not excuse her attendance. And the Court would hold soon after *Alderman*, in *Davis v. Alaska*, 415 U.S. 308 (1974), that the right of a juvenile offender to seal his criminal record must yield when the offender is a government witness and defense counsel wants to cross-examine about the offender's prior misconduct. Williams needs to establish a hierarchy of values, and he is invoking good law in doing so. He will soon play the other card—the government's ultimate burden of proof.

Q: We are talking about sanctions and protections to repair the two violations of the Fourth Amendment.

A: That is right. The difference in the cases, Your Honor, is that C is a defendant in a criminal proceeding who has a right not to be convicted by illegally obtained evidence.

In the case that you hypothesized A and B are not defendants. In this frame of reference, I say that in the hierarchy of values, the Court should place A and B's rights subordinate to C. If A and B were indicted, and they were seeking vindication of their constitutional rights, I would have a different answer for them, but I stand by what I said earlier, sir, having taken as the fact the unconstitutional invasion of all three, that is, between A and B and C, and we are talking about a common-law right to privacy, A and B against C, and that can be safeguarded in so far as practical for the vindication of C's rights by a protective order that inhibits both C and his counsel from making unnecessary disclosure of the contents of that conversation.

COMMENTARY

> If Williams cannot succeed in selling the hierarchy of values, he must rely on the protective order idea. It must therefore be worked in to every relevant answer.

Q: Just in a word, what is the violation of A and B's constitutional rights?

A: In a word, Your Honor, the government illegally and unconstitutionally listened to conversations which they believed were being privately held as has been said in Silverman against the United States.

Q: It is a *Katz* sort of case?

A: *Katz, Silverman, Wong Sun* and *Irvine.*

Q: Is that subject to C's consent?

COMMENTARY

> Irvine v. California, 347 U.S. 128 (1954).

A: No, sir, not by C's consent.

Q: If C suggested to the government that A and B were going to have a conversation, and they come and listen, even though A and B participate?

A: If I understand your question, are you asking whether C could give consent to the government to electronically monitor A and B's conversation without notifying them that their privacy was being invaded? I would say no, it must be where the parties to the conversation cannot reasonably foresee that they are going to be overheard in the normal course of things.

COMMENTARY

> Williams's position on this issue is not now the law, for consent of one party to a conversation will usually authorize overhearing it even though the other parties do not consent and have no reason to suspect that some other party has consented. *See* Tigar,

Foreword: Waiver of Constitutional Rights: Disquiet in the Citadel, 84 HARV. L. REV. 1 (1970). However, the point is not relevant in *Alderman.*

Now, with respect to the problem of standing that has been raised here,

─────────── COMMENTARY ───────────

Standing is the second issue. Williams signals that he is turning to that issue with a transition. The standing issue does not seem likely to succeed. The Court will in all probability hold that traditional property-based standing concepts are to prevail but that anyone will have standing to suppress overheard conversations of his or her own or where he or she was present and no party gave consent. One could take the California view, discussed earlier, and we did brief that. But for argument's sake it seemed wiser to take the more limited position that co-defendants and co-conspirators should have standing. Williams will develop that theme. It was adopted by Justice Fortas in dissent in *Alderman.*

it is our contention, and I have, I think, articulated that in response to Mr. Justice Fortas's question,

─────────── COMMENTARY ───────────

Williams identifies the justice who asked one of the early questions. The Supreme Court transcripts do not identify the justice who asks a given question, for fear that they will get it wrong. My own practice is to respond to questions by saying "Yes, Judge [or Justice or Chief Justice] X," and then continuing with the answer. I think this helps to direct the answer, and I know it helps me do what Williams is now doing—remembering which judge or justice asked a particular question so that I can refer back to it later in the argument.

One must, however, be careful to get the name right. In Gregory v. City of Chicago, 394 U.S. 111 (1969), counsel for the respondent city repeatedly referred to Justice Marshall (who was African-American) as "Mr. Justice Black." Justice Black was also on the Court at that time. The effect was not salutary for the advocate.

that Alderisio has standing with respect to conversations heard on his premises, notwithstanding the fact that he was not present.

I read page 21 of the Solicitor's brief as a concession of that position. I think a concession of this sort is necessary for the simple reason that if we are to make the fruits of an unconstitutional invasion of one's premises inadmissible, it follows clearly we must make the conversation seized on Alderisio's premises inadmissible against him.

COMMENTARY

The rule was clearly as Williams states it with respect to searches for tangible objects. Indeed, the law of standing is based to a large extent on property concepts when physical searches are at issue.

Q: The fact is, it was not Alderisio's premises or any premises he had an interest in. Then I gather you limit his right to the tapes of the conversations to which he was a party or conversations where he was present?

A: To answer your question as sharply as it was posed, Your Honor, yes, I would take that position, and I underscore that section of your question which said in which he had no interest.

COMMENTARY

This is a hostile question. This justice (and it may have been Justice White, but I cannot be sure) is accepting the government's newly minted view that Alderisio did not have a proprietary interest in the premises he often visited and where the bug was installed. The questioner is not really seeking information, but rather making a point. In oral argument, one must be unfailingly courteous to the judges, but one need not take the questions for any more than they are worth. Williams's first device is to defuse the question with "to answer your question as sharply as it was posed," which is not a prelude to being as impatient or even openly hostile as the question was. These words are uttered gently, with a smile. But the point is made.

Q: For myself at least the government has introduced something here which I did not know was an issue in the case, namely, that these were not Alderisio's premises.

COMMENTARY

Now another justice chimes in, with an implied rebuke of his colleague who asked the previous question and to open up the question of just who owns these premises. One must be alert for such clues. The justice is looking for agreement or reinforcement here.

Certainly, the original order was written on the premises of Alderisio in Chicago.

COMMENTARY

The justice is saying that the original *Kolod* order, 390 U.S. 136 (1968), was issued on the understanding—stated by the defense and not then contradicted by the government—that Alderisio had a proprietary interest.

A: As we developed the question of standing through the morning here, Your Honor, it is ultimately our position that a person agreeing within the purview of an electronic surveillance and Rule 41 is one against whom the search is directed whether it is identified or unidentified at the time of the search.

Q: I know, but still I want to be clear about this. If the fact is that these conversations with Alderisio that were illegally bugged were conversations on premises not his own or in which he had no interest, his right to suppression is limited to conversations of his own or conversations in his presence; is that right?

A: That is right, Your Honor, subject to one qualification which I am going to develop. I think that a co-defendant stands in the shoes of his co-defendant with respect to this right. A co-conspirator stands in the shoes of his co-conspirator with respect to this right.

So in the case, for example, of Alderman, against whom the government says it conducted no surveillance and whose premises it says it did not invade, we nonetheless say, if the Court please, that since this was an indictment in conspiracy and since the government took the procedural advantages that flow from the conspiracy case, namely, the imputation of the acts and declarations of Alderisio to Alderman and Alderman to Alderisio, and the unindicted conspirators to each, and since it takes the partnership theories and lays all of the duties of the partnership on each of the co-conspirators.

We say then that when you take that theory to the limits of its logic, you have to give them the rights of partners, also.

Q: Let's take and expand on the position of the courts. . . . The Fourth Amendment right across the board.

A: I suggest the time has come when the concept of standing must be expanded if we are going to fashion a rule that will deter electronic surveillance because I suggest that the rule for which the government contends is now archaic.

Q: I think I must have misunderstood you a moment ago. Did you say any person against whom electronic surveillance is directed has standing? Do you take a position as broad as that? Do you say if there were unlawful electronic surveillance directed against A that he has standing even though he may be a total stranger to the conversations and the premises and no co-defendant or co-conspirator is involved?

A: If neither his conversation is heard or his premises are not invaded, if he is not the subject matter of the conversation and if he is not a co-defendant with one whose conversations, premises or privacy were invaded, then I say he does not have standing.

Q: You inserted one word ingredient. You inserted, "If he is the subject of the conversation, even though it is between total strangers, then he is entitled to disclosure."

A: Yes.

Q: So that is another ingredient?

A: That is another ingredient, and I think that is the ingredient on which we part company with the government in this proceeding, as I understand their briefs.

I see that my time is up with respect to this case. The next case set is *Ivanov.* I hope to develop the question of standing fully in that companion case to this. So I will defer, with the Court's indulgence, my discussion of standing until that case is called.

* * * * * * *

MR. CHIEF JUSTICE WARREN: We will now call No. 11, Igor A. Ivanov, petitioner, versus the United States.

Mr. Williams, you may continue.

MR. WILLIAMS: Mr. Chief Justice, may it please the Court, petitioner Igor Ivanov, a citizen of the Soviet Union, an employee of Amtorg Trading Company, stands convicted of a conspiracy to commit espionage against the United States under Title 18, United States Court of Appeals of the Third Circuit. A petition of certiorari was filed here. Without detailing the intermediate pleadings between the filing of the petition for certiorari and this oral argument, suffice it to say that pursuant to the order in the *Kolod* case, the government conceded that certiorari should be granted, that there should be a remand to the district court for an in camera ex parte hearing with respect to electronic surveillance conducted in this case.

In the brief filed in this Court in *Ivanov,* the government says that conversations of each of the petitioners in these cases were overheard by the use of electronic surveillance equipment and footnoted is this statement, "In some of the instances, the installation had been specifically approved by the then Attorney General. In others the equipment was installed under a broader grant of authority to the FBI, in effect at that time, which did not require specific authorization."

Experience would indicate to us, I submit, that that is a concession of both wiretapping and eavesdropping in this case.

This case is significantly different from the case just argued at bar because the government avers in this case that there is a national security consideration to be weighted in the balance of competing and social interests.

I think it is equally significant, if the Court please, if I may say so at the outset of the argument, that the government by that reason does not ask for different treatment between *Alderman* and *Ivanov*. It asks for precisely the same treatment. It asks for in camera ex parte proceedings with respect to the logs, electronic logs, memoranda and records of the electronic surveillance in each.

Now, first of all, it is our position, if the Court please, that the Fourth Amendment to the Constitution does not make a division among the various kinds of crime. It does not draw a line of demarcation, and the founding fathers, when the Constitution was written and when the American Bill of Rights was forged, understood quite clearly that there is a difference in the various types of crime.

They gave recognition to this in Article III, Section 3, of the Constitution when they defined treason, and they prescribed the quantum and quality of proof necessary for a treason conviction, but they didn't make any exception in the Fourth Amendment with respect to spy catchers or subversive hunters.

COMMENTARY

This argument is being made early in 1969. Later that year the attorney general announced the legal position that national security electronic surveillance was an exception to the warrant requirement and could be conducted based on specific or even general authorization from the president of the United States. This position was then litigated over the next few years, resulting first in United States v. Smith, 321 F. Supp. 424 (C.D. Calif. 1971), then in United States v. United States District Court, 407 U.S. 297 (1972).

Here the issue is somewhat narrower, dealing only with whether national security excuses disclosure of electronic surveillance, not with whether such surveillance is lawful.

As a matter of technique, this is an argument from the text of the Constitution, considered as a whole. The argument from omission is not always strong, for there are many reasons why one part of an enactment will be silent and yet not be held to cover a given situation. Here, however, Williams is using a kind of shorthand, which one must do in oral argument. He is setting out the contention in its boldest form, waiting to see if there is a challenge from the bench. Had there been such a challenge, he could have pointed out that the Fourth Amendment was a specific response to British police action against alleged subversives, both in the colonies and in the mother country.

In oral argument, time is always limited. You must make some parts of your argument as assertions in outline form, just as Williams is doing here. If the judges do not follow up, they may simply regard your argument as not worth challenging, or they may not have thought about the issue. Assuming a well-prepared panel of judges—which one can do always in Supreme Court arguments and generally in federal courts of appeals—the wiser assumption is that your position is accepted.

If you have doubts on this score, then you can either refer to your brief for more explanation, or you can make the given part of the argument more fulsome.

It is next our position, if the Court please, if the Attorney General of the United States certifies to the Court that there is a national security consideration which should excuse the United States from making a disclosure with respect to the nature, the time, the place or the fruits of an electronic surveillance illegally conducted, we say he should be excused provided he consents to a dismissal of the prosecution under the time-honored principle of Coplon against the United States, which was decided in 1950, in an opinion by Judge Learned Hand, which was foursquare with the facts in the case: An alleged spy, a convicted spy, and the premise was articulated that there the government had a choice of making a full disclosure to the defendant for the vindication of her constitutional rights or dismissing it. The government dismissed.

COMMENTARY

United States v. Coplon, supra, and the case on which it relies, *United States v. Andolscheck, supra,* are the linchpins of the argument here. Obviously, there are some surveillances that are so embarrassing to the government that dismissal is preferred to disclosure. Sometimes the embarrassment would be revelation of investigative techniques and sometimes revelation of the overheard conversations themselves. Williams knows that the Court is familiar with this doctrine. Not only is it discussed in the briefs, but also the Court had cited *Coplon* and *Andolscheck* shortly before, for this very proposition. Dennis v. United States, 384 U.S. at 872–73 n.20.

Now, that case, and I think it is significant to note, has stood unassailed by the government for 18 years until argument was heard in this case last Term. That case was simply a repetition of the doctrine articulated also by the Second Circuit in the United States against Andolschek. So, if the Court please, it is reduced to essence that the concept of national security should not be the talisman for a pro tanto suspension of due process of law or of any of the rights guaranteed to an accused in a criminal case.

If, in the conduct of relationships between governments in our time, it has become the custom or it has become a necessity to engage in wiretapping or eavesdropping or dissembling or purloining or burglarizing or even killing, it is not our argument in this Court today that the Executive Branch should be manacled or impeded or harassed in the conduct of relationships with other governments. It is our argument here today that at least the federal courts should be a sanctuary in the jungle, and that these morals and mores should be not be imported into the American Judiciary System, and that the fruits of this kind of conduct should not become evidence in a criminal case brought by the sovereign power against an accused, nor should those derived from these kinds of conduct be available to the prosecutor in a criminal case brought by the sovereign power.

In essence, as I understand the government's position in this case, it is asserting its right to be let alone

---

COMMENTARY

Here he picks up Justice Brandeis's phrase, used in the quite different context of an individual's right to privacy, and turns it on its head. Brandeis wrote:

The makers of our Constitution . . . sought to protect Americans in their beliefs, their thoughts, their emotions and their sensations. They conferred, as against the government, the right to be let alone—the most comprehensive of rights and the right most valued by civilized men. To protect that right, every unjustifiable intrusion by the government upon the privacy of the individual, whatever the means employed, must be deemed a violation of the Fourth Amendment. Olmstead v. United States, 277 U.S. 438, 478 (1928) (dissenting opinion).

---

and to that we say Amen, so long as the evidence is not offered in a Federal criminal proceeding.

Q: That is not quite the issue, unless I misunderstood, Mr. Williams. The issue is how should it be determined whether the evidence is being offered or the fruits of the unlawfully obtained evidence is being offered. Perhaps I misunderstand, but I thought the government's position was not to depend on the use of such evidence, but that the government's position was to insist that whether such evidence is being used and the fruits thereof are being used, should be determined by the judge in camera. Am I wrong about that?

A: I think that is the government's position. The government's position is the same in this case as it is in the Alderman case, and we say just as it is impossible for this kind of determination to be made in the Alderman case, it is equally impossible for this kind of determination to be made in camera ex parte by the Judge even though the issue may affect national security.

But the government has argued in its brief at great lengths that we are seeking to impede the government in assuring the national security, and I say that we are not.

I say that we are not asking that any rules be fashioned to impede or harass the government in the conduct of its affairs with other governments, or in the conduct of its duty to preserve the national security.

We are asking for a much narrower rule.

COMMENTARY

Williams concedes the force of the government's national security concerns, and with rhetorical fervor that even the government's brief did not summon. He then makes the assurance that his is a modest proposal. Such an argument will often be suspect—that is what advocates will claim, after all. So Williams backs up his statement with two supporting themes: the general principle of adversary inquiry, and specific national security cases in which the right to such inquiry has triumphed over national security claims.

We are asking that this kind of evidence not be offered in Court, and we are saying that the same rules should pertain to this kind of evidence as pertains with respect to any other kind of evidence, that there should be a disclosure. A disclosure may be made under Rule 16 as the disclosure may be made as in any other kind of case to eliminate unnecessary dissemination of the information.

So, our position, if the Court please, is that the defendant has the right to disclosure under appropriate protective orders, and he has the right to disclosure to his counsel under appropriate protective orders, regardless of what the nature of the information may be and regardless of whether or not it is contended by the government that it affects national security, unless the government is willing to dismiss the prosecution in which case we agree that it should be excused.

Q: You don't mean the government is saying even if in Alderman's disclosure to the defense, protective orders to take care of the problem were held to be in that kind of case sufficient—you don't mean to say that nevertheless in a national security case there are other considerations of a national security case which argue for the in camera situation? You don't believe the government is making that distinction?

A: I don't read them as making that distinction, sir. I read them as asking for the same kind of proceeding in each case.

Q: They are, but you do not read it as saying even if we lose out in Alderman, nevertheless there are elements in the national security case which justify an in camera proceeding?

A: I don't read it that way. They may contend it orally. I read them as asking for the same kind of hearing, and I read them as saying the protective orders can be fashioned here just as in the *Alderman* case. If we are driven to the unhappy conclusion that the alleged spy goes free, then I think we can draw some consolation from the history of the last three decades; that in the three decades of recorded federal jurisprudence, during which there were three wars, we have only one instance of an averred spy going free in this frame of reference, and she was the defendant in the case to which I allude, the *Coplon* case, and I think we can also get a measure of consolation from the fact that of all the crimes in jurisprudence, the amount of recidivism that takes place in the area of espionage is by and large defused.

COMMENTARY

The first observation—about Judith Coplon—is true so far as we were able to find. The "recidivism" point is, I think, very funny. It drew a laugh in argument. The two references together are kindred to the "one-tenth of one percent" observation in *Alderman* about the potential danger to third parties from disclosure. Williams is trying to convince the Court that the alleged danger posited by the government is trivial. He is on fairly firm ground here, because foreign citizens like Ivanov caught in espionage plots are generally repatriated and not prosecuted.

More generally, this kind of sardonic humor is a powerful weapon that can be dangerous to its wielder. Judges will sometimes say something they think is funny, or ask a question that is ironic or in jest. Let them have the laugh. If the question contains the germ of something serious, answer seriously and with good humor, even if the jab was directed at you or your position. Justice Thurgood Marshall would often try to illustrate a problem with an advocate's position with humor. For example, in Gutknecht v. United States, 396 U.S. 295 (1970), when my opponent argued that the Justice Department would take care of injustices in the draft system by confessing error in appropriate cases, Justice Marshall said, "Oh, I see, the absolute discretion of the Selective Service board is all right because of the absolute discretion that you have to confess error." The appropriate response would have been to address the issue of discretion.

If you are the advocate, humor must be on target, in good taste, low key, and delivered with a straight face. It must appear to come spontaneously from something in the situation.

Q: Weren't there two others involved in that case?

A: Yes, sir, there are two petitioners in this case.

Q: Were there not involved in this whole episode others?

A: There were three others who were Soviet nationals who had status enough to go back to the Soviet Union with our blessing.

COMMENTARY

He means that there were five arrested. Butenko, an American citizen, was allegedly passing secrets. Ivanov was a chauffeur who was driving three Soviet agents to the meetings. The three had diplomatic status and could not be prosecuted. Ivanov was prosecuted, but was bailed into the custody of the Soviet United Nations Mission, and was eventually repatriated.

Now, Your Honor, with respect to the problems that this Court has propounded on standing in this case, and the Court has propounded some hard questions with respect to the subject of standing in this case, for the purposes of standing, we do contend in capsulized form that a person aggrieved within the purview of Rule 41 is one against whom the illicit search is directed, whether he is known or unknown at the time.

COMMENTARY

Williams is turning the corner, introducing a new subject with a transition. Rule 41 is FED. R. CRIM. P. 41(e), which provides that "[a] person aggrieved by an unlawful search and seizure or by the deprivation of property may move the district court for the district in which the property was seized for the return of the property on the ground that such person is entitled to lawful possession of the property."

We say, for purposes of standing, that the concept must be considered under the Rule describing an aggrieved person. We say, if the Court please, it must be considered against the background of an age in which electronic surveillance has become a widespread investigative technique, that we must consider in the light of the philosophical rationale for the federal exclusionary rule.

COMMENTARY

Williams is proposing a standing rule that contains two important limitations, to gain broader support for his position. First, he will speak only of standing to suppress unlawful electronic surveillance. This is a sensible limit, for electronic surveillance is different from a physical search in that it hears everything that goes on in a given area or on a given telephone. Indeed, it was persuasively argued that electronic surveillance could never be lawful even with a warrant because it is inherently the "general search" forbidden by the Fourth Amendment requirement of "particular" description. *See generally* Berger v. New York, 388 U.S. 41 (1967) (invalidating electronic surveillance orders as general searches). The Court's expressed concerns in *Berger* led to

the quite detailed limitations on electronic surveillance authorized by Congress in 18 U.S.C. §2510–20. *See* LaFave & Scott ch.
4 for a history of wiretapping and electronic surveillance case
law and statutory development. Williams picks up on these concerns to make an argument for expanded standing to suppress
the fruits of electronic searches when they are determined to
have been unlawful.

The second limitation that Williams will propose is that not
everyone against whom the fruits of surveillance is to be used
will have standing. Rather, the category will be limited to those
chosen by the government—as co-conspirators or co-defendants
of the person whose premises or conversations were invaded
and to those who are the "targets of prosecution" of the surveillance, as he explains a little farther on.

Now, the rationale of the federal exclusionary rule has
been articulated many times by many courts as being simply that the courts recoil at the philosophic concept that
the end justifies the means in the administration of criminal justice, that the exclusionary rule is designed to dis-
courage it and effect compliance with the acts of the
sovereign power with the law.

COMMENTARY

For a discussion of the rule's rationale and evolution, see Mapp
v. Ohio, 367 U.S. 643 (1961) and Justice Roger Traynor's analysis on which the Court relied in Mapp, People v. Cahan, 44
Cal.2d 445, 282 P.2d 905 (1955). *See* LaFave & Scott ch. 9 for a
general discussion of the background and scope of exclusionary
rules. Note that Williams moves from saying "government"—as
he usually does—to "sovereign power." He chooses the more
intensive words to call up the image of necessary restraint on the
exercise of that power.

It is our position that the rule on standing for which the
government contends is archaic and that it is ineffective
against this background. During the early evolution of
cases under the Fourth Amendment, by and large we were

concerned with cases where the defendant's constitutional rights had been invaded by virtue of the search of his
premises, and of seizure of his papers and his effects, so
that in the great majority of cases there was not a serious
problem of standing, but we have passed that era and we
now have an era where electronic surveillance is used in
the following manner, as illustrated in many ways in our
papers.

The government does not listen to the suspect. It does
not invade his premises electronically by planting an electronic bug there. Rather, in a very careful, selective manner, it listens to the conversations of his relatives and
friends and associates and it invades the premises of his
relatives and friends and associates, and it gathers criminal intelligence by this fact, which it indexes and comput-
erizes and makes dossiers until such time as it has by
utilizing these leads developed a situation where in an
indictment can be secured by the presentation of some of
this evidence, a grand jury, and subsequently a conviction,
can be obtained by the use of the same evidence.

And, the suspect, the defendant is left without a remedy
because the government contends he has not been victim-
ized because he was not heard and because no premises
in which he had a proprietary interest was invaded.

I suggest to the Court that the government's position on
standing in this case with respect to electronic surveillance
is like Solomon's approach to the baby. "Cut it in half,"
says the government. There are two competing social
interests: One, that the culprit should not go free. Society
has a major interest in this.

The other is that there should be a deterrence in illegal
methods of law enforcement. The government's proposal
would satisfy neither competing social interest.

Why? Because it says that a selected class of culprits
should go free—those who fall within their concept of the
term standing, but, on the other hand, the green light
should be flashed for a continuation of illicit electronic

surveillance because this kind of activity can remain tremendously fruitful and beneficial in the gathering of criminal intelligence without giving the ultimate victim a status to object.

Now, we say, if the Court please, that the time has come for standing to be given vis-à-vis electronic surveillance to the following:

1. To those whose conversations are illicitly listened to, and the government does not gainsay this.

2. To those persons whose premises are illegally invaded by electronic eavesdropping equipment, and as I read the government's brief, at page 21, in the *Alderman* case it clearly does not gainsay this because as I previously read to the Court, the government says it adheres to the position that a defendant, though not a participant, if the overhearing occurred on premises owned by him or in which he had some interest he has a standing.

Now, I suggest to the Court that one who is the subject matter of an overhearing illegal in nature must have standing if illicit electronic surveillance by federal agencies is to be deterred.

Finally—

Q: The subject matter of the conversation and so forth?

A: Yes, sir, and finally, I say this and this sounds very much like a simplistic approach to the problem and I assure the Court that it is not a simplistic approach to the problem. I assure you that consideration has been given to all of the social and legal interests in making the statement.

I believe that standing must be given to a co-defendant in a criminal case whether he be named as a co-conspirator or not. I say this first of all because it is hard to conceive that defendants can be joined in a criminal case in the federal courts under Rule 8, which provides for joinder of defendants unless there be what could have been averred as a conspiracy. Why? Because the rule provides that they must have been engaged in an act or a series of acts or transaction or series of transactions constituting an offense.

─────────────── COMMENTARY ───────────────

This is an accurate statement of FED. R. CRIM. P. 8(b), which is the sole measure of proper joinder in a multidefendant case.

Q: Suppose he is a defendant being separately prosecuted in connection with the same transactions and he is not a co-defendant?

A: That is why we are driven, Your Honor, in order to avoid this kind of circumvention, to say that the overall position of the defendant is that he has standing if the search was a search directly against him.

Q: So, you don't want us to understand your statement as a category precluding you from suggesting its expansion at a later date?

─────────────── COMMENTARY ───────────────

This is a question more often posed in Supreme Court argument than elsewhere. The justices want to know where the proposed rule will take them—by necessary extension or in the advocate's view. But one must always prepare for argument by considering the possible extensions of a rule for which you or your adversary contend. It is never enough to say, "That is not this case." You will invite a testy judicial response: "I know it is not this case. That's why I posed it as a hypothetical. Now, what is your answer?" So be prepared to show—if the rule is one for which you contend—where the logical and principled limits are.

Again, Williams is basing his standing category here on "person aggrieved" in FED. R. CRIM. P. 41(e). That is, he identifies a principled textual basis for his proposal. Many judges and justices take seriously the command that text must be the starting point of analysis. *E.g.,* Connecticut National Bank v. Germain, 503 U.S. 249, 253-54 (1992) ("We have stated time and time again that courts must presume that a legislature says in a statute what it means and means in a statute what it says there.")

A: I don't want, if the Court please, for anyone to do by indirection that which is inhibited directly. If the prosecutor, by the simple device of not joining two persons in the same prosecution, could subvert the proper concept of standing, then I would be opposed to that. That is why I suggest, Your Honor, as an umbrella under which to gather all of the kinds of electronic surveillance, the fruits of which should be excluded, the rule that a person aggrieved within Rule 41 is a person against whom the electronic surveillance was directed.

We all know that when an electronic surveillance is directed against a person, it is not only against him but it is against those engaged in the illicit enterprise with him whether identified or unidentified at that time.

When there is a monitoring, the government is not just interested in what it hears about "X," it wants to know about his business associates and friends and acquaintances.

Q: You don't go so far as to suggest that all rules of standards in this area should be abolished and the interest and deterrence of illegal enforcement activity should lead us to say that the government never uses anything that it has obtained. You don't go that far.

A: In this case I don't have to go that far.

COMMENTARY

This is not an evasion. He is asked—told, really—that he is not going that far. So he knows that he will face the "how far" issue more directly a little farther on.

Q: Where do you stop short?

A: I believe in *People versus Martin,* which was decided by the Supreme Court of California, is a proper ruling. It has been adopted by California. That abolishes all illegal evidence because I do not believe the Court lends itself to illegal conduct on the part of the prosecution.

Q: How far short of it?

A: But I believe it will be an adequate determination to illegal eavesdropping.

Q: How far short of it?

A: It is this far short, Your Honor, that before a defendant could come in and compel the kind of disclosure that we are talking about in this proceeding here this morning, he would either have to have been the participant in a conversation which was invaded or he would have to have been the owner or occupant or have a proprietary interest in premises which were invaded, or he himself would have had to have been the subject matter of the conversation which was illicitly overheard.

Finally, he would have to be a co-conspirator or co-defendant of the person who fell within the purview of that particular rule or standing.

Q: Whether or not named?

A: Whether or not named because I think we have to go that far because otherwise there can be a ready and easy circumvention of the rule. I do not contend, however, as the government suggests, a rule that would permit indiscriminate rummaging through the government's file to find some illicit conduct on behalf of some federal agency.

I am confining it to this, and I say the best capsulized summary that we can fashion to cover all of those things in one short business phrase, and I hope it is not an over-simplification, is to give standing to one against whom, whether identified at the time or not, the search of the government agents is directed.

Q: Plus his co-defendant?

A: I said that if the search is directed against him, he is the co-defendant?

Q: It was not directed against him, but he was a co-defendant.

--- COMMENTARY ---

This is difficult to follow, but Williams is relying on his quite sensible analysis of FED. R. CRIM. P. 8(b), which would not permit

> making someone a co-defendant who was not involved in the
> same common scheme or plan, whether or not charged as a con-
> spiracy.

A: Yes, sir, whether it was named or not.

Q: Suppose out in San Francisco the government illegally bugs a place and they hope to overhear a conversation in which John Jones's name is mentioned. They were
not looking for John Jones, but out of something they
heard, they look into John Jones, and find he has been
guilty of income tax evasion, and they prosecuted him for
that. Would he have standing?

A: It would have to be turned over to him under the
rule for which we have contended.

Q: Even though he was the subject matter, otherwise
the government was innocent?

A: Otherwise you cannot get effective compliance of
the rule outlawing electronic surveillance.

Q: That is why I asked you how far you are going to
abolish old rules or standards.

A: I am not asking that, Your Honor.

Q: I know you are not, but I wonder if it is not tanta-
mount to that.

A: I am asking the Court to fashion a rule of standing
which encompasses the interests which I believe need to
be served if we are to have an effective exclusionary rule
with respect to electronic espionage.

I say to the Court that it will be used because it will still
be fruitful and beneficial to federal agents. . . .

Q: It really sounds to me in the area of electronic surveillance what you are suggesting is that the only really
practical way to make deterrents meaningful is just to bar
the government from using any electronic surveillance
illegally obtained in any case.

A: Except that we are not going to stumble into the pit-
fall suggested by the Solicitor General that we are asking

to go through the Department of Justice and rummage through all of the files which can be classified as garnered illegally.

We are saying that before we have a right to have a disclosure of those materials, we must be in one of the categories which I have gone into.

Q: Take the case I have put to you. Jones, in fact, was come upon through this lead in the overheard sample conversations, but Jones knows nothing about this.

A: In all of this discussion we had today, and in all of the discussion we had last Term, and we are at the mercy of the good faith of the Department, which we do not impugn, that they will come forward under the doctrine of Kolod and say we heard John Jones by using an electronic surveillance conducted in San Francisco. Here is the conversation of Mr. Jones. Make the most of it, if you can relate it to your prosecution, we are willing to have any evidence gleaned therefrom stricken.

Of course, it goes without saying that Jones has no way to vindicate his constitutional rights.

Q: What you are saying is that Jones would not have any right to insist that the government turn over information to him as to whether or not it had obtained the information that way?

A: He would have the right to insist on it, but he would get it entirely dependant upon the good faith of the government.

Q: Does this mean that in every case the defense says we don't know where the government got its evidence, but maybe it got it through some lead through illicit electronic surveillance? We want the government to tell us what it did.

A: The government, under the Kolod case, has an obligation, as I understand, to come forward with any evidence which relates to the defendant, any evidence relating to the defendant which has been seized by electronic surveillance.

Q: Of course, the government had initially come out with the information, but what I am asking is in the Jones case does Jones's lawyer initiate some proceeding to have the government say whether any of this evidence came in?

A: If *Kolod* is complied with, the government would admit, but I would say out of an abundance of caution, it would behoove Jones's lawyer to ask the question of whether there was any eavesdropping, whether his premises were invaded or whether he was the subject matter of conversation of others.

Q: Then this would be standard procedure in every criminal case the government brings?

A: I am afraid it has to be if we are going to effectively deter electronic surveillance. I think the same results would apply to wiretapping cases.

Q: But in the non-wiretapping, non-bugging cases, you would not favor this?

A: No. I am confining all of my suggestions and contentions to the areas to which we are concerned, Mr. Justice Harlan, electronic eavesdropping or electronic surveillance.

COMMENTARY

The discussion here is about what procedure there will be to trigger a government search of its files for illegal electronic surveillance. Williams is describing the procedure that became law after *Alderman,* and was one of that case's salutary contributions to combating lawless law enforcement. Defense counsel would file a statement setting out reasons why unlawful electronic surveillance was thought to have occurred. The government would then be required to affirm or deny.

Later, in 18 U.S.C. §3504(a), the obligation to affirm or deny was codified. This provision was construed in Gelbard v. United States, 408 U.S. 41 (1972), which I argued.

Q: But can you make the same kind of rule on the basis of your argument?

A: Yes.

Q: But you don't want to go that far?
A: I am not asking the Court to go that far.

COMMENTARY

My son Jon is fond of the phrase "pigs get fat, hogs get slaugh-
tered." A thought to keep in mind when staking out positions in
lawsuits.

Q: It is right around the corner.
A: As did the Supreme Court of California. I am asking
the Court to go only so far as I have contended in cases
involving electronic surveillance.
Thank you very much.

* * * * * * *

From the last series of questions, one can see how the
standing issue will fare. The Court held, over Justice Fortas's
dissent, that standing should be restricted to those with a
personal or proprietary interest. Williams was pushed on this
issue, but did not retreat. He had come to put forward a
position on electronic surveillance that had been part of his
work in many cases leading up to *Alderman*. His view was
worked out carefully in a series of discussions at the office,
during the briefing schedule and in preparation for argument.

On the main issue, the Court reaffirmed *Kolod*. It held that
whenever there is illegal electronic surveillance the government must disclose its existence and leave it to adversary
inquiry whether or not the illegality tainted the prosecution's
evidence.

NOTES

1. 18 U.S.C. §§2510–20.
2. A "bug" is a listening device in a room. A "wiretap" is an inter-
ception of a telephone line. A bug picks up everything in the room
but would not hear the calling party in telephone conversations.

Wiretapping has been unlawful since the Communications Act of 1934. *See generally* Nardone v. United States, 308 U.S. 338 (1939). A "bug" placed without a warrant and statutory authorization is unlawful in part because physical trespass is necessary to install it—*see* Silverman v. United States, 365 U.S. 505 (1961) (a spike mike that penetrated only 1/4 inch into the dwelling wall was nonetheless a sufficient intrusion to merit Fourth Amendment protection) (a Williams case)—and more modernly because it invades a protected privacy interest in communication. Katz v. United States, 389 U.S. 347 (1967) (irrespective of property notions, the user of a phone booth is entitled to a Fourth Amendment–protected expectation of privacy, and therefore overhearing his conversations violates the Fourth Amendment).

3. For details, see the 10th Circuit opinion reversed by the Supreme Court in *Alderman,* 524 F.2d 504 (10th Cir. 1967).

4. This procedural history is recounted in the Court's eventual opinion at 394 U.S. 165 (1969).

5. On taint and fruit of the poisonous tree, see generally *Nardone, supra. Nardone* also developed the notion of "fruit of the poisonous tree"—that is, the taint to the government's case from use of the unlawfully obtained information. This doctrine was refined in Wong Sun v. United States, 371 U.S. 471 (1963) (argued by Edward Bennett Williams). *See generally* LaFave & Scott ch. 9.

6. This case was argued before the electronic surveillance provisions of 18 U.S.C. §§2510–20 became effective and well before the Foreign Intelligence Surveillance Act, 50 U.S.C. §§1801–25 was adopted.

7. 390 U.S. 136 (1968).

8. People v. Martin, 45 Cal.2d 755, 290 P.2d 855 (1955).

9. *E.g.,* Silverman v. United States, *supra,* and Wong Sun v. United States, *supra.*

Conclusion

> You certainly know this simple, beautiful, and inflam-
> matory notion. Every time you stand before a jury in a
> criminal case, you are drawing all over again the most
> important line the law can draw—between the idea of
> reasonable doubt and the reality of some poor soul on
> trial for his life or his liberty. And you take on the
> sacred duty to persuade that jury to set aside intuition
> and prejudice and walk that line.

Kevin McCarthy and I put these words in the mouth of Dan
O'Connell.[1] He is not reported to have said them, but he
might have.

These words are true of every case that goes to trial. While
in criminal cases the stakes are higher, there are consequences from every jury verdict that weigh more or less
heavily upon the litigants. This book began with some
thoughts from classical rhetoric. One might have made the
same points from contemporary experience. It seemed right,
however, to remember that what we do as advocates traces
deep roots in our cultural tradition. When we accept this, we
then understand that the elements of classical discourse are
truly the windows on modern persuasion.

Experience, after all, has a certain transient quality, and
few of us accumulate enough of it in a single lifetime to be
appropriately confident that we always know what we are

doing. Without the guidance from the past, we might make the mistake of which Mark Twain spoke:

> We should be careful to get out of an experience only the wisdom that is in it—and stop there; lest we be like the cat that sits down on a hot stove-lid. She will never sit down on a hot stove-lid again—and that is well; but she will never sit down on a cold one any more.

Another theme of this book is that the advocate's aspirations and craft are linked. Edward Bennett Williams was a great advocate because he deeply studied the advocate's rhetorical tradition, because he took law seriously as an intellectual discipline, and because at the center of his being he had a moral code. At Frank Lloyd Wright's studio in Arizona, there is this quote from that great architect. It could apply to lawyers as well:

> Consider that you, as young architects, are to be the pattern-givers of civilization . . . you must be the way-showers. As no stream can rise higher than its source, so you can rise no more or better to architecture than you are. So why not go to work on yourselves, to make yourselves, in quality, what you would have your buildings be?

I close near where I began. What is the advocate's duty? This is what I wrote in the *Texas Law Review* about being appointed in the Oklahoma City bombing case to represent Terry Nichols.[2]

* * * * * *

The editors have asked for an Essay, a sort of travelogue of the distance between Austin and Oklahoma City, home and away, sanity and madness, hope and despair. They hinted vaguely that I might want to answer criticisms of my representing Terry Lynn Nichols. I am not responding to those hints, because I do not need to, at least not in a publication by and for lawyers. I was appointed by the court. Almost everyone I meet has been warm, supportive, and understanding. The man who ably keeps my boots repaired told me last week that he well understood what I was doing. "If people who get arrested did not have lawyers, then anybody the police suspect would be railroaded off to jail. It would be a police state."

By similar token, you will not find much in this Essay about the "facts" of the Oklahoma City tragedy. Trials are the place for evidence. The media, even a law review, is not the place for me to try this lawsuit.

The reader will, however, detect some passion and even anger in the words below. To accept a great challenge requires, at least for me, a passionate commitment to fulfill it. In litigation as in love, technical proficiency without passion is not wholly satisfying.

The call came on Thursday, May 11, 1995. I had spent the day talking about appellate practice at the Thurgood Marshall Building in Washington, D.C. The audience members were federal public defenders, who do a difficult job with too little recognition, working every day to see that the line between the state and human liberty is drawn fairly.

Chief Judge David L. Russell of the Western District of Oklahoma had called my home. My eleven-year-old daughter took the message. When I checked in from Washington National Airport, my daughter said I should call the judge.

Chief Judge Russell and former Chief Judge Lee West (before whom I had appeared some years ago) said they wanted to appoint me to represent Terry Lynn Nichols, the forty-year-old father of two who was being held as an accomplice in the April 19, 1995, Oklahoma City bombing.

I confess I had not followed the details in the media. I knew the government did not claim that Mr. Nichols was present in Oklahoma City on that day. I also knew that the case had been characterized as capital by the Attorney General and the President.

Judge Russell said he first had the idea of appointing me when he remembered a videotape of a mock closing argument in a capital case that I had done as part of the Smithsonian's annual Folklife Festival in Washington, D.C., nearly a decade ago. He said he had checked me out with lawyers and judges, mentioning Judge Patrick Higginbotham of the Fifth Circuit by name.

When a judge tenders an appointment in a criminal case, only the most compelling reasons should make a lawyer try to avoid the assignment. We daily proclaim our commitment to the adversary system. While we have the right to pick and choose among clients who come to our doors, the indigent defendant facing death at the state's hands has a powerful claim on us. Were it not so, our protestations about the adversary system would crumble into hypocrisy and cynicism.

Judge Russell's story of how my name came to mind is probably incomplete. The Administrative Office of the U.S. Courts has statutory responsibility for advising judges on appointments in federal capital cases, and that office has said that there was a "short list" of advocates being considered for appointment. Some lawyers had gone on national television to say they would not take such an appointment.

The charges against Mr. Nichols might make this a capital case. Hence, he is entitled to at least two experienced lead counsel. I was lucky that Ronald G. Woods, a University of Texas graduate with thirty years' experience as prosecutor and defense counsel, agreed to accept appointment along with me. Ron Woods has seen law practice as few lawyers have. He was an FBI agent, an assistant district attorney, an assistant United States Attorney, the United States Attorney for the Southern District of Texas, and a lawyer in private practice. I have opposed him when he was in government service, and worked with him during his time in private practice.

During my eleven years at the University of Texas, I have been counsel in many challenging pro bono and appointed cases. Law students have worked alongside me, with the consent of the dean, and have received course credit for their work. Using pro bono cases as a learning ground for students may be reason enough to accept such responsibility. In addition, the law professor's obligation of public service demands some form of contribution to the community.

There is more. I remain a defender because I am dismayed and angered by what I see around me, and I think that as a lawyer the only way through the present terrible time is to fashion and refashion a certain image of justice.

I am not speaking now of the tragedy of April 19, 1995. I am visited every day with the sense of loss felt by all the people of Oklahoma, which is one reason I think it unfair and unreasonable to ask them to pass dispassionate judgment on those events. Nor am I conjuring up the image of the President and the Attorney General rushing before the television cameras to call for the death penalty, as though no fact that could ever be found would stand in the way of deliberately taking another life as a means of doing justice for the ones already lost.

I am not talking of the storm of publicity, nor of a sense that this is a "historic" case. Every lawyer in the Oklahoma City case knows that our work will be judged, now and in time to be. It is important not to be self-conscious about that knowledge. None of us can make a bargain with history, saying, "Well, if I act in this way, can I guarantee that I will be regarded in a certain way twenty years hence?" We can only do the next right thing as best we see it. History, the past and the present, informs us, teaches us. History yet to be written cannot turn us from our honestly determined duty.

In deciding to act, one steps into a space between past and future. The past—the suffering and tragedy—are established events, to be understood as well as one can. Stepping into the moment now is a search for something called justice. Justice or injustice, in the now and in the future, is part of a process. The past events cannot be unraveled or undone, but one can perhaps prevent people's attitudes towards those events from becoming an excuse for injustice.

I am talking of a prosaic, down-to-earth notion of justice. Something like Camus was describing when he said that our chance of salvation is to strive for justice, which is something that only the human species has devised. Justice, as Camus also reminded us, must be more than an abstract idea; it must be a reflection of compassion for one's fellow beings. In the name of Justice, the abstract idea writ large, great wrongs have been done. Jordan and Carol Steiker have given us a compelling essay about a death row inmate weighted down by abstract and yet inhuman justice. The inmate, Karla Faye Tucker, had a T-shirt that said, "Kill them all. God will sort them out." This is one version of a cry attributed to the papal legate who presided over the massacre of some 15,000 men, women, and children at Beziers, near Marseille, in 1209. It seemed that some of these people had been adjudged (and there is the word again—derived from the same root as justice itself yet separate from it in its essence) heretics.

Today, and close by, legislators are busy terminating and trimming programs of legal assistance for the poor. The most visible casualties are the Resource Centers that have valiantly struggled to represent—and to help volunteer lawyers represent—defendants charged with and convicted of capital crimes. The most despised, the most endangered defendants may be without counsel.

Yet their cases, as history teaches us without any reason for doubt, are the ones most likely to have excited governmental passion in ways that make judgment fallible.

Do you doubt this statement about fallible judgment? Consider the Haymarket trial, in which innocent men were railroaded, and only those who escaped the noose could be pardoned years later. Sacco and Vanzetti were swept up in the xenophobic hysteria fomented by the federal government, most visibly in the person of Attorney General A. Mitchell Palmer. More recently, a Cleveland auto worker spent years in a death cell convicted of being Ivan the Terrible of Treblinka; not only was he innocent of that charge, but our own government had defrauded the federal courts to get him extradited to Israel for trial.

In each of these cases, there were victims of crime. It was no honor to them, nor proper solace to those who mourned them, that their deaths became an excuse for crimes committed in the name of the state—in the name of justice.

Yet, in cases like these that may arise in the future, and that are now pending, there are not to be lawyers, unless something is done very quickly.

This is not to speak of the civil claims of people who simply want access to the justice system to present or protect their theoretically valid rights. These folks are to lose many of the lawyers provided by legal services offices.

In Alabama, the newspaper reports, the chain gang is back. There is no social need for it. The state gets all the gravel for its roads from commercial quarries. But rocks are being shipped at state expense to prisons, so that men in prison can be chained together and break the rocks into smaller rocks. Nobody has any proof that this degradation of humans deters anyone from crime, and there is no hint that the rock-breakers acquire a skill or do some useful labor.

Alabama's atavistic adventure is simply one example in a growing list of savageries committed in the name of justice. In 1993, 2.9 times as many people were behind bars in America as in 1980. The prison population continues to increase; sentences are longer. Yet the proportion of violent offenders among the prison population declines, telling us that prison is becoming the remedy of choice for nonviolent crime. The statistics become grimmer in the inner cities, where incarceration rates for African-American males are multiples of the already high national average. In the United States, we incarcerate a far higher percentage of the population than any country in the world, and that includes the former Soviet Union and pre-democracy South Africa.

I doubt many people feel safer knowing that prison sentences are longer and more readily handed out. To say this is not to endorse a vague commitment to finding the "social causes of crime" and doing nothing until we make the discovery. The drive for ever-sterner sentences handed out in proceedings where defendants have ever-fewer rights is simply an abandonment of rational discourse. The political success of such proposals is partly due to a gap in criminological theory. Criminologists try to tell us why people commit crimes and to describe the patterns of criminal behavior. They have had little to say about how to make people safe from criminal behavior.

It is possible to accommodate the perceived need for public safety with the dignity of all persons, but doing so will require a rational search based upon familiar values. That is, indeed, one of the most important tasks now facing us.

To look beyond our shores, we must all share a sense of horror at the waves of ethnic violence—and the incipient pogroms—that wash over nations on several continents. These tortures and murders are being inflicted by groups possessing state power, and therefore claiming a legitimate monopoly on the instruments of violence. The perpetrators are pleased to call what they are doing "justice."

For me, the question is "What personal responsibility do I, as one trained in the law, living the law, have right now?" Responsibility from where, from whom? Responsibility how determined? Responsibility to whom? When one says responsibility, one inevitably summons up some "other" or "others," present and not present, from the past, and in some time to come. One summons up a dialectical image of process. This sense of the other, the not-present, is eloquently evoked by Jacques Derrida in his series of lectures published as *Spectres de Marx.*

Derrida moves from considering continuity to confronting the idea of justice. Just now, I used the term "justice system." That is a mistake. It is the system-called-justice. It is called-justice in the same sense that the papal legate was sent to Beziers to dispense "justice." The "system" is an abstraction, a machine for putting a name, the name "justice" or "judgment," on results. The "system" is not "justice" because the system makes "justice" into an abstraction. When I say "justice" I do not mean a name-giver. I mean what Camus meant—an idea that unites uniquely human values based upon compassion.

When I speak of a prosaic and down-to-earth idea of justice, I mean simply that one can deduce principles of right from human needs in the present time. That is, I reject the cynical, or stoic, or "no-ought-from-an-is" idea that one set of rules is just as good as another. I reject the notion, as Professor Martha Nussbaum has characterized it, "that to every argument some argument to a contradictory conclusion can be opposed; that arguments are in any case merely tools of influence, without any better sort of claim to our allegiance." Rather, again borrowing from Professor Nussbaum, my notions of justice "include a commitment, open-ended and revisable because grounded upon dialectical arguments that have their roots in experience, to a definite view of human flourishing and good human functioning." One element of such views is that "human beings have needs for things in the world: for political rights, for money and food and shelter, for respect and self-respect," and so on.

By hewing to a basic definition of justice, I mean to confess a certain hesitation, perhaps humility. In times as turbulent as these, with opinions swinging widely and violently from side to side, I want to return to the most basic skills and values I know and possess. I want to live my lawyer-life in the search for, and fidelity to, this "justice" as I understand it.

I will try to derive truths from the past and present, and from a sense of responsibility to those who will come after, but I am making decisions for myself and not as an apostle of others or with a claim to lead. If the ideas appeal to you, there is plenty of work to do and all are welcome.

The sense of hesitation, and of personal quest, is also evoked by Derrida in his lectures. He begins with a translated passage from the first act of Hamlet. Hamlet sees the spirit of his father, and learns how and why his father was murdered. "The time is out of joint," Hamlet says, "O curs'ed spite, That ever I was born to set it right!"

Derrida conjures with the spirit, and with various translations, of this passage to show us that thinking of justice drops us into the stream of history, the flow from past to future. In the past are the events that put time "off its hinges," or that "turn the world upside down." But to say that things are "wrong" implies that from that same past there is some idea of how things are "right-side up," or "on their hinges." This past-given sense, which is encompassed in an ideology that we can study and know, is not simply about carpentry or gravity. It is about subjective but verifiable principles of human flourishing.

And then in the present is our action, which tends into the future, towards the "set it right." To make a personal commitment to that path is not to pretend to be Prince of Denmark. It is simply to have understood the text in a certain way, and to have drawn from it certain lessons—as well as certain warnings about excessive or obsessive commitment.

This last observation is important. If the time is out of joint, the remedy is surely not to swing off one's own hinges, to become "unhinged." "And what if excessive love bewildered them till they died," Yeats wrote of the Easter martyrs, and again warned us that "Too long a sacrifice can make a stone of the heart." But the dangers are not, for me, a reason not to step into the stream.

So to return to the theme, the system-called-justice dispenses "judgments" that bear the name "law" or "right"—in French "loi" and "droit." But the term "droit" or "right" rarely goes out alone. Sometimes it is modified with an eye to justice, as in "human rights" ("droits de l'homme"). More often, it is qualified (and particularly in French) by words that give it an arid and abstract quality, like "civil right" as something the "law" recognizes, or " droit criminel" as the French would say "criminal law" and refer by those words to the system of penal rules enforced by the state. So we do best by sticking to a certain, more basic and yet more ample, sense of the term "justice."

As law students, we studied the branches of the common-law system: contracts, torts, property, criminal law, civil procedure, constitutional law, and whatever else our law schools required. "What branches of learning did you find at Harvard?" Emerson said to Thoreau, who replied, "All of the branches and none of the roots."

We had our chance to study the roots. Most of us did so, and from that study can come an informed judgment that the time is out of joint. Our study, and our passports to the places where the system-called-justice does its judging, adjudges, gives judgments, give us unique access. I will not say our study and our passports give us a responsibility. We must each figure that one out for ourselves.

For me, I will take my knowledge and my passport and try to advocate, in the places I am admitted, for just principles and just results. I will remember that I am lucky enough to be "admitted" to classrooms and lecture halls and street corners and byways and law journals and newspapers, as well as to places where more formal advocacy is done in the system-called-justice.

In making this decision, I am borne up by the example of my friends. Dullah Omar, a lawyer in South Africa, struggled for so many years against apartheid generally and for Nelson Mandela's release specifically. He came to be Minister of Justice in the new South Africa. His struggle, and his decisions in it, were the product of experience, the result of stepping into the stream and not of standing beside it lost in thought.

If I see the time is out of joint, and want to help "set it right," how shall I decide to use my energy in this, the sixth decade of my life? I am not alone on the path, so I must protect the well-being of my family in whatever I do.

Beyond that, I take my knowledge and passport to places I think I am best suited to be, not as compared to anybody else but only to how well or not-well I would do in other places where I might be.

Today, the system-called-justice poses its greatest threat to justice properly-so-called in the criminal-law system. Criminal trials, particularly famous ones, are intended to be didactic. That is, the state uses the criminal system-called-justice not only to take away liberty and life, but to announce and enforce social priorities.

Taking lawyers away from people sentenced to death announces a priority—to kill inmates without ceremony, in a way that says that poor people's claims of innocence, claims for justice, are not important.

In the Oklahoma City cases, we have already witnessed some announcements of priorities. Custodial interrogations of the defendant and his family were done without semblance of process or legality. Government agents felt free to leak theories of the defendant's complicity, only to leak contradictory stories a few days later. It seemed that many people in government had decided that the stakes were high enough that the rules didn't matter.

I have seen this arrogance of power before. A federal judge asked me in oral argument why the government would commit the frauds I had alleged in an effort to condemn John Demjanjuk for a crime he did not commit. I recalled simply the rhetorical excess in which the entire government case had come to be enfolded, and summoned up Ruskin's words that there is no snare set by the fiend for the mind of man more dangerous than the illusion that our enemies are also the enemies of God.

To spare a life that might be wrongly taken, or shelter a freedom that might be wrongly abridged, is already a significant participatory act. One must bring to bear the sense of justice, and the skills learned because one is an advocate.

There is more to it. The state sees its system-called-justice as didactic, and arranges matters in the service of that goal. When the system delivers someone from the state's power, the lesson taught is not the one intended, but is a lesson nonetheless. Because the initial decision to make the system-called-justice didactic in a particular way is the state's to begin with, these deliverances have a significance all out of proportion to their number. The opportunity to weigh in that balance is an additional benefit of participating.

When the colonial newspaper editor John Peter Zenger was charged with seditious libel, no doubt colonial Governor Cosby thought to teach Zenger, his cohorts, and his supporters all a lesson. When the tables were turned, and Zenger acquitted, a far greater and longer lasting lesson was taught. When George IV sought to rid himself of his wife, Queen Caroline, by charging her with adultery in the House of Lords, her vindication had more force than the opposite result could ever have had.

When a South Carolina jury refused to condemn Susan Smith to death for killing her children, its members were expressing a community sentiment about justice, and their verdict sounded out louder than a plea-bargained life sentence would have.

These lessons—unintended from the state's perspective—redeem, refine, and announce justice and reaffirm the human commitment to it. These reaffirmations in turn help to validate norms and principles of justice, in commands and procedures. The time is out of joint, swinging on its hinges, turned upside down, dishonored; the dominant theme in every reading of Hamlet's cry is flux, change, uncertainty. "The time," the good old boy would say, "is like a hog on ice." In such a time, an image of justice—of which the human species is the only one to conceive—and of participation in a process fixed between the no-longer-there and the yet-to-be, is a guide to behavior. The option of doing nothing, a "kind of silence about injustice," as Brecht said it, is itself a participation.

So I participate because I have an inkling, and am given a means to validate it step by step.

In telling about stepping into the stream between past and future, I make clear why I part company with those who criticize my representation of this or that person. I owe those detractors no duty of explanation. My private reasonings are mine to share or not as I should wish. By focusing on some purported obligation of personal justification, these misguided souls are missing the entire point of the journey. I am not trying to set an example. I am trying to understand how to live my life. Je voudrais apprendre à vivre enfin.

I can say I am not trying to set an example. I realize that by making some public expression—for the lawyer as for the artist—one is condemned to signify. Neither the artist nor the advocate can plausibly claim to be tracing figures on the inside walls of his mind, for his own delectation.

But in a time out of joint, the surest signifying is done in a context provided by events. For the advocate, the event is a cry for justice, not usually spectral but from a flesh and blood human being.

I know, of course, that the rigged didactic of the criminal trial has false elements. In the courtroom arena, there is a symbolic equality of defense and prosecution. We understand that in fact the balance of resources almost always tips in favor of the government, and this is particularly so in high-profile cases where high officials have announced an intention to take the defendants' lives. The defendant is not given a choice whether to participate in the unequal contest. The inequality is just another device of the system-called-justice. The lawyer's job is to expose the device, deploying the signs of justice against the signs of system-called-justice. The signs of justice include empowering the jury, calling on the tribunal to respect its oath, exposing contradiction—bringing out solid reasons why the judge and jurors should go beneath the surface of things.

About 90 percentt of criminal cases are disposed of on pleas of guilty, so the 10 percent of cases that are tried bear all the semiotic weight. The trial-court struggle over what will be taught covers the entire range of symbols. On one side, we see the government's reassuring sense of power and knowledge, of things as they should be, that we will be safer if another creature is jailed or put to death. On the defense side, the symbols are of individual responsibility for results; the image is one of courageous individuals standing up to superior force and using their intellect, power, and insight.

Maybe when time is rejointed, back on its hinges, right-side up, we will see more equal struggles over liberty. I can hope so.

My purpose in Oklahoma, and in whatever venue to which the case is moved, is not to justify myself. That would be an arrogant, foolish, pointless act. I am and will be there to try and see that the system-called-justice respects and renders justice properly-so-called. I am there to see that done for a fellow creature whose life I am to shelter.

Where am I then? To borrow again from Derrida, Ou suis-je enfin? Where am I finally? Not "finally" in the sense of an end, but of a moment between past and future, and about to push ahead again like feeling one's way forward in the dark. On a mountain road in the coal black night, C. S. Lewis wrote, we would give far more for a glimpse of the few feet ahead than for a vision of some distant horizon.

I am in that moment that has fascinated writers for centuries. The place between. "Your sons and daughters shall prophesy, your old . . . shall dream dreams, your young . . . shall see visions." I am old enough to be the dreamer evoked by this passage from Joel 2:28. My dreams are of things recollected, which I flatter myself to call old truths and insights. The visions and prophesies are of the future, where those who will live there longer than I will reap the harvest of this moment in time.

NOTES

1. In our play, WARRIOR BARDS (1989).
2. Michael E. Tigar, *Defending: An Essay,* 74 TEX. L. REV. 101 (1995). The sole footnote in the essay reads:

I thank Professor Ellen T. Birrell for reviewing drafts of this Essay and helping me—again—with the concepts of semiotics. There are no footnotes, save this one. The quotations from Martha Nussbaum are from her article, *Skepticism About Practical Reason in Literature and the Law,* 107 HARV. L. REV. 714 (1994). The Jacques Derrida work is SPECTRES DE MARX (1993). The English translation is SPECTERS OF MARX (Peggy Kamuf trans., 1994). The Derrida paraphrase towards the end of the Essay is my translation from page 14 of the French original. The Kamuf translation of the Derrida passage I am paraphrasing seems a bit wrong to me. He writes *"Ce qui suit s'avance comme un essai dans la nuit. . . ."* Jacques Derrida, SPECTRES DE MARX 14 (1993). The English text has it: "What follows advances like an essay in the night. . . ." Jacques Derrida, SPECTERS OF MARX xviii (Peggy Kamuf trans., 1994). *Essai* means a tentative exploration, and *"s'avance"* means to take oneself forward; neither subtlety is captured in the English text. I have derived some insights from Kenneth B. Nunn, *The Trial as Text: Allegory, Myth and Symbol in the Adversarial Criminal Process,* 32 AM. CRIM. L. REV. 743 (1995). Recent figures on incarceration rates are from Adam Walinsky, *The Crisis of Public Order,* ATLANTIC MONTHLY, July 1995, at 39, 47. I agree with Mr. Walinsky's view that more police patrols and other devices devoted to preventing crime are one good way to make people feel safer and to end the drive to put more and more people in prison.

I have read Professor Freedman's response. Monroe H. Freedman, *The Lawyer's Moral Obligation of Justification,* 74 TEX. L. REV. 111 (1995). The transcript of our debate twenty-five years ago, and the videotape of our more recent encounter at Hofstra, are available to anyone who wants to look at them. My remarks at the latter encounter were directed at the points Professor Freedman is making. For the present discussion, that is enough to say.

Table of Cases

Index